The Ancient City

PETER CONNOLLY
HAZEL DODGE

The Ancient
City

Life in Classical Athens & Rome

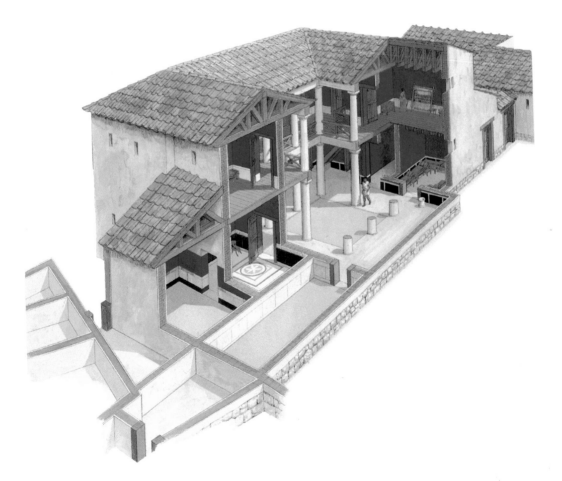

OXFORD UNIVERSITY PRESS

Oxford University Press, Great Clarendon Street, Oxford OX2 6DP

Oxford New York
Athens Auckland Bangkok Bogotá Bombay
Buenos Aires Calcutta Cape Town Dar es Salaam
Delhi Florence Hong Kong Istanbul Karachi
Kuala Lumpur Madras Madrid Melbourne
Mexico City Nairobi Paris Singapore
Taipei Tokyo Toronto Warsaw

and associated companies in
Berlin Ibadan

Oxford is a trade mark of Oxford University Press

Illustrations © Peter Connolly 1998
Text © Peter Connolly and Hazel Dodge 1998

First published in 1998

Design: Herb Bowes Graphics

A CIP catalogue record for this book is available from the British Library

ISBN 0-19-917242-0
US library edition 0-19-521409-9

1 3 5 7 9 10 8 6 4 2

Printed in Italy

CONTENTS

PART I   ATHENS

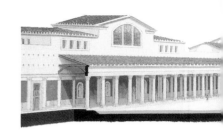

PART II   ROME

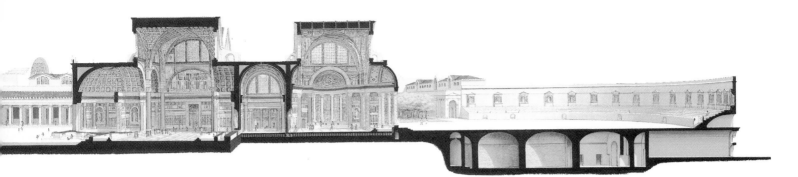

ATHENS

Athens was the shining star of the ancient world, dominating almost every field of human endeavour. A person wandering around the bustling Agora, the market place and political centre of Athens, in the fifth century BC might expect to rub shoulders with the sculptor Phidias, the dramatists Sophocles and Euripides, the comedy writer Aristophanes and the historian Thucydides. They might visit the small shop belonging to Simon the cobbler, just beyond the south-west corner of the Agora, and find the philosopher Socrates teaching a class of young boys with names such as Plato and Xenophon. Never in history have so many great people been alive at the same time, let alone living in the same town.

These people were the product of the first and perhaps the only real democracy that has ever existed. There were no political parties, no professional politicians. All decisions were taken by popular vote. Anyone could address the assembly of the people. Persuasion was the only political muscle allowed. Any unpopular or discredited politician could be banished for a time. No one could defy the will of the people and expect to get away with it.

Of course it had its bad side too. Unjust and stupid decisions were taken – Socrates himself was condemned to death by one of Athens' democratic law courts, but in true Athenian style he was given the chance to escape and go into exile. It was his refusal to leave his beloved Athens that cost him his life. Women and slaves did not have the vote, but this must be seen in the context of the age in which they lived. We must not judge ancient societies by late twentieth-century standards. The Athenians would be horrified by what we call democracy. Slavery was common to all ancient societies. It was nowhere condemned, not even in the Old and New Testaments. To its credit, Athens was well known for an over-liberal attitude towards slaves. Women were expected to live a sheltered life as wives and mothers, in conditions not unlike those of many non-western cultures today. The play-wrights Aristophanes and Euripides both advocated raising the status of women. We may agree with them, but it is debatable whether many Athenian women would have supported their views.

THE GOLDEN YEARS

The fifth century BC was the century of Athens – an age of startling brilliance unequalled before or since. Yet Athens rose to greatness only after long centuries of recovery from the Greek Dark Ages, and even in the fifth century war and disaster were seldom far away.

Before the eighth century BC, Athens is lost in the mists of time. The names of several legendary kings of Athens have come down to us: in particular Erectheus, the first king, who was believed to have established the worship of the goddess Athena on the Acropolis, and Theseus, killer of the Minotaur, who (according to the Greek historian Plutarch) unified Attica.

But in general little has survived in Athens from the Bronze Age. Traces of a Mycenaean palace, part of the defensive walls and an underground cistern have been found on the Acropolis, and a few tombs in the Agora – but little else.

Oligarchs and tyrants

Mycenaean palace civilisation collapsed throughout Greece soon after 1200 BC, leading to depopulation, large-scale migration, loss of literacy, loss of artistic skills and the breakdown of overseas trade networks. This is often conventionally referred to as the 'Dark Age' of Greece. It was not until the eighth century that city states began to emerge, governed not by kings but by aristocratic councils (oligarchies).

The Athenians overthrew their monarchy in about 950 BC. The succeeding centuries were

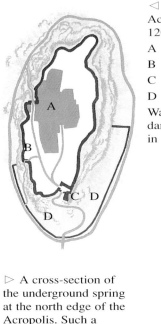

◁ A plan of the Acropolis in about 1200 BC.
A Palace
B Underground spring
C Main gate
D Lower town
Walls are shown in dark brown and roads in grey.

▷ A cross-section of the underground spring at the north edge of the Acropolis. Such a spring was essential if the citadel was to survive a siege.

▽ The Acropolis, the citadel of Athens, as it might have appeared in about 1200 BC. The area of the later Agora, in the foreground, was used as a cemetery. The Areopagus appears on the skyline on the extreme right.

dominated by a power struggle between the aristocracy and the lower classes which gradually led to a limited democracy. But the pace of reform was slow, and in 560 BC the popular leader Pisistratus seized power and became dictator (*tyrannos*). He and his sons dominated Athens until 510 BC.

The population had expanded rapidly over this period, greatly increasing the city's revenues. A large temple was built on the Acropolis to house the sacred wooden statue of Athena Polias, guardian of the city, and the building of a huge temple to Zeus, chief of the gods, was started on the flat ground to the east of the Acropolis.

War with Persia

The Greek colonies established on the eastern coast of the Aegean from about 1050 BC had been absorbed into the vast Persian empire in the mid-sixth century BC. Athens helped the colonies in an effort to throw off the Persian yoke, and when this revolt was finally put down in 494 BC, the Persians launched a punitive raid against Athens.

The Athenians called for help from the other Greek states and advanced to meet the invaders. They won a stunning victory in 490 BC at Marathon, 30 kilometres north-east of Athens, before the other states had mobilised. This success so boosted Athenian pride that they began building a great temple to Athena on the Acropolis.

The Greeks knew they had gained only a breathing space. Alliances were forged and command of the Greek forces was handed over to the Spartans, renowned throughout Greece for their military prowess. But constant conflict with trading rivals, particularly the island of Aegina, some 30 kilometres (19 miles) away in the Saronic Gulf, had prompted the Athenians to build up a large navy, and this was to be decisive in the coming war.

Thermopylae and Salamis

In 480 BC a huge army under the Persian king Xerxes crossed the Dardanelles into Europe. A small Spartan army made a heroic attempt to stop their advance at the narrow coastal pass of Thermopylae, but the Persian army broke through and descended on Athens. The population was evacuated and the Greek army withdrew to the easily-defended isthmus of Corinth, while their fleet was beached on the island of Salamis.

When the Persian fleet sailed into the Saronic Gulf, the Spartan admiral wanted to withdraw to the isthmus. The Athenian commander, Themistocles, unwilling to desert the many Athenian civilians who had taken refuge on the island, persuaded him to stay. The following dawn Themistocles lured the massive Persian fleet into the narrow channel between Salamis and the Athenian coast and inflicted a devastating defeat on it.

Glorious Plataea

The Persian king returned home in disgust, leaving his general Mardonius to continue the campaign. Realising that without naval supremacy he could not hope to dislodge the Greeks at the isthmus, Mardonius withdrew to the plain of Boeotia, some 50 kilometres (31 miles) north-west of Athens. The following summer the Spartans led the combined Greek army over the mountains to Plataea. They met the Persian army in the foothills and annihilated it. Mardonius himself was killed, the Persian camp stormed, and enormous booty was taken. In the same year, the Greeks destroyed the Persian navy, which had landed at Mycale in Ionia.

The Confederacy of Delos

The Greeks vowed to continue the war against Persia until all Greeks were free. The maritime

△ The Acropolis about 480 BC. The partly-built earlier temple of Athena stands on the southern edge, with the archaic temple of Athena Polias to the left.

▽ A marble *kore* (draped female figure), one of the many sixth-century statues found on the Acropolis.

△ A fragment of the pediment of the temple of Athena Polias.

states, of which Athens was the most powerful, agreed to maintain a fleet, under the overall command of the Athenians, specifically to wage war against the Persians. Each state was to supply ships in proportion to their resources. This league became known as the Confederacy of Delos, or the Delian League.

The oath of Plataea

With a mixture of exhilaration and sadness the Athenians reoccupied their city. It had been burned by the Persians. Scarcely a stone was left standing.

11

It was said in later years that the Greeks had made a vow at Plataea. The oath is quoted by the Athenian statesman Lycurgus, writing towards the end of the fourth century BC:

I will rebuild none of the shrines burnt and overthrown by the barbarians; I will allow them to remain as a memorial to barbarian impiety for future generations.

The Athenian shrines and temples lay in ruins for thirty years, though a temporary shrine must have been erected on the Acropolis for the sacred wooden statue of Athena, which had been evacuated to Salamis. For the moment the reconstruction of the city itself was all-important.

New defences

Determined that their city should never again be abandoned, the Athenians gave priority to building a wall round the whole populated area. The Spartans protested on the grounds that such a wall would upset the balance of Greek power. But Themistocles, by a mixture of diplomacy, duplicity and prevarication, managed to gain time for the walls to reach a defensible height. He also persuaded the Athenian assembly to strengthen the city's defences by fortifying the port of Piraeus.

A conflict of ideologies

Sparta, a landlocked state, was ruled by an oligarchy with two constitutional monarchs. Every aspect of the state was sublimated to the military. Sparta had conquered most of southern Greece, reducing the population to the status of subjects (*perioikoi*) or slaves (helots).

Athens was a democracy, dependent on trade and imported food, particularly grain, for survival. Athenian military power was mainly naval. Rivalry with Sparta was intense.

In 464 BC Sparta was devastated by an earthquake. Some Spartan subjects revolted and the Spartans called upon their allies for help. Athens sent 4,000 troops, but the Spartans so distrusted them that they sent them back. The insulted Athenians withdrew from the alliance.

In about 460 BC the Athenians openly defied Sparta by supporting Megara against Corinth (both cities were members of Sparta's Peloponnesian League). Four states used the Saronic Gulf as an outlet to the Aegean: Aegina (the traditional enemy of Athens), Megara, Corinth and Athens itself. In the ensuing war the Spartans were too involved with their own problems to intervene. The Corinthians were repulsed and Aegina, which had sided with Corinth, was captured, leaving Athens in control of the Gulf.

Walls to the sea

Faced with certain Spartan retaliation, the Athenian assembly took the crucial decision to build two long walls from the city to the coast, one to the port at Piraeus, 6 kilometres (3¾ miles) away, and the other to Phaleron, 5 kilometres (3 miles) away. These formed a triangle with the sea as its base and Athens at the apex. Now, as long as the Athenians controlled the sea, no enemy could starve them into submission.

With unbounded confidence, the Athenians went on the offensive. They seized control of Boeotia and Phocis, securing their northern borders, and at the same time the Athenian fleet pounced on the port of Naupactus on the north side of the Gulf of Corinth. Corinth was now in a stranglehold. The Spartans were harried by naval raids on the coasts of southern Greece. But the Athenians suffered a major defeat aiding an Egyptian revolt against Persia and, their resources over-stretched, agreed to a truce in 451 BC.

Peace with Persia

Two years later, in 449 BC, tired of constant Athenian interference, Persia granted independence to the Greek cities of Asia Minor. With the war over, the Confederacy of Delos should now have been dissolved, but the Athenians refused to allow it. Most members of the Confederacy had opted to pay a levy rather than supply ships. Now levy became tribute, and the Athenians felt free to dispose of the funds in any way they wished. Urged on by the great Pericles, they voted to use it to rebuild their temples.

A disastrous war

Aware that war with Sparta was inevitable, Pericles evolved a strategic response. The Spartans were invincible on land and could not be prevented from invading Attica, but Athens could respond with seaborne attacks on the

▽ A map illustrating the war with Sparta. The islands of the Aegean and virtually all the coastal towns were members of the Confederacy of Delos. Thessaly and parts of western Greece also sided with Athens. Most of the states of southern Greece were members of the Spartan Peloponnesian League. Boeotia and Macedonia also sided with Sparta.

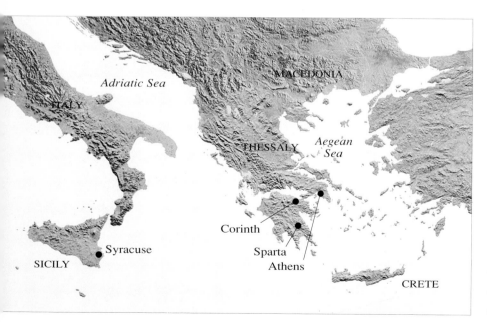

A The large mercantile harbour of Kantharos.

B The main naval harbour of Zea.

C The smaller naval harbour of Munichia.

Athens was totally dependent on food brought in by sea. The Long Walls to Piraeus and Phaleron enabled the Athenians to keep contact with their fleet even while besieged. Only the defeat of the fleet forced them to capitulate.

territory and colonies of Sparta and its allies. Pericles thus hoped to convince the Spartans that they could not win a war.

Once again Corinth was the cause of war. This time it was Corcyra (modern Corfu), another ally of Corinth, that asked Athens for help. The Corinthians responded by assisting an Athenian ally, Potidaea, to secede, and by 431 the whole of Greece was involved. When the Spartans invaded, the Athenian forces withdrew within the city walls and sent a naval expedition to attack the north-west coast of the Peloponnese. As Pericles had predicted, Sparta suffered more. But the next year Sparta received an unexpected ally. Plague struck Athens, killing thousands in the crowded conditions behind the walls, including Pericles himself.

A change of strategy

On the death of Pericles, the demagogue Cleon became the Athenian leader. After capturing 120 Spartans on the island of Sphacteria, he became convinced that Sparta could be defeated in the field. Athenian disasters began immediately. An invasion of Boeotia was crushingly defeated. Sparta offered peace, but the Athenians refused. Only another massive defeat, in which Cleon himself was killed, forced the Athenians to the negotiating table. Generous Spartan terms left Athens no worse off than before the war.

The Sicilian expedition

The brilliant but unstable Alcibiades then persuaded the Athenians that their hopes of gaining an empire might be realised by a campaign to conquer Sicily.

Nicias, who had negotiated the peace with Sparta, opposed the expedition but the people voted in favour. Three generals were elected: Alcibiades, Lamachus and Nicias. In the event Alcibiades was recalled to stand trial for sacrilege, Lamachus was killed in action and Nicias led the Athenian forces into their greatest disaster, an unsuccessful siege of Syracuse which cost more than 200 triremes and 20,000 troops in 415-13 BC.

Final humiliation

Sparta meanwhile reopened the war in Greece itself, and was soon reinforced by the Syracusan fleet. The Athenians managed to struggle on for nine years, even regaining the initiative on occasion, but in 405 the whole Athenian fleet was captured by the Spartan admiral Lysander at Aegospotami in the Dardanelles. Lysander sailed into the Saronic Gulf and blockaded Piraeus. The Athenians still held out for several months but, facing starvation, they surrendered in April 404 BC.

The Corinthians demanded the traditional practice of killing all the men and selling the women and children into slavery, a practice to which the Athenians themselves had resorted during the war. But the Spartans remembered Salamis and demanded only that the Long Walls and the Piraeus fortifications be dismantled, the Athenian navy be restricted to twelve ships and that the Athenians accept an oligarchic government of thirty pro-Spartan aristocrats, who became known as the Thirty Tyrants.

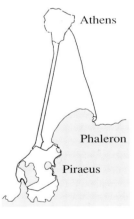

△ The Long Walls. A second wall to Piraeus, parallel to the first, giving the city a defended corridor to the port, was built during the war with Sparta. This made the wall to Phaleron redundant, and there is no evidence that it was ever used.

THE KEYS TO SURVIVAL

Early fifth-century Athens was a vulnerable city. After driving the Persians out, the Athenians concentrated on strengthening their military defences and securing supplies of food and water.

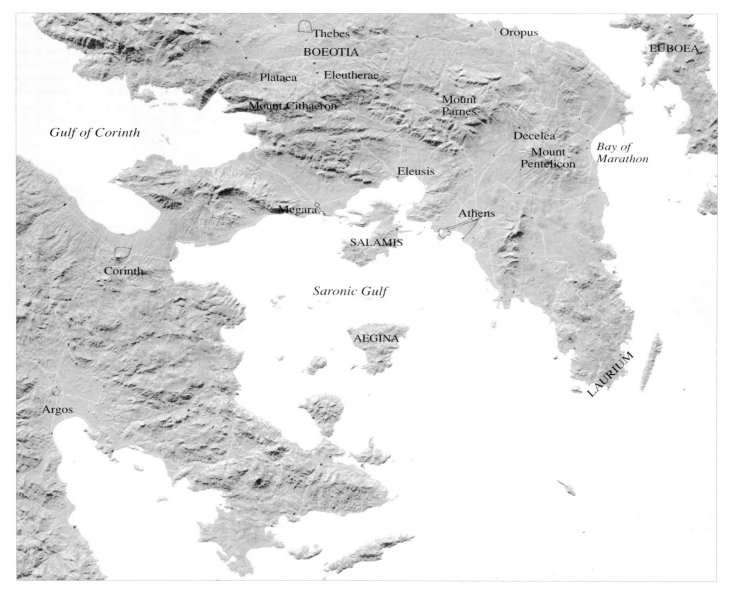

△ The boundary of the territory of Athens (Attica) followed a line from a point just west of Eleusis to the summit of Mount Cithaerum, and then eastwards to Oropus. The main enemies of Athens were Aegina, Megara and Corinth, all competing for trade into the Saronic Gulf, and Thebes in Boeotia.

Estimating the Athenian population is not easy. The roll of Athenian citizens included free men from Piraeus, the port of Athens, and all the villages and farms of Attica. Based on historical sources, a reasonable estimate of total Athenian military strength may be 45,000, all citizens being liable for military service from the age of 18 to 61. Including their families would suggest a total of about 180,000. There were also about 20,000 resident aliens (metics or *metoikoi*) who with their families might add another 80,000.

The number of slaves is far more difficult to assess. There is no way of knowing how many poorer families had slaves. But the wealthy

Nicias had a gang of 1,000 slaves which he hired out to work in the silver mines at Laurium. Many farms used slaves, and most families had domestic slaves. But there may also have been many families who owned no slaves. It seems reasonable to suggest that there may have been as many slaves as free people, and that the total population of Attica may therefore have been as much as half a million.

Food supply

Attica did not have the farming capacity to feed such a population. The main extra sources of grain were Euboea, the great island to the east

△ A typical well-head, showing wear marks from the rope being pulled against its upper lip.

▽ A vase painting showing a youth drawing water from a well.

of Attica, Thrace and the north coast of the Black Sea. A strong navy was essential to safeguard supplies from the latter two sources. During the great war with Sparta one of the most decisive developments was the establishment of a Spartan garrison at Decelia, to the north-east of Athens, which cut the overland supply route from Euboea.

Water supply

Most houses had their own wells or cisterns for collecting rainwater, but relied on the public fountains for extra water. The women of the family collected water each morning.

The tyrant Pisistratus and his sons had brought water into the city from the hills north-east of the city, through rock-cut conduits and pipes. Pipes feeding a fountain were uncovered during excavations in the south-east corner of the Agora, the ancient market place, north of the Acropolis. These pipes were made of fired clay with round inspection holes.

The fountain at the south-east corner of the Agora dates from about 530 BC and must have been one of those established by the tyrants. It had basins measuring about 6 by 3 metres (20 by 10 feet), at either end of the 18-metre

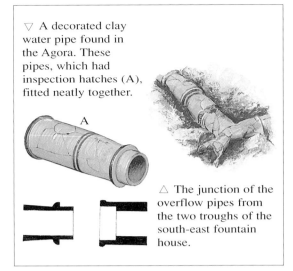

▽ A decorated clay water pipe found in the Agora. These pipes, which had inspection hatches (A), fitted neatly together.

△ The junction of the overflow pipes from the two troughs of the south-east fountain house.

(60-foot) building. The western basin served as a reservoir from which water could be drawn by dipping in a pot. The eastern end probably had spouts set into the wall, from which jugs could be filled. Such fountains are often shown on vase paintings. Surplus water was carried to the drains through similar clay pipes.

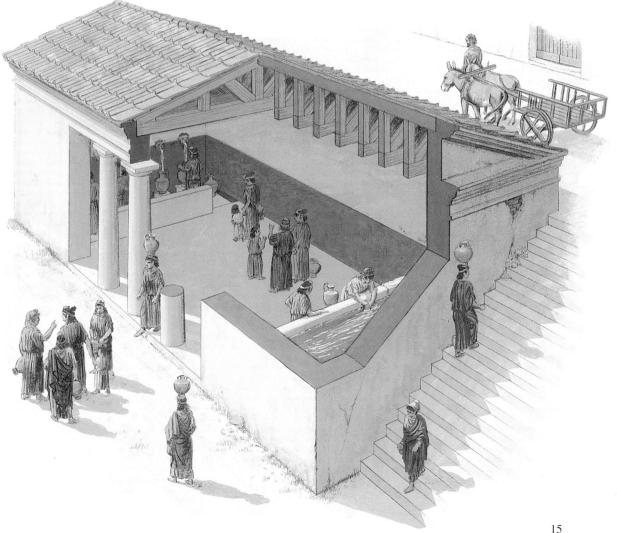

▷ A reconstruction of the spring house in the south-east corner of the Agora. Fresh water was channelled here from a spring on the slopes of Mount Lycabettus in the sixth century BC. Only the foundations of the building remain.

△ An Athenian vase painting showing two women collecting water from the spring house. Note the pad worn by the woman on the left to enable her to carry the water jar on her head.

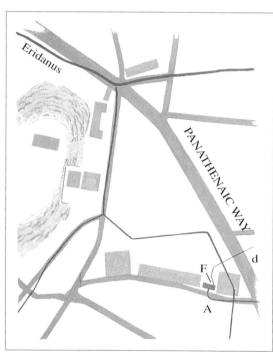

▷ A plan of the Agora, showing the drains (shown in red) under the Agora carrying rain-water to the Eridanus stream. The south-east fountain house (F), with its aqueduct (A) and separate overflow (d), was built before the main drains.

▽ The covered channel of the main drain, south-west of the Agora.

The great drain

A series of drainage channels was discovered during the Agora excavations. The main stone-lined channel down the west side of the Agora was built early in the fifth century BC, primarily to convey rainwater into the Eridanus, the stream at the north end of the Agora. Around the end of the fifth century two branches were constructed converging from the south-east and south-west, draining water from the slopes of the Acropolis, Areopagus and Pnyx.

No public lavatories have been found in classical Athens. Two are known from the Roman period in the Agora, one in the south-west corner on the western branch of the great drain and the other at the south-east entrance. A particularly fine example was built at the east entrance of the Roman market, to the east of the Agora.

The old walls

Thucydides, renowned as the most reliable of ancient historians, wrote his history of the Peloponnesian War in the later fifth century BC. He states unambiguously that Athens had a circuit wall before the Persian invasion. He claims that after the Persian sack of Athens 'only short sections of the circuit were left standing'. A further passage, describing the murder in 514 BC of Hipparchus, Pisistratus' son, implies that there was a gate on the Panathenaic Way just beyond the north-west corner of the Agora. The natural course for such a wall would have been along the summit of the Kolonus Agoraeus, the low hill on the west side of the Agora, on which the Temple of Hephaestus stands. However, no trace of a city wall dating from before the fifth century BC has been found, despite the fact that virtually the whole south-western section of the ancient city has been excavated. The archaeological evidence suggests that the only wall in existence at the time of the Persian invasions was the old wall around the west end of the Acropolis.

The fifth-century walls

By contrast, we have copious evidence for the walls erected immediately after the Persian defeat in 479 BC. Some 200 metres (656 feet) of the city wall, including the Dipylon and Sacred gates, were uncovered during the Kerameikos excavations, and many other stretches of it have been found, enabling scholars to draw up a complete plan of the walls with a reasonable degree of certainty.

The new walls were about 2.5 metres (8 feet) wide with a stone base rising about 1 metre (3 feet) above ground level. The base was composed of an inner and outer stone face laid in fairly regular courses, the space between being filled with rubble.

The excavations in the Kerameikos confirm the haste with which these walls were erected;

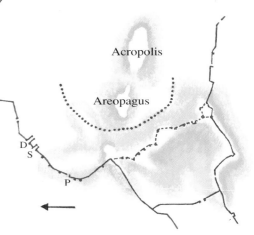

the stone base was built of any materials that came to hand, including tombstones. On the eastern side of the city column drums from the unfinished temple of Zeus were used.

The upper part of the wall, rising a further 7 or 8 metres (about 25 feet), was made of mud brick faced with plaster. The walls were reinforced at strategic points with towers about 5 metres (16 feet) square.

Constant rebuilding

The wall was rebuilt several times over the centuries. Each time, because the ground level had risen, the brickwork was demolished and a new stone base was built on top of the previous one. The wall visible today appears to be entirely of stone, but in fact it represents these consecutive stone bases built one on top of the other.

The wall was first rebuilt in 394 BC, when Athens had recovered from defeat by Sparta. When this was replaced in a similar way 90 years later part of the mud brick superstructure was encased inside the new stone base.

The original wall was damaged, possibly by an earthquake, during the first half of the war with Sparta. It was repaired and strengthened, probably during the Peace of Nicias (421–416 BC). At about this time a low stone wall (*proteichisma*), fronted with a moat, was built 7 to 8 metres (about 25 feet) in front of the main wall to protect it from enemy sappers. The troops defending this low wall would normally have withdrawn through postern gates in the main wall if the *proteichisma* was in danger of being overrun. A postern gate about 1.5 metres (5 feet) wide was discovered next to the south tower of the Sacred Gate.

The gates

The walls were pierced by about fifteen gates and a number of small posterns or sally ports. The two gates uncovered in the Kerameikos were the most prestigious and probably the

△ The walls south of the Sacred Gate.

▽ The wall south of the Sacred Gate, with the mud brick superstructure found inside the later stone foundation.

▽ A section through the wall showing its successive foundations.

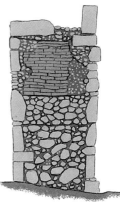

△ A reconstruction of the Dipylon (left) and Sacred gates as they might have appeared in the fifth century BC, before the forward defences (*proteichisma*) and moat were added.

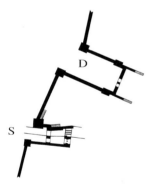

△ A plan of the Dipylon (D) and Sacred (S) gates.

▽ A plan of the Piraeic Gate; (A) at the time of Themistocles, (B) in the fourth century BC.

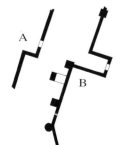

most strongly fortified on the whole circuit. They are both of 'courtyard' type, set back from the line of the wall so that an enemy approaching the gates had to pass between two towers and across a small courtyard flanked by walls with a sentry walk on top before reaching the gate. The more northerly Dipylon ('double gate') has the largest 'courtyard' (22 metres/72 feet by 41 metres/135 feet) in Greece. The fact that it was used for the Panathenaic procession, with the Panathenaic Way passing through it, is probably the main reason for its size. The enormous crowd of participants, including cavalry and chariots, must have waited in the courtyard and outside the gates for the call to take their place in the procession.

The Sacred Gate was also used for a procession, that to Eleusis, but it was also the outlet for the Eridanus, flowing under the Sacred Way. The design of the gate was modified several times and the Eridanus re-channelled, but the plan remained basically the same, with the Eridanus lapping the north wall of the courtyard and the Sacred Way hugging the south wall.

The birth of a naval power

A secure overseas grain supply for Athens demanded a strong navy, and a strong navy demanded a secure base. The architect of Athenian naval power was Themistocles. As early as 493 BC he had begun developing and fortifying the rocky promon-tory of Piraeus with its three natural enclosed harbours. Prior to this, Athenian warships had been beached in the bay of Phaleron, open to the weather and to enemy attack. The failure of a fleet of fifty Athenian warships to carry the day in a conflict with Aegina in 484 BC had emphasised the city's lack of a truly powerful navy.

Themistocles persuaded the humiliated Athenians to use a rich strike of silver made at Laurium in 483-82 BC to build up their navy. This decision, taken at great personal sacrifice by the people who would otherwise have shared out the money, meant that when the Persians invaded in 480 BC Athens was able to launch a fleet of 200 warships.

The wooden walls of Athens

On the eve of the Persian invasion ambassadors had been sent to the oracle at Delphi to seek guidance from the priestess of Apollo. The oracle's reply, 'Put your trust in wooden walls', was characteristically elusive.

Themistocles convinced the assembly that the advice meant they must put their trust in their wooden ships. (One must wonder whether he had bribed the priestess to give such a response.) In any event, he convinced the Athenians that their only hope of salvation lay in evacuating the city and fighting the Persians at sea.

The fortification of Piraeus

With the city itself secure, Themistocles persuaded the Athenians to complete the development and fortification of Piraeus. Piraeus had a landlocked harbour, Kantharos, on its northern side and two smaller harbours, Munichia and Zea, on the southern side. The fortifications narrowed the entrances to the harbours so that they could be closed by chains. The remains of ship-sheds have been found around all the harbours.

The fortifications were finished by 476 BC. Later, as increasing numbers of people, particularly foreign traders, settled in the port, the architect and town planner Hippodamus of Miletus was called in to lay out the town on a rectangular grid.

The price of greatness

Themistocles was one of the two outstanding leaders of Athens. His strategy at Salamis won him the admiration of all Greeks – all, that is, except the Athenians. With the Persians defeated, the threat their invasion had posed seemed less real, and many Athenians blamed Themistocles for the destruction of the city. His obsession with Piraeus made many forget what he had done for Athens. Soon after the completion of the fortifications he fell out of favour and was exiled.

Ship-sheds

Remains of ship-sheds for sheltering and repairing the triremes have been found at all three harbours. Zea, the larger of the two southern harbours, was the main military harbour with 196 ship-sheds. The smaller Munichia harbour had 82. The remainder of the fleet must have been housed on the southern side of Kantharos, the much larger mercantile harbour to the north, where 94 ship-sheds have been found. In the fourth century BC, when Athens again became the predominant naval power, there were 372 ship-sheds.

The installations in the Zea harbour appear to have been arranged in units of four, each shed being separated from the next by a row of columns. The sheds, which were somewhat over 40 metres (131 feet) long, were actually covered slipways, up which the triremes could be hauled or winched clear of the water.

The arsenal of Philon

Some of the equipment for the fleet was stored aboard the ships or in the ship-sheds themselves, but most was kept in large storehouses.

△ An aerial view of modern Piraeus.

The Arsenal of Philon is the best known of these storehouses. It was built behind the Zea ship-sheds, opposite the entrance to the

△ The same view as it might have appeared in 430 BC. Munichia harbour is in the foreground with Zea in the centre and Kantharos in the background.

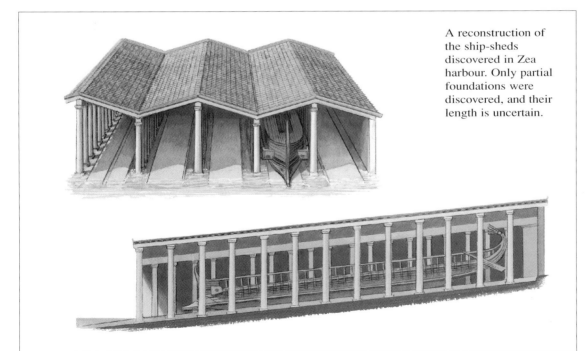

A reconstruction of the ship-sheds discovered in Zea harbour. Only partial foundations were discovered, and their length is uncertain.

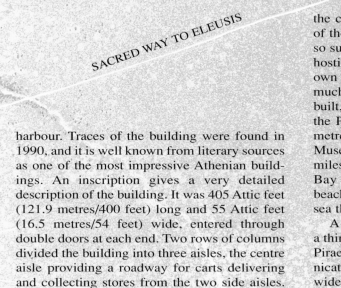

SACRED WAY TO ELEUSIS

harbour. Traces of the building were found in 1990, and it is well known from literary sources as one of the most impressive Athenian buildings. An inscription gives a very detailed description of the building. It was 405 Attic feet (121.9 metres/400 feet) long and 55 Attic feet (16.5 metres/54 feet) wide, entered through double doors at each end. Two rows of columns divided the building into three aisles, the centre aisle providing a roadway for carts delivering and collecting stores from the two side aisles. Each pair of columns formed a separate store-room lined with shelves for ships' cables and equipment, while sails were kept in large chests on the floor.

The long walls

When the Athenians came to the defence of Megara in 460 BC they quickly grasped the defensive weakness of the town, nearly 2 kilometres (1¼ miles) from its harbour at Nisaea on

the coast. The building of walls on either side of the road joining the town to the port proved so successful that as soon as there was a lull in hostilities the Athenians decided to equip their own city with a similar defensive system, on a much larger scale. Initially two walls were built, one 6 kilometres (3¾ miles) long from the Pnyx Hill to Piraeus and the other 5 kilometres (3 miles) long from the foot of the Museion Hill to Phaleron, 5 kilometres (3 miles) south-east of Piraeus. This left open the Bay of Phaleron, where ships were still beached, but as long as Athens controlled the sea this was not a risk.

A few years later, on the advice of Pericles, a third wall was built to the south of the wall to Piraeus and parallel to it, enclosing a communication corridor about 167 metres (550 feet) wide between the city and the port. Much easier to defend, this corridor made the Phaleron wall irrelevant and there is no evidence that the original wall was ever used. The line of the two Piraeus walls is fairly well established by remains along its route, but the line of the Phaleron wall is mainly conjectural.

The Long Walls were demolished as part of the peace agreement in 404 BC, but the two walls to Piraeus were rebuilt early in the fourth century BC.

An aerial view looking west across the Athenian plain from above Mount Lycabettus, with the island of Salamis in the background. The Sacred Way to Eleusis, which entered the city through the Sacred Gate, gave access from Athens to all parts of Greece.

A, B, C The three great suburban gymnasia of Athens:

A Academy

B Lyceum

C Kynosarges

THE CRADLE OF DEMOCRACY

Athens was the world's first democracy, though Athenian democracy differed in many important respects from our own. The popular assembly, open to all citizens, met in the Agora, which may therefore be considered the cradle of democracy.

Fifth-century Athenian democracy was concerned above all with the limitation of power. It was a democracy in the sense that all matters were decided by the vote of the citizen assembly, the *ekklesia*. Because women, non-Athenians and slaves were excluded from citizenship, however, they did not participate in the *ekklesia*. Athenian democracy was therefore less truly representative than our own. But it was also in some ways more powerful. Democracy had evolved in Athens as a means of limiting the powers first of the king, then of the aristocracy, and finally of popular leaders (tyrants). Most public offices were allocated by drawing lots, and any person becoming too powerful or ambitious could be banished for ten years. The chief aim of the system was to prevent any individual or group from gaining too much power, and to eliminate corruption. This aim was central to every aspect of government and the administration of the law in classical Athens.

The Agora

It was only natural that the Agora or market-place should also be the political and legal centre of the city. Here were found the municipal offices and the law courts. But here also were the shops and stalls of the traders, and the fountain where the women came each morning to draw water, to do their washing and to meet. Here too were the stoas, the open-fronted covered buildings where business could be done, where friends could meet, and where philosophers would expound their views; the Stoics actually took their name from these buildings.

Most Athenian men with time on their hands would spend it in the Agora in discussion with friends. The Agora was planted with plane trees soon after the retreat of the Persians, to provide more shade. Each summer, at the time of the festival of Athena, the Agora was turned into a sports stadium, with a racetrack running down the centre and temporary stands erected for the spectators.

The Persian destruction

The Persians had destroyed most of the buildings in the Agora. The civic buildings had been at the foot of the Kolonus Agoraeus, the low hill bordering the Agora on the west.

△ A boundary stone discovered in the south-west corner of the Agora. The inscription reads 'I am the boundary of the Agora'.

▷ The west side of the Agora, where the main civic buildings stood, with the temple of Hephaestus looking over them from the Kolonus Agoraeus, the low hill west of the Agora.

△ A reconstruction of the Painted Stoa. This meeting place was built in a prime position on the northern boundary of the Agora, looking up the Panathenaic Way to the Acropolis. It gave protection from the north wind and from the high summer sun, but made the most of the low winter sun.

The Bouleuterion, the meeting house of the Council of 500, was not beyond repair. It appears to have been patched up and used for another sixty years before being replaced by a new building. The Royal Stoa in the north-west corner of the Agora, the Heliaia or law courts, and the fountain house in the south-east corner were also patched up. These were the essentials for life to continue.

The excavation of the Agora undertaken by the American School of Classical Studies at Athens began in 1931 and is still continuing. It is a triumph of modern archaeological techniques and it was only as a result of painstaking analysis that sense could be made of the maze of foundations that have been uncovered. The Agora today provides a bewildering snapshot of over 1500 years of constant building and rebuilding.

The Painted Stoa

Soon after the retreat of the Persians a new stoa, the Painted Stoa, was erected at the north end of the Agora. This was to become the most famous of all the stoas. Archaeological and literary evidence suggest that the front was a simple colonnade of Doric columns, while a row of Ionic columns inside supported the roof.

This stoa received its name (*poikile*, 'painted') from the series of large paintings which decorated its walls. These were painted on wooden panels by the three great Athenian painters of the day, Polygnotus, Micon and Panaenus. The paintings depicted the great Athenian military events: Theseus' war with the Amazons, the Trojan War, the victory over the Spartans at Oenoe and the Battle of Marathon. These were still in place when the Greek travel writer Pausanias visited Athens 600 years later. The stoa was also hung with victory trophies such as shields. A shield captured from the Spartans during the Peloponnesian War was discovered during the excavations.

Some forty years later another stoa, dedicated to Zeus Eleutherius (the Deliverer), was built just to the south of the Royal Stoa. It was also built in the Doric style, but with projecting

△ A Spartan shield taken at Pylos in 425/4 BC and exhibited as a trophy in the Painted Stoa. The inscription reads 'The Athenians from the Lacedaemonians [Spartans] at Pylos'.

▽ A reconstruction of the Agora in about 400 BC, seen from the east. A plan of this same area is shown on p. 27. In the bottom left hand corner is the Mint, with the south-east fountain house behind. Next to this is the South Stoa. The Pnyx assembly platform is above the stoa to the left and the Hill of the Nymphs above the stoa to the centre. The circular building in the centre is the Tholos, with the old Bouleuterion to the right of it.

wings. A third stoa, the Stoa of the Herms, also stood in this area, but no trace of it has yet been found. It was probably just west of the Painted Stoa.

The evolution of democracy

Aristotle wrote a detailed description of the Athenian constitution. Together with the works of the Athenian historians, this allows us to understand the stages by which democracy evolved in Athens.

In about 950 BC the Athenian monarchy was replaced by aristocratic rule (oligarchy). Three aristocratic magistrates (archons) were elected every ten years: the *basileos* or king archon, who took over the religious duties of the king; the *polemarch* who led the army, and the 'eponymous archon' (so called because the

decade for which he held office was named after him) who had jurisdiction in civil matters. Over the succeeding centuries the power of the aristocracy was gradually restricted, and more power devolved to the citizens. In 683 BC the power of the archons was limited by making the office an annual one. Their power was further reduced by increasing their number to ten. These reforms were made by the aristocracy themselves to limit the power of individuals.

Although they were elected by the assembly, the archons were always members of the aristocracy. After their year of office they entered the Council of the Areopagus, which acted as an advisory body to the archons. It was extremely conservative, its members holding office for life. It also acted as a court for trying murder, attempted murder and arson.

The reforms of Solon

The late seventh and sixth centuries BC were a time of great political upheaval as the aristocracy and the common citizens struggled for power. In about 594 BC the moderate and universally respected aristocrat Solon was elected archon, to bring about a reconciliation between the commons and the aristocracy. Solon passed laws limiting the power of the old aristocracy. He also passed laws to protect the poor from oppression by the rich, and established law courts where people could be tried by their fellow citizens. But his most significant reform was the creation of the *boule*, a body of 500 representatives of the citizens who took over from the Council of the Areopagus the task of preparing the agenda for the popular assembly.

Tyranny

Civil disorder continued, however, until Pisistratus seized power as popular leader or *tyrannos*. This term is hard to translate. Originally a non-Greek word, it meant something like 'chief' or 'boss', but came to be applied specifically to leaders of revolutionary movements against aristocratic power: the English word 'tyrant' is not equivalent. Pisistratus died in 527 BC and his son Hippias ruled, with increasing despotism, until his brother was murdered in 514 BC and he himself was ousted in 510 BC.

The aristocracy was unable to regain power. Cleisthenes, the archon for 508/7 BC, abolished the old tribal organisation of Athenian society and divided the citizens into ten new tribes, each of which supplied fifty men for the *boule*

▽ The new Bouleuterion is behind the old one. The temple on the hill is the Temple of Hephaestus on the Kolonus Agoraeus. To the front and right of the temple is the Stoa of Zeus with the Royal Stoa next to it. The Altar of the Twelve Gods is in the larger enclosure in front of the two stoas. The Panathenaic Way passes next to these, running towards the Dipylon and Sacred gates in the distance. The Painted Stoa is to the right of the road.

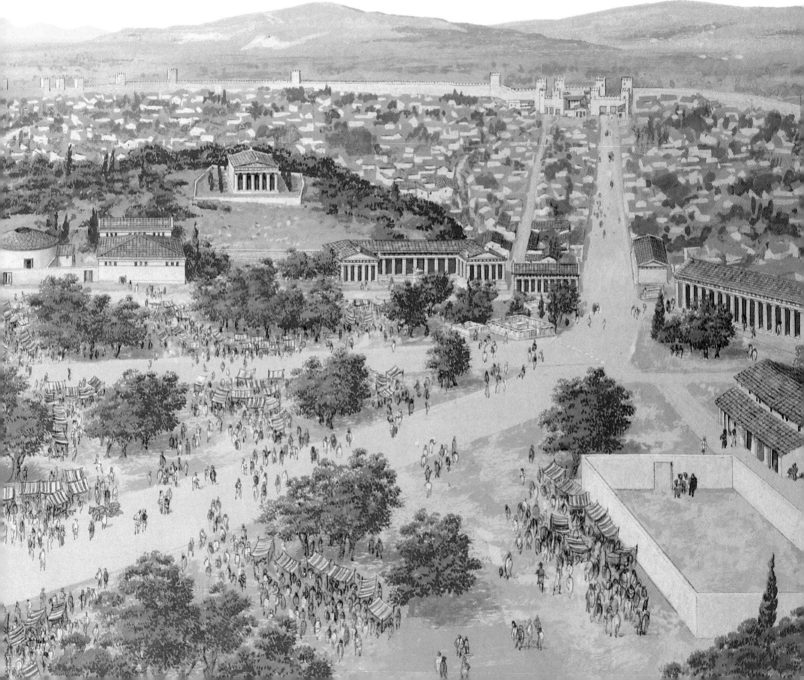

▷ A reconstruction of the round Tholos building, with the old Bouleuterion to the right and the new Bouleuterion behind it. The Temple of Hephaestus is in the background.

△ A reconstructed plan of the Tholos building, showing a possible arrangement of the 25 dining couches.

see p. 26). Cleisthenes also introduced the system of ostracism (see p. 28).

Democracy established

In 487 BC a law was passed specifying that candidates for the archonship were to be selected by lot, rather than elected. This broke the hold of the aristocracy over the office of archon, and reduced the power of the Council of the Areopagus. This system of appointment by lot was eventually extended to most of the formerly elected offices. Further laws passed twenty years later reduced the Council of the Areopagus to a law court for murder trials.

▽ The remains of the Tholos building.

▷ An antefix 30.6 cm (1 foot) high, from the roof of the Tholos building.

▽ Eave tiles from the roof of the Tholos building with an antefix in place. The main part of the roof was covered with diamond-shaped tiles.

The rise of Athenian imperial power was also important. Tributes and levies allowed state payments to be made for the performance of civic duties. This allowed poorer citizens to participate equally in politics. By the middle of the fifth century power resided largely in the assembly of the people (the *ekklesia*).

The *boule*

The 500 members of the *boule* were selected by lot and held office for a year. A member could only hold office twice, and not in successive years. Each tribal group was on duty for thirty-six days at a time, working three shifts, with a minimum of seventeen members at hand night and day to handle any urgent business. They had to call an assembly at least four times during their thirty-six days, and they had to prepare the agenda for the assembly. The members of the *boule* were paid, and those on duty were fed at public expense.

The Bouleuterion, where the *boule* met, was a square building some 23 metres (75 feet) wide. Practically nothing now survives above the foundations, but the building may have had tiers of benches on the north, west and east

sides. Towards the end of the fifth century BC a new building was erected immediately to the west of the old one. Again only the foundations survive. It was smaller than the old building, measuring about 16 by 22 metres (52½ by 72 feet), and it is hard to see what advantage this had over the older building, which was still standing.

The Tholos and the Eponymous Heroes

A third building in this area of the Agora is equally enigmatic. This is a round building 18.32 metres (60 feet) in circumference. It has been identified as the Tholos, where the fifty

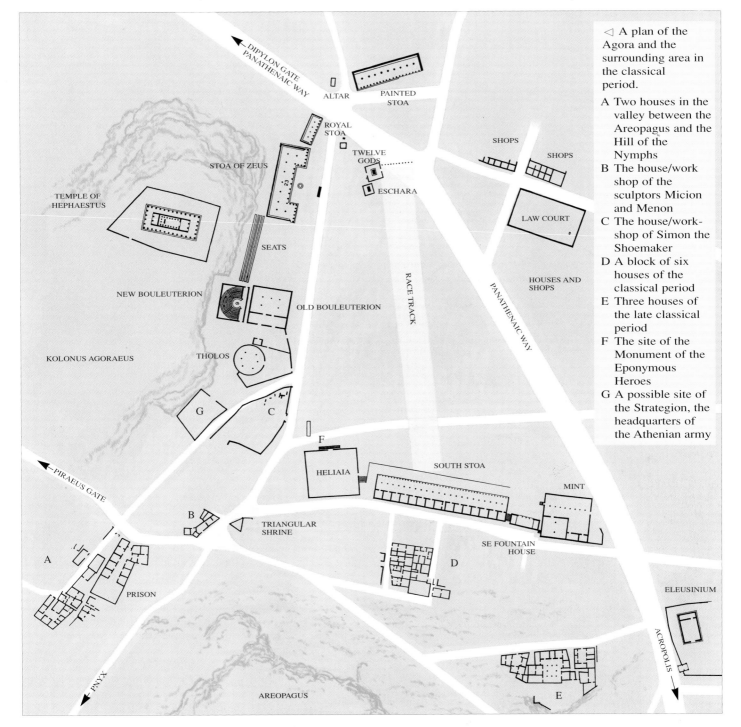

◁ A plan of the Agora and the surrounding area in the classical period.

A Two houses in the valley between the Areopagus and the Hill of the Nymphs
B The house/work shop of the sculptors Micion and Menon
C The house/work-shop of Simon the Shoemaker
D A block of six houses of the classical period
E Three houses of the late classical period
F The site of the Monument of the Eponymous Heroes
G A possible site of the Strategion, the headquarters of the Athenian army

THE ANCIENT CITY: ATHENS

duty members of the *boule* ate at public expense. The problem is that only about twenty-five dining couches could be fitted into the space available.

The Tholos also housed the official weights and measures. Several standard models, such as a marble tile used for checking the size of terracotta tiles, were set up in front of the building.

One further structure in the Agora can be included among the buildings associated with Athenian democracy: the monument of the Eponymous Heroes. This was

△ An *ostrakon* with the name Themistocles scratched on it. This is one of over a thousand *ostraka* found during the Agora excavations.

set up in honour of the heroes who gave their names to the ten Athenian tribes established by Cleisthenes in 508/7 BC. Members of each could find notices concerning their tribe displayed on the monument base beneath the appropriate hero. Other more general notices were also displayed here.

Ostracism

Ostracism was a uniquely Athenian system. Recognising that it would be difficult to prove before a court that a particular individual posed a threat to democracy, Cleisthenes devised a system by which, if a sufficient number of people believed it to be so, the individual concerned could be banished for ten years.

If necessary an *ostrakophoria* could be held once a year, in the winter. On an agreed day a wooden barrier was erected around the Agora with ten gates in it, one for each tribe. Voting, which was supervised by the archons and the members of the *boule*, was done by writing the name of the offender on a broken piece of pot (*ostrakon*). More than 6,000 votes had to be cast for an ostracism to take place. Once sentenced, the offender had ten days to move his place of abode out of Attica. No confiscation of property or other penalty was imposed.

Many *ostraka* were found during the excavation of the Agora and the Kerameikos. Some examples bore such names as Aristeides, Cimon, Miltiades, Themistocles and Pericles.

The *ekklesia*

A minimum of 6,000 citizens had to be present before an assembly could take place. The *ekklesia* met on average once every nine days, though there could be additional emergency meetings. When an assembly was due the police, using a long rope covered in red powder, started from the north end of the Agora, driving the people up to the place of assembly. Any eligible citizen found outside the assembly with red marks on his clothes was liable to punishment. Women, slaves, resident foreigners (*metoikoi*) and children were not eligible.

The assembly was held on a great artificial platform still visible on the slopes of the Pnyx, a hill to the west of the Acropolis. The assembly had originally been held in the Agora, but shortly before the Persian Wars it had been transferred to the slopes of the Pnyx, and it finally moved to the specially-built platform towards the end of the fifth century.

The speakers addressed the assembly from a platform near the top of the hill. The *ekklesia* could only discuss matters prepared by the *boule*, but it could order the *boule* to bring a particular matter before it at its next meeting. Any citizen could express an opinion at the assembly and a vote was taken by a simple show of hands.

▽ A plan and elevation of the artificial Pnyx assembly platform constructed in 404/3 BC. The earth platform was supported by a massive stone retaining wall. It had two stairways leading up to it. The speaker stood on the dais (A) to address the assembly. The area was enlarged in 330-326 BC, as shown by the red line.

A Speaker's dais
B Steps to the original platform
C Remains of steps to the enlarged platform

◁ A view of the Pnyx during excavations carried out there in the 1890s. The Pnyx itself is on the left, while the hill of the nymphs is on the right.

The Herms

Numerous fragments of Herms were found during the Agora excavations. A Herm was a rectangular column with a phallus halfway up and a head of the god Hermes at the top. Most had rectangular protrusions at the shoulders on which garlands could be hung. They were religious figures, set up to mark entrances, roads and street corners. There were so many at the north-west entrance to the Agora that the area was known simply as 'the Herms'. The most famous Herm, carved by Alcamenes, stood at the entrance to the Acropolis.

One night in 415 BC a group of young men were alleged to have mutilated many of the Herms, possibly while drunk. The episode may have been set up as a political smear: Alcibiades, one of the commanders of the army campaigning in Sicily, was suspected of being involved. He was recalled and sent into exile, a contributing factor to the greatest Athenian military disaster.

Law and order

The law was an essential part of democracy and the Athenians went to great lengths to ensure fairness and stamp out corruption.

The main Athenian court was the Helaia, which may have sat in the south-west corner of the Agora. The Helaia heard all cases other than those concerning state officials and murder. State officials were tried by their peers in the *boule*. Very serious crimes against the state were tried by the assembly.

Murder was tried by various courts, depending on the circumstances of the crime. The main murder court was that of the Areopagus, which judged premeditated or attempted murder, and arson where life was endangered. It could inflict the death penalty for murder, or exile with confiscation of property for lesser offences.

Manslaughter

Cases of manslaughter and incitement to murder were tried at the Palladium. The maximum sentence this court could inflict was a period of exile. Cases of homicide which the king archon (*basileos*) considered justifiable or having mitigating circumstances were heard at the Delphinium, with the king archon presiding.

There was also a rather strange but typically Athenian court for trying a citizen who was already in exile for manslaughter and had subsequently committed first degree murder. The trial was held by the sea with the accused offering his defence from a boat.

The scapegoat

The fifth and last murder court was held outside the Prytaneum. This was a religious court, concerned with cleansing the state of the defilement caused by a murder when the culprit was unknown. It was presided over by the king archon and the ten tribal 'kings'. It condemned the unidentified culprit and pronounced solemn sentence on a scapegoat animal, or an object which had been the cause of the death, and cast it into exile. A similar religious response to crime can be found in many ancient societies.

Trial by jury

The development of the law and its administration in Athens had run parallel to the development of democracy. A concern for limiting abuses of power was central to both. All lawbreakers were tried by a jury selected from the citizens. But the Athenians also relied on wide participation to limit corruption. Juries were enormous: the minimum size was 201, the normal size 501, and 1001, 1501 and even 2001 jurors were not unknown. The extra one was to avoid an evenly split decision.

The selection of juries

The method of selecting jurors and judges was extremely complicated. Its aim was to prevent the accused or his accusers identifying the jurors in advance and bribing them. Aristotle outlines the method in *The Athenian Constitution*. Each citizen was on jury service for a year. He was issued with a bronze ticket (*pinakion*) bearing his full name (personal

△ A Herm. Remains of several of these guardians of entrances were found during the Agora excavations.

name, father's name and his deme, or tribal subdivision) and an official stamp. On the day of the trial those on jury service assembled in the Agora at dawn. A magistrate placed their *pinakioi* in a basket according to tribe, which he could identify from the deme marked on each.

The allotting device

The magistrate then placed the tickets in the allotting device. Pieces of these devices were found during the excavations in the Agora. The device consisted of a rectangular stone block with ten vertical columns and numerous horizontal rows of tiny slots, into which the tickets were fitted. Alongside this grid was a bronze tube with its top in the form of a funnel, and with a crank at the bottom.

The tickets of the first tribe were placed in the first column. The second tribe's tickets were inserted in the second, and so on. A number of white marbles equal to one tenth of the

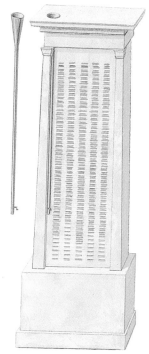

△ A reconstruction of an allotting device, with the trumpet-shaped tube for the black and white marbles shown separately.

▷ Part of an allotting machine found in the Agora.

△ A reconstruction of a fifth-century water clock belonging to the Antiochid tribe, found in the Agora. It ran for approximately six minutes. These clocks were used to time speeches in the law courts.

number of jurors required was mixed with black marbles up to the total number of complete horizontal rows of tickets. The marbles were then tipped into the funnel. The magistrate released them one at a time with the crank. If a white marble came out first, the first row of tickets, one from each column, was selected. If a black marble came out first the candidates represented by tickets in the first row were dismissed. The crank was then turned for the second row, and the process was continued until the required number of jurors was selected. The tribes were thus equally represented in all juries.

Each selected juror was then given a bronze disc telling him which court he must attend. He returned this after the trial and was paid for his jury service. Judges were selected in a similar way and probably voted with the jury.

The police

The Athenians had no police force in the modern sense, but they did have a corps of Scythian archers. These were public slaves who were more like court ushers than crime fighters.

The law was enforced by a group of magistrates known as the Eleven or the Criminal Commissioners, who were assisted by slaves. The Eleven were responsible for arresting malefactors and running the state prisons.

The trial of Socrates

The most famous Athenian trial was that of the philosopher Socrates. Socrates was a free thinker who fell foul of the Thirty Tyrants because of his liberal views. In the backlash that followed the overthrow of the Tyrants he then fell foul of the democrats, because one of his ex-pupils, Critias, was a member of the Thirty. The charges against Socrates were brought by a religious fanatic named Meletus.

There was no public prosecutor in Athenian courts; any citizen could bring charges. To limit false accusations, any accuser who failed to win one fifth of the jurors' votes was heavily fined. In court the accuser put his case and the accused defended himself. Each was allowed a fixed time, measured by a water clock, to make his speech.

The presiding magistrate was normally one of the three main archons. The *basileos* or king archon presided when the case concerned homicide or religion, the civil archon if it was a civil case brought by a citizen and the *polemarch* in cases involving non-citizens. Six junior archons (*thesmothetae*) presided over cases where the material interests of the state were involved. The magistrate collected sworn statements of witnesses and recorded the details of the accusation and of the defence.

The formal charge against Socrates was one of failing to worship the state gods and 'introducing new and unfamiliar religious practices and corrupting the young'. The prosecutor demanded the death penalty.

Socrates argued that the charge itself was contradictory, and almost certainly succeeded only in confusing the jurors. On the other hand, the case put by Meletus was made more difficult by an amnesty proclaimed after the democratic counter-revolution of 404/3 BC, which covered the events in question. Nevertheless he managed to obtain a guilty verdict.

The decision

The jurors took no formal part in the proceedings, though they would often show their sympathies. Their job was simply to vote guilty or innocent. They cast their votes as they left the court, dropping a token (a pebble or shell) into a receptacle for guilty or for innocent.

This method of voting had the drawback of revealing which way each juror had voted. A new system was introduced during the fourth century BC, using a small bronze device like a child's top, a disc with a rod through the middle. The rod was either solid for innocent or hollow for guilty. Each juror was issued one of each. He held one between the thumb and forefinger of each hand, concealing the ends of the rod. As he filed past the two urns he cast his decision in the first, discarding the remaining token in the second. Several of these tokens were found during the Agora excavations.

Punishment

In general the punishments were mild, consisting of fines, confiscation of property, loss of civic rights or exile. Imprisonment was usually for foreign residents (*metoikoi*) or those awaiting execution. Flogging, branding and the pillory were used for slaves. Capital punishment was reserved for premeditated murder and other serious crimes, and took various forms. Poisoning, stoning and beheading were all practised, as was a form of crucifixion. The last entailed being fastened to a board with iron clamps and left to die. In 1915 a grave was found at Phaleron containing the skeletons of seventeen people who had been executed in this way. They still had the iron clamps around their necks, wrists and ankles. The Athenians executed the rebellious Samians in this way in 439 BC, but put them out of their misery after ten days by clubbing them to death.

At the end of his trial Socrates was asked to suggest what his sentence should be. Everyone expected him to suggest banishment, especially as the prosecution had demanded the death penalty. But Socrates could never agree to leave his beloved Athens. He suggested a fine. The jury, who had hoped he would voluntarily go into exile, were exasperated and sentenced him to death by poisoning, using hemlock.

The execution

Socrates was taken to the state prison, which might be identified with a building just beyond the south-west corner of the Agora. This building, some 17 metres (56 feet) wide and 40 metres (131 feet) long, is divided along its length by a corridor with five square cells on the right and three on the left. The corridor leads through to a walled courtyard at the rear. There is a complex of four rooms to the left of the entrance which may have had an upper floor. These were possibly offices. Thirteen small medicine bottles were found in one of these offices which may have been used for hemlock.

The philosopher's friends bribed the guards to let him escape, but he refused as it would imply he was guilty. At sunset the executioner gave him hemlock to drink. According to Plato, he walked around the cell until his legs began to go numb, then lay down on the bed while the numbness gradually spread through his body. In fact, hemlock causes vomiting and severe convulsions before death: Plato clearly wished to dignify the death of his teacher, friend and hero.

△ A ballot box found in the law court in the north-east corner of the Agora, and two bronze ballots marked *psephos demosia* (public ballot). The ballot with the hollow axle was for guilty and that with the solid axle for innocent.

◁ Three of the medicine bottles found in the prison. These may have been used to hold the hemlock for executions.

◁ A reconstruction of the prison just beyond the south-west corner of the Agora.

DAILY LIFE

Life in fifth-century BC Athens offered the individual every opportunity to develop his full potential as a citizen – but only for freeborn males. The lives of girls and women were governed by restrictions which we would find very oppressive.

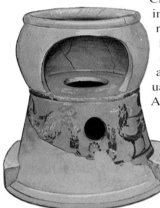

△ A terracotta high chair reconstructed from pieces found in the Agora.

▷ A red-figure vase painting showing a mother with her baby in a high chair.

Childbirth in fifth-century Athens was cloaked in ritual. The father's family smeared pitch round the house when labour started, symbolically advising friends and neighbours of the event as well as ritually isolating the mother and her helpers. The ancient origin of such ritual acts may have been as obscure to classical Athenians as to us.

Babies were delivered by the women of the family. A midwife was called only in cases of serious complications. The new-born baby was wrapped in the traditional swaddling clothes, a long strip of linen, to restrict its movements. The father hung an olive branch at the front door of the family house to proclaim the birth of a boy, or a strip of cloth for a girl.

Unwanted babies

The Athenians did not favour large families. In a society in which inheritance was usually divided equally among surviving sons, splitting the family wealth between numerous sons, and daughters requiring dowries, was to be avoided. While an Athenian father would normally bring up all his sons as a civic duty, he might dispose of an unwanted daughter. Killing a baby was unlawful, but exposing a new-born baby to die was not forbidden. Abortion, too, was not illegal, though an abortion could not be performed without the express permission of the father. The philosopher Aristotle advised that abortions should be performed only before the foetus had received life and feeling.

An exposed child was usually left out in a clay pot. It was sometimes rescued by a childless woman and passed off as her own, but more often such a baby was rescued to be brought up as a slave. The famous courtesan Neaera was such an exposed baby. She was rescued by a woman who was renowned for being able to recognise future beauties by their features at birth.

The celebrations

The *amphidromia* was held about a week after the birth. This was the ritual cleansing of the mother and any member of the family who had come in contact with her during her labour. Once purified, she could return to her normal duties as a wife. It also marked the formal acceptance of the baby into the family. The father carried the baby symbolically around the hearth, and from this point it became illegal for the family to reject the child.

A banquet was held ten days after the birth. The family brought presents for the baby, including amulets which were hung around its neck as protection against evil. The father now announced the baby's name. A boy was usually given the name of his paternal grandfather. His full name would consist of his given name, his father's name, his deme (the local subdivision of his tribe) and occasionally also his tribe itself. The philosopher Socrates' full name was Socrates son of Sophroniscus of the Alopece deme. He was of the Antiochid tribe.

▽ A black-glazed terracotta feeding bottle for a baby.

Infancy

Poor women had to care for their own children, but if a couple were reasonably well off they might have two or three slaves, one of whom might be an experienced nurse. So the mother would have been spared the more arduous chores of motherhood. The baby would probably have been breast-fed by the nurse.

Toys and games
A Terracotta rattle in the shape of a pig
B Terracotta toy chariot
C Knucklebones and dice found in the Agora

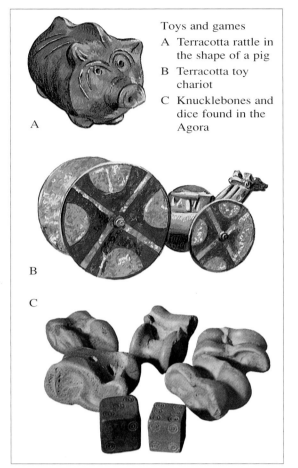

A

B

C

Athenian vase paintings show babies sitting in a type of high chair. One was found during the Agora excavations. It was made of terracotta and had a hole in the middle of the seat so that a chamber pot could be placed underneath it (babies' nappies were not used). In Aristophanes' *The Clouds*, Strepsiades, who has more than usual to do with his young son,

tells him that he understood all his baby talk:

> Wah-wah meant you wanted a drink... ma-ma meant you were hungry... and as for ca-ca – well, the moment you said that I had you out of the house and held you at arms' length.

Early childhood

The young child would have learned nursery rhymes from its mother. If she was educated she might have read stories such as Aesop's fables. Socrates could still remember these in his death cell at the age of seventy.

Many toys have been found in excavations. Rattles and balls were very popular. Vase paintings show children playing in chariots. Many dolls have been found. These are usually made of terracotta, with articulated arms and legs. Terracotta dolls of course are more likely to survive than those made of wood or cloth, and no doubt these also were common. As children grew older they would have learned to play knucklebones and dice. There were also team games. A bas-relief in the Athens Archaeological Museum shows boys playing a game very similar to hockey.

Off to school

When he was about seven a boy from a wealthier family would be taken out of the care of his nurse and placed in the charge of a *paidagogos*, a slave who accompanied him everywhere. The *paidagogos* taught him good manners and could punish him if he was naughty. He took his charge to school, often attending classes to make sure the boy did his work, and even tested him afterwards.

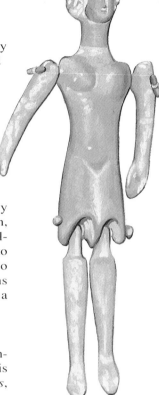

△ A terracotta articulated doll found during excavations in Athens.

▷ An Athenian red-figure vase painting showing a boy practising writing with a stylus on wax tablets.

◁ An Athenian red-figure vase painting showing a boy playing with a hoop.

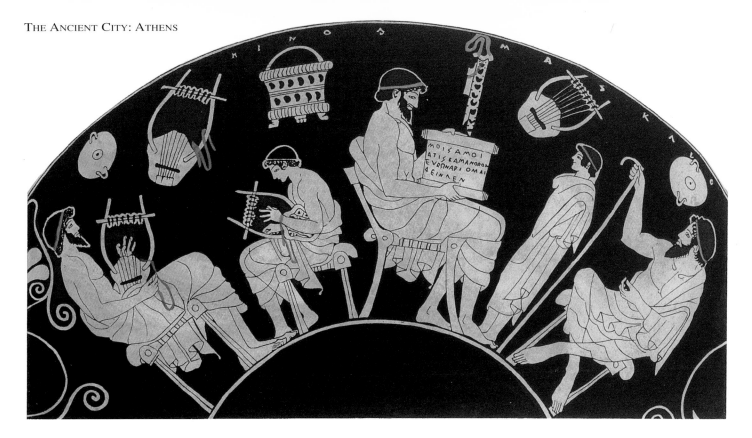

△ An Athenian red-figure vase painting showing teachers instructing boys in music and reading.

All except the poorest boys went to school. Classes took place from about half an hour after daybreak until about half an hour before dusk. There was a law forbidding children from being taken to and from school in the dark.

Reading, writing and arithmetic

Classes were held in the private houses of teachers. The boys were taught basic reading, writing and arithmetic. They also had to learn verses from the great poet Homer, and quoted him aloud in a group.

There were no desks. Vase paintings show boys sitting on stools holding wood-backed wax writing tablets. They wrote on the wax with a stylus, a sort of bone or metal pencil pointed at one end and flattened out in a leaf shape at the other. Many of these have been found. The flattened end was used for smoothing out the wax to make corrections. Occasionally they were allowed to write properly, with a reed pen and ink on papyrus. All books were written on papyrus, and rolled up in scrolls rather than bound in pages.

After two or three years, pupils were introduced to music. The boys were taught to sing and to play the lyre and the flute. Ancient Greeks loved to sing, accompanying themselves on the lyre. The pupils were also introduced to more complicated lyric poetry.

A healthy body

Physical education took precedence over all other activities from about the age of twelve. The boys now came under the authority of the *paidotribes*, an austere man with a purple cloak and a long two-branched stick, who taught gymnastics and other physical exercise. The boys were divided into two groups by age. Classes were held in a *palaistra*, an open-air sports ground surrounded by a colonnade under which the boys did their academic lessons. There were also rooms behind the colonnade for changing and bathing and a shop where they could buy oil and fine sand needed for exercising.

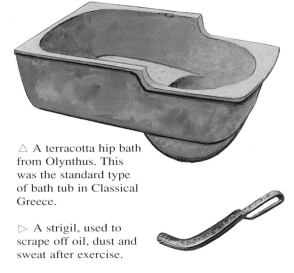

△ A terracotta hip bath from Olynthus. This was the standard type of bath tub in Classical Greece.

▷ A strigil, used to scrape off oil, dust and sweat after exercise.

The boys stripped totally to exercise. They washed down, rubbed themselves with oil and sprinkled themselves with fine sand or dust as a protection against chills. After limbering up to music they performed such sports as throwing the discus and the javelin, running, jumping and wrestling.

Wrestling

The *palaistra* was named from wrestling (*pale*). The boys had to break up the earth to soften it before wrestling. The object of the sport was to throw one's opponent to the ground.

After exercising, the boys went to the bath house to clean up. Each boy had a strigil, a metal scraper to remove the oil and dust, and also a sponge to wash down. No gymnasium has been fully excavated in Athens. There is a round bath house outside the Dipylon Gate. A similar bath house forms part of the gymnasium at Eretria on the island of Euboea. These were furnished with hip baths. They had no integral heating system and relied on braziers for heat.

Education for girls

We do not know how much education Athenian girls received. Middle and upper class girls learned to read, write and probably play the lyre from a female tutor at home. They only performed physical exercises at festivals, and probably never in public as Spartan girls did. The Athenians were deeply shocked by this. But the Spartans regarded physical health in girls as an important factor in producing future generations of warriors.

Military service

Athenian boys remained at school until they were eighteen. Then they underwent military training for two years. Boys from wealthier families were fitted out with expensive hoplite armour – round shield, helmet, greaves and body armour plus spear and sword. The family had to pay for this except in the case of a boy

△ A reconstruction of an Athenian bath house. No bath house has yet been discovered intact at Athens. The reconstruction is based on ancient Greek bath houses elsewhere.

▷ An Athenian hoplite putting on his armour. This consisted of a cuirass, usually made of layers of linen, a helmet, greaves and a shield. His main weapon was a spear but he also carried a sword.

whose father had been killed in battle. Each youngster was given basic training, learning how to hold a shield so that it protected his companion on his left as well as himself. He learned the standard drill manoeuvres involved in fighting in formation (the phalanx), open order, close order, doubling and weapons handling. Much of his training was spent in the frontier forts on the borders of Attica.

Men's clothing

Most Greek clothing was made of wool, but flax was also used, as was a coarse cloth called *sakkos* made from animal hair. Greek clothing was not tailored. It was made from rectangular pieces of cloth.

Greek men wore no underwear. The basic article of clothing was the tunic. There were two types. The *exomis*, worn by slaves and those doing manual work, was fastened at the left shoulder with a pin or knot, leaving the right shoulder bare, and was tied at the waist with a girdle. The *chiton* was a more refined version, fastened at both shoulders. Children wore a short tunic without a girdle.

The Greek man also wore a *himation*, a large rectangular piece of woollen cloth which he draped over his left shoulder, bringing the back end round under his right arm and across his front. It was then either passed back over his

△ Athenian men's hair styles based on vases and sculptures. Young men usually wore their hair fairly short. Older men often had long hair and beards.

▷ The younger man is wearing a *chiton*. The older man wears a *himation* over his *chiton*. He has sturdy walking boots and wears a felt hat (*petasos*).

▷▷ Men's clothing shown on Athenian vases. The top figure shows a man wearing a refined tunic (*chiton*). The man next to him is wearing his tunic folded down to the waist. The figures in the middle show various ways of wearing the *himation*. The figure at the bottom is wearing a cloak (*chlamys*), sturdy boots, and broad-brimmed felt hat (*petasos*).

◁ A reconstruction of women's dress. The figure on the left is wearing the long tunic. The figure on the right wears a long tunic covered by a *himation* and a head-scarf. The figure in the centre has her *himation* wrapped round her.

◁◁ Figures from Athenian vases showing women's dress. The top figure wears the Doric *peplos*. The two below wear the more fashionable long Athenian tunic. The lower figures show ways of wearing the *himation*.

▽ Women's hairstyles.
A Worn in a pony tail.
B Worn up in a bun with ribbons.
C Enclosed in a head-scarf.

A

left shoulder or draped over his left arm. The surplus material hung down, covering his body right down to the lower leg. In cold weather it could be wrapped completely round the body, even covering the head.

Common also was a type of cloak, the *chlamys*, often worn by soldiers. This was made of a thicker material. It was draped round the shoulders and fastened at the throat with a clasp.

Vase paintings show men wearing footwear varying from light sandals, no more than a sole and two or three straps, to sturdy boots.

Women's dress

Women wore a woollen or linen tunic falling to the ankles. Linen was more luxurious than wool. The material was held by two pins at the shoulders, but more elaborate versions were joined at several points to form sleeves.

Women also wore the *himation*, often draped in a very similar way to the men. They are usually shown with bare feet, but this may be an artistic convention. Sometimes one can discern light sandals.

Hairstyles

In artistic representations, young men are often shown clean-shaven with short cropped hair, but they are also depicted with hair down to their shoulders or longer. Older men have beards and often very long hair.

Women invariably have long hair, but it is often pulled back in a bun or pony tail, with ribbons holding it in place. Head-scarves covering

B

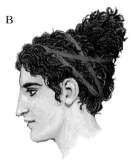

C

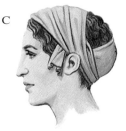

△ An Athenian red-figure vase painting showing a bride surrounded by friends bearing presents and by winged *erotes*, one of which she is holding like a baby. The little girl on her left is giving her a *lekanis*, a bowl with a lid used to hold cosmetics or small valuables. One woman, the second figure to the bride's right, carries a *lebes gamikos*, a wedding bowl with a high stand, in her right hand.

△ A *lebes gamikos* from Athens. These bowls on high stands were made exclusively for weddings.

all or part of the hair were also very fashionable. Hats are sometimes shown on the vase paintings. They are generally worn by men, in particular a broad-brimmed flat felt hat (*petasos*) resembling the shape of a sunflower.

Marriage

Marriages were arranged. The couple may not even have met, as Athenian girls lived very sheltered lives. Most men seeking a wife were in their twenties. A boy under eighteen had to ask his father's permission, or his father could arrange a suitable marriage for him.

A girl was usually fourteen or fifteen when she married. Her father did not have to seek his daughter's agreement to the marriage. All Athenian middle class girls were brought up in seclusion, and the daughter's opinion would have been thought meaningless. As Xenophon put it, '[my bride] would have known nothing of life, for until she entered my house she had lived under the most restricted conditions, trained from her childhood to see as little as possible, and to ask the minimum of questions.'

The betrothal

The bride's father agreed to the match and the betrothal took place. This was an arrangement between the suitor and the girl's father; she was not expected to attend. The betrothal was a verbal contract:
'I give you this girl that she may bring children into the world within the bond of wedlock.'
'I accept her,' the groom replied.
'I agree to provide her with a dowry of ... '
'I accept that too, with pleasure.'

The agreement was sealed by shaking hands. It is generally accepted that men wanted to make what used to be called a 'good' marriage. They did not expect to find love in the modern sense. An Athenian declared in court:

We have courtesans for pleasure, concubines to perform our domestic chores, but wives to bear us children and to be faithful guardians of our homes.

The girl could not question her father's authority, though he might seek her approval. And she might try to persuade him.

From girl to wife

A girl was legally married from the day of her betrothal, but a day was named when her father formally gave her away. Marriages usually took place at the time of the full moon. The month of Gamelion (January) was the most popular as this was sacred to Hera, the queen of the gods and patroness of marriage. The very name Gamelion means the month of marriage.

The ceremonies started on the eve of the wedding day. Sacrifice was made to Zeus, Hera, Artemis, Apollo and Peitho, the protectors of the marriage bed. The bride sadly collected mementoes of her childhood, her dolls, her toys and her clothes, and offered them to one of the wedding goddesses. An anonymous but moving record of such a dedication survives:

Timarete, daughter of Timaretos, before her wedding, has dedicated her tambourine, her pretty ball, the net that shielded her hair, her hair, and her girl's dresses to Artemis of the Lake, a virgin to a virgin, as is fit. Daughter of Leto, hold your hand over the child Timarete, and protect the pure girl in a pure way.

Then the women of the bride's family went in torchlight procession to the Fountain of Callirhoe to bring back water for her ritual bridal bath. This was both a physical cleansing and a religious purification. At his own home the groom also received a ritual bath.

Below left: An Athenian red-figure vase painting showing the bride dressing for the wedding. A girl is fastening her special bridal sandals, while a maid brings in a decorated box, possibly containing the wedding veil. Two *lebetes gamikoi* stand in front of the door and a *loutrophoros* can be seen behind the chest in the middle.

▽ An Athenian vase painting showing the bride after the wedding, accompanied by the women of both families. The woman at the far left is arranging flowers in two wedding bowls (*lebetes gamikoi*) received as presents for the bride. Another woman is arranging flowers in a *loutrophoros*, the tall vase in which the water for the bride's ritual bath was carried.

The wedding day

Both families decorated their houses with branches of olive and laurel for the wedding day. The groom, wearing a garland and anointed with myrrh, went with his family and his best man to the bride's house in the afternoon. A sacrifice was offered to the gods, and then they all sat down to a banquet. The bride was surrounded by her friends. She wore her best clothes, her head was covered by a veil and crowned with a wreath. Her matron of honour (*nympheutria*) sat by her side. The men sat separately.

△ A red-figure vase painting showing a wedding procession. The bride and groom are in a chariot following the *proegetes*, the leader of the procession. Women follow the chariot carrying the wedding presents. Two figures, one probably the bride's mother, carry torches. Torches were an essential part of the procession; an unmarried couple living together were said to have had a wedding without torches.

▽ A painting of a woman playing a cithara.

The food was traditional, including sesame cakes, a symbolic guarantee of fertility. A young boy went round the guests offering them bread and repeating the ritual formula 'I have avoided the worse; I have chosen the better.' The guests now presented their wedding gifts to the bride.

Vase paintings of wedding scenes are reasonably common. These emphasise the importance of marriage as an institution, but we have little evidence of what Athenian women thought of their position within marriage.

The procession

As night fell the bride's father gave his daughter to the groom. This was probably the moment that her veil was removed and the groom saw her face, perhaps for the first time. A procession was formed to convey the bride to her husband's house. The bride and groom were ushered into an open carriage driven by one of the groom's friends. The bride carried a sieve and a gridiron, symbols of her domestic duties. The carriage set out with the bride's relatives following on foot carrying torches and singing the marriage hymn to the accompaniment of flutes and lyres. The groom's mother and father went on ahead and waited at the door to receive the couple. His father wore a myrtle wreath and his mother carried a torch. The groom helped his bride down from the carriage and the crowd showered her with nuts and dried figs as she entered the house, where she was offered a piece of wedding cake made of sesame with honey and a date or quince, all symbols of fertility.

The groom led his bride straight to the bridal chamber his parents had prepared. He closed the door and a friend stood guard while the guests noisily sang the nuptial hymn, making as much noise as they could to ward off the evil influences. The following day the bride's parents, accompanied by flute players, brought gifts. It was probably now that the dowry was presented.

A woman's place

Men spent most of their time outside the family home, either working, performing civic duties, exercising at the gymnasium or simply socialising. Athenian men also did the shopping, though in wealthier homes this was done by trusted slaves.

Evidence is limited, but the life of a typical Athenian woman seems restricted by modern western standards. She was not only largely confined to the house, but at times also to her own part of the house, an area known as the *gynaikeion*. A wife's duty was to cook, weave and raise children. She was not expected to have a social life with her husband. Women were not specifically forbidden to go out, and could visit women friends in their homes. But respectable woman would not make such visits alone: she would be accompanied by at least one female slave.

It was customary for women to collect the water from the fountain and this was a popular place for the women to socialise. But in wealthier homes water was collected by female slaves. Poorer women may thus have had more freedom in some respects. Many poorer women also worked or kept stalls in the market.

For women only

There were certain religious festivals exclusively for women. The *Thesmophoria*, for example, was a festival specially for married women. Women may have attended the theatre, but there is much conflicting evidence. Respectable women were probably expected for the most part to stay at home, and those women who did attend were almost certainly of the lower classes. Evidence from Plato suggests that women did go to the theatre in the fourth century.

The dinner party (*symposion*) was an important social event in fifth-century Athens, but even though these parties normally took place at home, wives were not invited. Courtesans, female flute players and female dancers (these were usually foreigners or slaves) were sometimes present, but such parties were not considered suitable for respectable women.

A

B

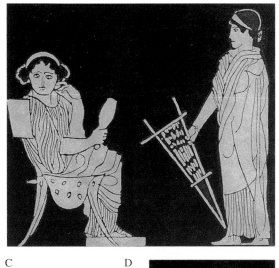

C

D

Scenes from domestic life shown on Athenian red-figure vases.

A Penelope, the wife of Odysseus, sitting at the loom.

B Preparing wool for spinning; the seated woman is rolling the coarse died wool on her leg as a preliminary to spinning.

C The seated woman is holding a roll of wool while the standing woman holds an embroidery frame.

D A maid carrying wedding presents.

E Women airing clothes.

Actual evidence of the lives and thoughts of the women of ancient Athens is very limited. It is therefore unwise to speculate on how Athenian women felt about their lives. However, there must have been many husbands and wives who loved each other, despite social attitudes which we would find restrictive.

E

△ The Sacred Way to Eleusis where it begins in the Kerameikos, just outside the walls of Athens. This area was a popular burial spot and graves have been found along all the roads leading from it.

▷ A red-figure vase painting showing women laying out a corpse on a bier.

Divorce

Divorce was easy for men but very difficult for women. A husband had the absolute right to divorce his wife without justification. If his wife was proved to be adulterous he was compelled by law to divorce her. He would also be expected to divorce a barren wife, as producing children was the prime purpose of marriage. A husband divorcing his wife had to return her dowry, and this may have saved many marriages.

Continual violence was probably the only real grounds on which a woman could sue for divorce. Euripides' *Medea* includes the comment that 'women have no right to repudiate their husbands'.

Sickness

Medicine came of age in classical Greece. The father of true medicine, Hippocrates, was born in about 460 BC on the island of Cos. His dictum: 'I shall administer no poison to any person, even at their request; I shall never administer abortifacients to a woman. Whatsoever house I enter, I shall go there for the healing of the sick, and abstain from all wilful wrong-doings or misdemeanours, and in particular from any seduction of women or boys, slave no less than free', has been the oath of doctors ever since.

There were many private doctors, but Athens also had a health service operated by doctors appointed and paid for by the state. These men were selected after declaring their qualifications before the *ekklesia*. Doctors performed quite sophisticated operations, as can be seen from instruments found in excavations. There were specialists such as dentists, who used lead or gold fillings, and oculists using eye-baths. There were also, of course, faith healers, practising in the sanctuary of Asclepius, the god of healing, on the south slope of the Acropolis next to the Theatre of Dionysus. Many dedications have been found thanking the god for miraculous cures.

Old age and death

The Greeks had great respect for old people, and sons were legally obliged to care for their ageing parents. When parents died the sons were also compelled by law to give them a proper funeral.

The family laid out the body, anointing it with oils and clothing it in clean garments. They then bound the body in waxed cloths, leaving the face uncovered, and placed it in a coffin. A coin was often placed in the mouth to pay Charon the ferryman who took the body across the river Styx into Hades. The body was placed on a bier in the entrance of the house for a day before the funeral.

Before sunrise the following day the body was taken out of the city. It was usually carried by the male relatives. The bier was accompanied by a procession headed by a woman holding a libation jar. She was followed by the male mourners and behind them came the female relatives. All were usually dressed in black or grey. Sometimes professional mourners were hired to add grandeur to the occasion. Flute players followed the procession.

The body was carried along one of the roads leading from the city to the family plot, where it was either buried or cremated, both rites being practised in Athens. The ashes and bones from a cremation were collected in a cloth and placed in an urn. Libations of wine and oil were poured to the deceased and the procession returned to the house of mourning. The mourners were compelled to go through lengthy purification ceremonies before they could enjoy the funeral feast. The following day the house itself was purified with sea-water and hyssop. Like the Jews, the Greeks believed a corpse defiled all who came into contact with it, and all had to be ritually cleansed.

△ The painting from the *lekythos* on the right. It shows two mourners at a tomb. Note the *lekythoi* on the steps of the tomb and hanging on the wall at the back.

◁ A white-ground *lekythos*, the commonest type of vase used for funerals.

▽ The mass of fourth-century grave monuments along the Street of Tombs in the Kerameikos.

WORK

Fifth-century Athens achieved great heights in many fields. Poetry, sculpture, painting, politics, philosophy and history were all outstanding, but so too was the work of Athenian potters, gem engravers and bronzesmiths. Their products were in demand all over the Mediterranean world.

Well over half the population of Attica drew its livelihood from the land. Most were smallholders, tilling the soil with the help of one or two slaves. A smaller number managed their farms, employing others to do the manual work. At the top of the scale was the absentee landlord who lived in Athens and employed a farm manager.

The main crops were wheat, barley, olives and grapes. But cabbages, onions, lentils, peas, garlic and figs were also grown. More exotic fruit and vegetables were imported from neighbouring states.

Arts and crafts

The city itself was famous for its workshops and factories producing goods of exceedingly high quality. Many of the artisans who produced these goods were Greeks who had moved to Athens, and more than half must have been slaves.

The area to the north-west of the Agora, the Kerameikos (from which the word 'ceramic' is derived) was famous as the Potters' Quarter. The vast majority of storage vessels and domestic appliances in use in ancient Greece were made of fired clay. Cookers, grills, baths were all made by potters. The quality of Athenian vase painting is astounding. Some of the figured scenes are among the finest pieces of drawing ever produced.

The hill that borders the west side of the Agora, the Kolonus Agoraeus, and the area to the west was famous for its blacksmiths and bronze workers. The temple on the hill was dedicated to Hephaestus, the god of fire and metalworking. Nine foundries have been discovered clustered around the temple, and another ten or so have been found in the area.

Forges are shown on several painted vases. The furnace, which is as high as a man, was raised to the required heat by a bellows made of goatskin. The Greeks and Romans melted the softer metals – gold, silver, copper and tin – but were unable to produce high enough temperatures to melt iron. Iron artefacts were therefore not cast but wrought – that is, made by heating the iron ore and beating the impurities out of it.

△ Scenes from an Athenian red-figure vase showing vase painters at work. This illustration is unique in showing a woman vase painter.

▷ A red-figure painting showing a carpenter at work with an adze.

△ A red-figure vase painting showing a bronzesmith's work-shop. The tall furnace is typical of this period. Large bronze statues were cast in pieces and brazed together.

◁ Two customers watching a statue being polished.

Carpenters and leather workers

Carpenters and leather workers are shown on several vases. Although virtually no remains of wood or leather goods have survived from ancient Athens, there is no reason to suppose that their quality was any less than that of the more durable products produced by other craftsmen. Highly decorated chests and other furniture are shown on vases and in sculpture. There had been disastrous deforestation in Attica, and by the fourth century BC most good quality wood had to be imported.

The cobbler's trade is shown on several vases. One sixth-century example shows a client standing on the cobbler's bench with his right foot on a piece of leather so that the shoe-maker can cut it to size.

Slavery

Slavery is abhorrent to us today, but was a common feature of the ancient world. It was practised in classical Athens, and was not an institution that any Athenian would have thought to question. It is quite likely that a typical Athenian regarded owning slaves in much the same way as we might look on own-ing a car. Only the poorest families owned no slaves at all.

◁ A red-figure painting showing a cobbler at work, with his tools and products hanging on the wall behind him.

△ A sixth-century black-figure vase painting showing a cobbler cutting the sole for a shoe.

Slaves, both male and female, were usually prisoners of war. It would be misleading to compare slavery in ancient Athens with that practised in the Confederate States of America or elsewhere in the nineteenth century. Slaves in Athens came from all levels of society and usually did jobs in keeping with their education and ability. While it is true that slaves worked in appalling conditions in the silver mines at Laurium, they were probably treated no worse than free men doing similar jobs in Europe as recently as 200 years ago.

Athenian slaves were generally treated better than those of any other ancient society. The Athenians were in fact criticised by the Spartans for being too lax. Slaves were often paid in Athens, especially when they were let out to work for other people. In such situations they were allowed to keep part of their wages, and might ultimately buy their freedom.

Domestic slaves

Domestic slaves were often treated as members of the family. A new female slave was received into the home with showers of nuts and figs as if she were a bride. Masters often went to court in defence of a slave who had been maltreated. Socrates encountered a son who was suing his own father for causing the death of one of the son's slaves.

An enormous number of artisans were slaves. There is no evidence to suggest that they were worse paid than free men. They had fair conditions of work and stood a good chance of being able to buy their freedom. Among female slaves those who played the lyre and the flute or danced at dinner parties would have received tips and were expected to buy their freedom. Fifth-century Athens was in many respects a remarkably liberal society, and most owners would have treated their slaves liberally.

Shops

The Agora was the main shopping centre of Athens. There were many permanent shops around the perimeter, but the majority of sellers set up stalls, barrows or tables within the Agora itself, probably under awnings. Many craftsmen sold their wares directly from their workshops. Potters, cobblers, lamp-makers and the like would display their wares on shelves outside their workplace. Farmers would bring their produce to sell direct to the public in market stalls. There were also many middle-men (*kapeloi*) who bought from factories, workshops or farms and marketed their goods to the public. And there were of course imported goods, which had to be handled by such retailers.

Each type of produce was sold in a particular area of the Agora. A shopper could say to a friend 'I will meet you at the fish' or 'at the perfume'. Each stall holder had his allotted spot, for which he paid a fee to the authorities.

Market inspectors

Shopkeepers were not renowned for their honesty, and inspectors (*metronomoi*) were appointed to ensure fair trading. A long stoa was constructed next to the fountain at the southern end of the Agora in the latter part of the fifth century BC. This appears to have had

△ A red-figure painting showing a slave carrying two amphorae.

Athenian weights and measures found in the Agora.

A–C A set of official weights marked with different emblems to denote their weight; the basic unit of weight was the *stater* (795 grams).

D An official liquid measure.

E–G Official dry measures used for grain, vegetables and the like.

All these measures have *demosion* printed on them to show they are official.

an official function. Fair trading inspectors may have operated from here and from the Tholos, as official weights and measures were found in both places. Standards for the *stater* (about 795 grams), the quarter *stater* and the sixth of a *stater* have been found. Dry measures holding three *choinikes* and one and a half *choinikes*, together with containers for nuts and grain, have also been found. All were marked with the word *demosion*, indicating that they were official measures.

Until recently the Athenian cubit was assumed to be about 45 centimetres long, but in the 1980s a metrological relief was found on the island of Salamis which gave a visual representation of the standard Attic measurements. The Attic cubit was 48.7 centimetres, the foot 30.1 centimetres and the span 24.2 centimetres.

Banking

Bankers may also have used the South Stoa, setting up their changing tables beneath its double portico. They lent money at extremely high interest rates of 12 per cent or more per month. The official mint was just beyond the fountain. It was built at about the same time as the stoa, and may be connected with it.

Coinage had been introduced in the sixth century BC and an enormous number of coins from all subsequent eras have been found during the excavations. The basic Athenian unit of currency was the drachma, weighing 4.36 silver *grazes*. Coins of two and four drachmae are common finds. There was also a ten-drachma piece. This was the largest Athenian coin and is fairly rare. The *mina* (100 drachmae) and the talent (6,000 drachmae) are purely accounting figures. There were coins valued at one, two and three obols, the obol being one sixth of a drachma, and there were also subdivisions of the obol. All coins had Athena's head on the obverse and the owl, sacred to Athena, on the reverse. Athenian coins were popularly referred to as 'Laurium owls', after Laurium in southern Attica where the silver was mined.

△ A metrological relief discovered on the island of Salamis. This shows the official Athenian measurements. The cubit, the length from elbow to tip of fingers, shown at the top is 48.7 centimetres. The foot is 30.1 centimetres, and the span, from tip of thumb to tip of little finger, is 24.2 centimetres.

◁ An Athenian silver two-drachma coin with the head of Athena on the obverse and the sacred owl on the reverse.

◁ An official roof tile measure found in the Agora. It was used for checking the size of curved Laconian tiles.

F

G

THE HOUSES OF ATHENS

History has left us with a poor impression of Athenian houses, of squalid slums with mud brick huts along narrow alleys. Excavation has shown this to be an exaggeration. Athens had many narrow streets, little town planning and many small houses, but several houses discovered in recent excavations are large, airy and quite luxurious buildings.

Excavations beyond the south-west corner of the Agora along the valley between the Areopagus and the Pnyx have revealed several houses and workshops. Seldom more than the foundations survive, and these have usually been overbuilt with later houses. A small house immediately next to the Agora (it actually had an Agora boundary stone resting against its east wall) belonged to a fifth-century BC shoe-maker called Simon who may have been the friend of the philosopher Socrates mentioned by Xenophon. When the philosopher wanted to talk to pupils who were too young to go to the Agora he would meet them at Simon's leather working shop 'near the square'. Pericles also seems to have been a regular visitor. Many bone eyelets and studs were found in the house,

Semi-detached houses

A little further up the valley, just south-west of the prison, are two semi-detached houses. The larger, to the south, measures 14.4 by 18.4 metres (47¼ by 60¼ feet). In common with all the houses so far discovered in Athens, it was also built round a courtyard. It had ten rooms, eight of them opening onto the courtyard, and a corridor leading from the front door to the courtyard. Room 5 also opens onto the street with no access to the house itself, suggesting that it might have been a shop or workshop. It

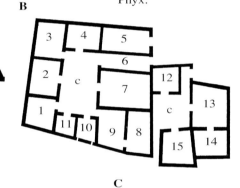

▽ Plans of Athenian houses of the classical period; c indicates the courtyard.

A The house-workshop of the sculptors Micion and Menon.
B Two semi-detached houses in the valley between the Areopagus and the Hill of the Nymphs.
C The hill house on the Pnyx.

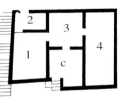

▽ A reconstruction of the house-workshop of the sculptors Micion and Menon just south-east of the Agora.

△ A reconstruction of the hill house (Kourouniotis' House) on the Pnyx.

but unfortunately Athens does not have the right climate for the preservation of leather. Only fragments of the walls survive, but the house appears to have consisted of a courtyard with rooms along three sides.

A slightly better-preserved house just to the south was occupied by a series of sculptors, the earliest, in about 475 BC, named Micion. This house again appears to have consisted of a courtyard with rooms on three sides.

seems probable that there was an upper floor at least above rooms 3, 4, 5 and 7, with stairs on the south side of the courtyard leading up to a balcony in front of the room above 4.

The other house is smaller. It had only four downstairs rooms, three of them opening onto its courtyard. It too has two corridors leading from the front and back doors to the courtyard. A pillar in the courtyard in front of room 12 supported a balcony which gave access to at least two upstairs rooms. The balcony would have been reached by stairs from the courtyard. Although little more than the base of the walls remain of these houses, details such as doors and windows can be filled in from vase paintings and from the excavations at such sites as Thoricus and Olynthus.

Hill houses

Several houses have been found on the Pnyx and the Hill of the Nymphs which conform to a pattern. They are all cut into the hillside, with four or more rooms grouped on three sides of a courtyard. The best example is that on the north-east slope of the Pnyx. It is cut so deeply into the slope that the rear rooms were semi-basements with rock-cut walls more than a metre high. Room 1 was a dining room (*andron*) with sufficient room for seven couches. This house probably had an upper floor.

A block of houses

Immediately behind the South Stoa on the lower slopes of the Areopagus is a block of houses very similar to a Roman *insula*. It measures roughly 25 by 22 metres (82 by 72 feet) and contains six houses, two square ones on the east side and four narrower ones on the west. They are all courtyard houses and probably all had upstairs rooms. Houses A and B have single pillars to support a balcony. The rear room

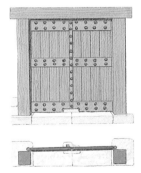

◁ A reconstruction and ground plan of a front door at Olynthus.

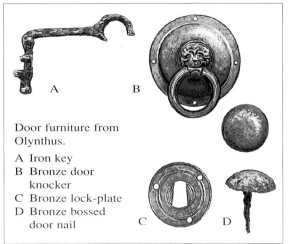

Door furniture from Olynthus.

A Iron key
B Bronze door knocker
C Bronze lock-plate
D Bronze bossed door nail

△ A reconstruction of the two semi-detached houses in the valley between the Areopagus and the Hill of the Nymphs.

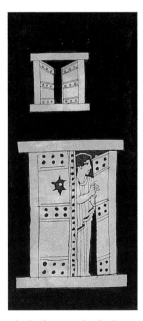

△ A shuttered window and a door shown on vase paintings.

of house B has five storage jars (*pithoi*) embedded in the floor, identifying it as a storeroom. All the houses are built of mud brick on a low stone socle and roofed with terracotta pantiles.

A late classical house

Halfway up the slope to the Acropolis, just to the west of the Panathenaic Way, three houses of the late classical period have been discovered. Only the scantiest remains of the original houses have survived but it has been possible to draw tentative plans (see page 51). The three houses are cut into the hillside. The two smaller ones have six and eight rooms, but the middle house is much larger, about 25 by 19 metres (82 by 62½ feet) overall. It has ten ground-floor rooms and a spacious courtyard, probably surrounded by a portico which supported a balcony. Access to the balcony was by a stairway, possibly from the north-east corner of the courtyard.

The house was entered from an alleyway. The front door opened into a corridor leading into the courtyard. At the opposite side of the courtyard was a room with a mosaic floor. This was clearly an important reception room, with a back room opening off it. The only room that can be identified with certainty is the room to the south of the corridor, which was the men's dining room. The *gynaikeion*, the women's quarters where the wife, daughters and female servants lived, would have been on the upper floor.

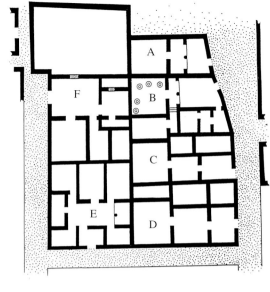

As there is no trace of plastering or wall painting, this house offers the opportunity to reconstruct a decoration scheme incorporating all that is known about classical wall decoration.

Wall decoration

Fragments of painted plaster have been discovered at many Greek sites, and the practice of plastering and painting walls is known to go back to the Bronze Age. Probably the most

◁ A block of six houses of the classical period behind the South Stoa.

▷ A cut-away section of the largest of the three late classical houses south of the Agora just west of the Panathenaic Way. The *andron*, the only identifiable room, is to the right of the entrance corridor. This hypothetical reconstruction shows the rooms decorated in the various styles of the classical period. In such a house the women's quarters were upstairs.

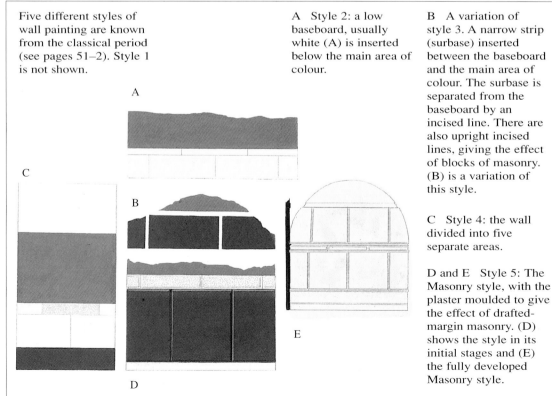

Five different styles of wall painting are known from the classical period (see pages 51–2). Style 1 is not shown.

A Style 2: a low baseboard, usually white (A) is inserted below the main area of colour.

B A variation of style 3. A narrow strip (surbase) inserted between the baseboard and the main area of colour. The surbase is separated from the baseboard by an incised line. There are also upright incised lines, giving the effect of blocks of masonry. (B) is a variation of this style.

C Style 4: the wall divided into five separate areas.

D and E Style 5: The Masonry style, with the plaster moulded to give the effect of drafted-margin masonry. (D) shows the style in its initial stages and (E) the fully developed Masonry style.

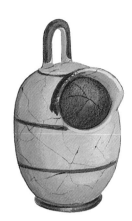

▷ The leg of a wooden Greek chair or stool found at Olympia.

△ A chamber pot (*amis*) found in the Agora.

▷ A portable terracotta lavatory seat found at Olynthus.

△ A reconstruction of the bathroom alongside the chimney well in the House of the Comedian at Olynthus. The floor is decorated with a simple black and white pebble mosaic.

▷ Various articles of furniture shown in Athenian vase paintings. Chairs have seats made of webbing. Similar webbing is used for beds and couches. A typical dining couch with table is shown at the bottom.

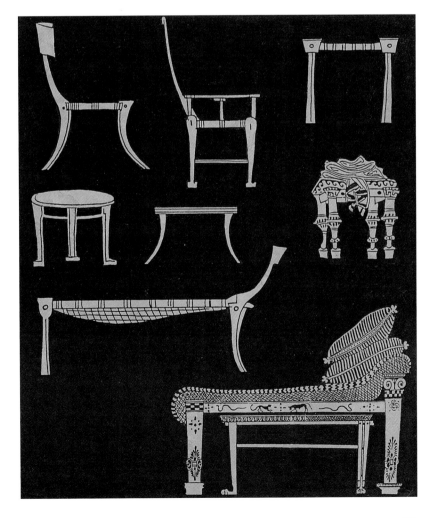

the Agora excavations, and a portable lavatory seat was found at Olynthus.

Furniture

Furniture was sparse and was moved from room to room as required. Tables were either round with three legs or rectangular with four. Chairs, stools, beds and couches are often shown on vase paintings. They were generally made of wood with seats made of webbing. Every household also had chests in which clothes and linen were kept. These were often brought with the bride as part of her dowry, or given as wedding gifts. These chests often had quinces or other dried fruit in them to perfume clothes. Vases, particularly *lebeti* (elegant vases specially made as wedding gifts), incense burners and tripods formed part of the furniture of wealthier houses. There were also lamps to provide light, and braziers for heating.

TEMPLES OF THE GODS

The most important feature of classical Greek religion was the sacrifice, which was performed outside temples or shrines dedicated to particular deities. Some of the temples in Athens are among the finest buildings ever created.

Ancient Greek religion was polytheistic. Twelve main deities (the pantheon) were familiar to all Greeks, but each of these was recognised in a wide variety of different aspects, often associated with a particular place, community or activity. There were also many minor deities, as well as semi-divine heroes. The gods combined supernatural and human characteristics, and no god was either wholly good or wholly bad. The Greeks had no concept of a Devil; at worst, the gods were simply indifferent to humans.

Classical Greek religion was above all a matter of behaviour, not of belief. Ritual was a central part of both public and private life, and the religious calendar (of which a number survive) was a sequence of days on which the proper sacrifices had to be made. There was no church in our sense of the word, and performance of the correct rituals was a practical means of obtaining the help of the gods in the present life. The Greeks had no generally accepted idea of heaven, hell or the afterlife.

The Greek pantheon, with their most common attributes, were: Zeus, the king of the gods (originally the sky god), his wife Hera (goddess

▷ The Panathenaic procession passing through the Propylaea, the gate of the Acropolis. The ceremonial boat, on which the new tunic (*peplos*) for Athena may have been hoisted as a sail, would probably have been parked alongside the Clepsydra fountain at the bottom left of the picture.

The tiny temple to Victory is to the right of the approach ramp, the Propylaea with its six-column front is straight ahead, and the Pinakotheke is to the left. Beyond the gateway to the right is the Parthenon, the temple of Athena Parthenos (the Virgin); in the centre is the small Erechtheum, and above the left side of the gateway is the house of the *arrephoroi*, the young girls who helped make the tunic for Athena.

△ The *omphalos* (navel) discovered at Delphi. This was a symbol of Apollo and marked the centre of the universe, which the Greeks believed to be at Delphi.

▽ A model showing the Sacred way from Athens to Eleusis. The procession, said by Herodotus to be 30,000 strong, set out at dawn from the Eleusinium, just below the Acropolis, and arrived at Eleusis, some 25 kilometres away, at dusk.

of marriage), Poseidon (god of the sea), Hades (god of the underworld), Apollo (god of prophecy and music), Athena (goddess of wisdom and war), Artemis (goddess of nature), Aphrodite (goddess of love), Hermes (the messenger of the gods), Hephaestus (god of fire and metalwork), Ares (god of war) and Demeter (the goddess of corn and fertility). Other important deities were Dionysus, the god of wine and the performing arts, and Asclepius, the god of healing.

Athena, guardian of Athens

Although Zeus and his two brothers Poseidon and Hades always headed any list of gods, individual cities usually held one deity in particular esteem. In the case of Athens it was Athena who held the pride of place. There were temples to Athena in her different aspects in various places in the city, including the great Parthenon on the Acropolis. But other gods also had their temples and shrines. Hephaestus, god of the forge, had his temple on the hill to the west of the Agora, in the area where the smiths worked.

Oracles and Mysteries

Two centres of particular religious importance were outside Athens, however. One of these was the famous temple of Apollo at Delphi. Here, in a cavern filled with sulphurous smoke, the priestess, the *pythia*, seated on a tripod,

answered practical questions about the present or future, usually in such obscure terms as to make almost any interpretation seem correct. Nevertheless, the oracle was consulted regularly by Athenians of all social ranks, and indeed by Greeks from all over the country. The popularity of this practice emphasises both the power and the practicality of Greek religion.

The Mysteries of Eleusis

The second of these sanctuaries was that of Demeter and her daughter Kore, or Persephone, at Eleusis. According to myth, Hades, the god of the underworld, had carried off Kore (Persephone) to his kingdom. Demeter protested, and a compromise was agreed by which Kore would spend six months of each year with Hades and six months with her mother. Though a shrine to Demeter and Kore known as the Eleusinium was built on the Panathenaic Way below the Athenian Acropolis, the main sanctuary remained at Eleusis. The Eleusinian Mysteries (as the rites performed there were known) were unusual in Greek religion in that they made direct reference to the afterlife. Nonetheless, the cult became famous throughout Greece, and an important part of Athenian public religion. Surviving evidence of the cult is from much later Christian sources, which were hostile to older religions and given to wilful misinterpretation of their practices, so the reconstruction which follows is very tentative.

Eleusis

Sacred Way

Sacred Way

Athens

Salamis Channel

Piraeus

Phaleron

The procession to Eleusis

Once a year, in the month of Boedromion (September/October), a great procession walked from Athens to Eleusis for the initiation ceremonies. On the 14th of the month the sacred utensils were brought to the Eleusinium at Athens and the chief priest, the hierophant, announced the beginning of the mysteries, warning the impure, murderers and those who did not speak Greek to keep away from the ceremonies. All Greek-speaking people were eligible for initiation, including women, slaves and foreigners. On the 16th of the month all the initiates went down to the bay of Phaleron together and purified themselves by bathing in the sea, taking with them sacrificial pigs (the animal most sacred to Demeter).

Early on the morning of the 19th the procession assembled at the Eleusinium and set off on the 25-kilometre walk to Eleusis. The procession was led by the priestesses carrying the sacred instruments. The crowd, carrying bundles of branches, danced along in a state of euphoria, stopping at a certain point to chant ritual obscenities associated with the Kore myth. The procession reached Eleusis by nightfall. None but the initiates was allowed to enter the great hall of the mysteries, the Telesterium.

The Telesterium

The Persians had destroyed the Telesterium, but the Eleusinian cult was so important that it was rebuilt immediately after the war. The new building proved inadequate and Pericles had it rebuilt again on a much grander scale. The new hall was 55 metres (180 feet) square, with stepped terraces on all four sides from which several thousand initiates could watch the

△ The sanctuary of the goddess Demeter and her daughter Kore at Eleusis, as it might have appeared in the fifth century BC. The Telesterium, the Great Hall of the Mysteries, is in the centre. The procession entered by the gate at the top of the picture.

◁ Inside the Great Hall of the Mysteries. The Hall was more than 50 metres (164 feet) square, with a roof supported by twenty columns. The *anaktoron*, the hidden room, is in the centre, with the throne of the hierophant to the left.

▷ A bull being led to sacrifice, shown on the Panathenaic frieze from the south side of the cella (that is, inside the colonnade) of the Parthenon.

◁ A typical stone altar discovered in Athens (National Archaeological Museum, Athens).

▽ A sixth-century painted wooden tablet found near Corinth, showing a sacrificial scene. The worshippers, crowned with wreaths and carrying olive branches, approach a blood-spattered altar. The procession is led by a young woman carrying the sacrificial basket on her head and the jug of wine in her right hand. A boy, followed by musicians, leads the victim, a sheep.

ceremonies. The roof was supported on twenty square pillars. In the centre was a separate, free-standing room, the *anaktoron*. At the west corner of the *anaktoron* was the throne of the hierophant.

The initiates crowded into the hall, the darkness relieved only by the torch-bearers. Suddenly a doorway at the west corner of the *anaktoron* opened and the hierophant emerged, in a flood of light which symbolised the return of Kore from the world of daylight, to take his place on the throne. We know very little of the initiation ritual itself, the initiates being sworn to secrecy under pain of death. The rites ceased when the Christian Emperor Theodosius forcibly closed the sanctuary towards the end of the fourth century AD.

Initiation

The new initiates (*mystai*) were probably brought in blindfolded and put though a ritual that progressed from blind terror to sublime joy as Kore was summoned up from the underworld by the hierophant striking a gong. An ear of corn was cut in silence. The new initiates had fasted since the previous evening, and broke their fast with the barley drink (*kykeon*) sacred to Demeter. The ceremony continued with dances and rejoicing, and a sacrificial feast the following day.

The whole ritual, which has much in common with harvest festivals, clearly had its origin in primitive farming rituals propitiating the gods and thanking them for a successful harvest. But it extended beyond this to take in the whole cycle of death and rebirth. Like Christianity, it promised recompense for the hardships of this world – at least for the initiates – in a happier time after death.

Priests

The Telesterium at Eleusis was built as an assembly hall. It was quite different from the normal Greek temple built simply to house the cult image of the god. Sacrifice, the most important rite of Greek religion, was offered on an altar outside the temple.

Priesthood was normally only a part-time job. Family religious observance was conducted by the father, and most public sacrifices by civic officials. Major religious ceremonies performed on behalf of the Athenian state were conducted by the king archon. Each sanctuary had its own priest or priestess who was responsible for seeing that everything was in proper order. The priestess of Eleusis was the only official who actually resided at the sanctuary there.

Some religious appointments were the prerogative of certain families. The hierophant at Eleusis was always selected from the Eumolpidai family and the priest of Athena Polias from the Eteoboutadai family.

Priests usually had long hair and wore a head band and garland. They dressed in expensive robes of white or purple with a special waistband and carried a staff. Priestesses are usually shown carrying a key. The priestess of Athena wore an *aegis*, a sort of armoured cloak covering her chest and shoulders, in imitation of the goddess. She was often to be seen in the streets in full regalia.

Children were often consecrated for a period of temple service. Two girls (*arrephoroi*) were selected to serve on the Acropolis, where they helped weave the sacred tunic (*peplos*) of Athena and looked after the holy olive tree. They were discharged after a year's service.

Sacrifices

The sacrifice was the central activity of all Greek religion, public or private. Sheep, goats, pigs and even poultry could be sacrificed (the animal had to be domesticated, not wild). The sacrifice par excellence was the ox, though particular animals were considered appropriate to particular gods.

A typical public sacrifice might proceed roughly as follows. A public procession, usually with music, would set out leading the victim to the sacrificial altar. The victim would be decorated with ribbons, with its horns gilded. The procession would be led by a man or woman carrying a basket containing the sacrificial knife, hidden beneath barley grains. A jug of water and an incense burner would also be carried.

On arrival before the altar, the procession would form up around it. The participants would wash their hands in water from the sacrificial jug. The victim would also be sprinkled with water. It would automatically shake its head, which was taken as a sign of its willingness to be sacrificed.

Taking the knife from the basket and keeping it out of sight of the victim, the priest would cut some hair from its forehead and throw it

◁ A sacrificial procession shown on an Athenian vase. A garlanded man carrying a libation bowl leads a group of men escorting two bulls to the sacrifice.

▽ Two men with an incense burner on a tall stand. Apollo, with the *omphalos* in front of him, is seated on a throne within his temple.

61

△ The Acropolis seen from the Hill of the Nymphs. The stone structure to the left is the Pinakotheke, with the Propylaea immediately to the right. Next to this is the small temple of Victory, with the Parthenon to its right.

into the flames on the altar, together with grains of barley. The slaughterer would stun the animal, then cut its throat, to the sound of a ritual scream (*ololuge*) from the women present. The animal was almost always held with its head up, so that the blood spurted up and fell down on to the altar and into a basin. The blood would then be poured on to the top and sides of the altar.

The animal would then be butchered. The heart and other entrails were removed first and spit roasted, to be eaten by those nearest to the altar. The animal was then skinned and cut up. The thigh bones were removed, covered in fat and sprinkled with incense, then burned on the altar as an offering to the god. The priest would pour wine over the offering, the alcohol making the fire flare up. When the flames had died down, the rest of the meat would be cooked (almost always by boiling in cauldrons) and eaten. The communal eating of the cooked meat was an important part of the ritual.

Rebuilding the Acropolis

The peace treaties with Sparta and Persia in the mid-fifth century BC recognised the Athenian empire and the right of the Athenians to coerce their allies. The treasury at Delos was moved to Athens in 454 BC, and subscriptions paid there now became tribute to Athens, providing the city with an enormous sum of money.

The Acropolis had lain in ruins for thirty years. The oath of Plataea was considered to have been fulfilled, and Pericles persuaded the assembly that the surplus money should be spent rebuilding the Acropolis with a grandeur befitting the foremost state in Greece.

Work began in 447 BC on the temple that was to become the most famous in the world, the temple of Athena Parthenos (the Virgin). It became known simply as the Parthenon. The temple was converted into a church of the Virgin Mary in the Middle Ages and later into a Turkish mosque. Although the centre was blown out in a disastrous explosion in 1687, much of the building remains to this day.

▷ An aerial view of the Acropolis as it might have appeared at the beginning of the fourth century BC. Besides the important sanctuaries on the summit, many shrines dating back to the Bronze Age were located along the sides of the hill.

A Parthenon
B Erechtheum
C Propylaea
D Pinakotheke
E Temple of Athena Nike (Victory)
F ramp
G The house of the *arrephoroi*
H Clepsydra fountain and the Court of the Pythion
I Eleusinium
J Agora
K Areopagus
L Theatre of Dionysus
M The unfinished Temple of Zeus

▷ The Propylaea, seen from the Areopagus. The Pinakotheke is on the left, with the later Monument of Agrippa to the right of it. The south columns of the monumental gateway can be seen to the right of this, with the steps leading up to it.

▽ A section through the Propylaea, showing the northern half. The Pinakotheke is on the left. The gateway was approached by a broad ramp which was probably stepped. Visitors passed through a temple-like entrance composed of six Doric columns. Inside the Propylaea the central passageway was flanked by Ionic columns. Five portals led to a back porch which echoed the Doric architecture of the front.

The Great Gateway

A monumental gateway, the Propylaea, was built at the top of the slope leading to the west end of the Acropolis. The annual procession celebrating the birthday of Athena would pass through the Propylaea on its way to the Parthenon.

The gateway was built after the Parthenon (437–432 BC), when resources were beginning to dry up. Relations with Sparta had become very strained, and war seemed inevitable. As a result, the Propylaea was never finally completed.

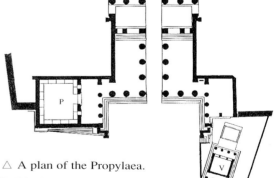

△ A plan of the Propylaea.

P Pinakotheke
V Temple of Athena Nike (Victory)

◁ Inside the Pinakotheke, the picture gallery. The slightly raised platform around the sides of the room, similar to those found in dining rooms, suggests that the gallery was also used for official banquets.

The design itself (by the architect Mnesicles) was fraught with problems as it had to take into consideration the sloping site of the former entrance to the Mycenaean citadel, and the existence of many shrines in the immediate area. There were shrines to Athena Hygiaea (the Healer), to Aphrodite and Demeter, and others. Further up the slope was the precinct of Artemis Brauronia which also had to be considered. All of these had to be incorporated into the area of the monumental entrance, either as niche shrines or small temples. The most famous temple now to be seen in the immediate area is the small temple to Athena Nike (the Victorious), known as Nike Apteros (Wingless Victory). This, however, was built after the Propylaea.

Building the Gateway

The Propylaea was built with a temple-like facade of six Doric columns at either end. The gateway was approached by a massive ramp a little over 20 metres (65½ feet) wide. This ramp, which rose 25 metres (82 feet) over its 80-metre (262½-foot) length (the same incline as the steepest part of the Panathenaic Way), was probably stepped, possibly with a 3-metre (10-foot) wide passageway up the middle for sacrificial animals. The two centre columns had a wider spacing to allow for the passageway. The passageway passed through a short colonnade of Ionic columns and emerged in a back porch with six Doric columns. The architraves

over the colonnade were reinforced with iron bars, a very early example of metal reinforcement in building. Pedestrians using the stepped ramp on either side of the passageway had to climb five steps to pass through the columns along the front and a further five steps to enter the rear porch. From here the visitor would see the great bronze statue of Athena, which towered above the Propylaea and could be seen from several miles out to sea. The porch also offered the first close-up view, albeit partial, of the Parthenon.

Two wings of unequal size flanked the front of the Propylaea. That to the north, the Pinakotheke, was a picture gallery and perhaps a ceremonial dining room, with space for seventeen couches. The travel writer Pausanias, visiting Athens in the second century AD, some 600 years after its construction, describes several of the paintings, though many had disappeared by his time.

The area to the south of the gate was restricted and there was only room for an anteroom to the temple of Athena Nike. Pausanias also describes a statue of Hermes, called the Hermes of the Gateway, somewhere in this area. No trace of this statue can be found today, but there must have been a Herm at the gate.

Materials

The Propylaea and the Parthenon were built of white Pentelic marble, quarried on the slopes of Mount Pentelicon, 13 kilometres (8 miles) north-east of Athens. It has been estimated that 22,000 tons of marble was used.

The blocks of marble were cut to size at the quarry, leaving small projections (*ancones*) on the sides for handling. They were transported either in ox carts, on sledges or by the use of fitted wooden discs with which they could be rolled. The attachment of a wooden frame made it possible to pull them. This may have been the only way that the larger blocks could be moved up the steep slope to the Acropolis.

Examination of the stone blocks used on the Acropolis has revealed the various methods by which they were raised and manoeuvred into position. The commonest method of lifting was by looping ropes around the *ancones*. These *ancones* can be seen on the south-east corner of the Propylaea where, in their haste to finish the building, the workmen neglected to remove them. It is also possible to see many holes and slots in the Parthenon stones which were used to lift and lever the blocks into position.

Cranes

No pictures of classical Greek cranes have survived, but we know from the fourth-century BC philosopher Aristotle that both the pulley and the windlass were in use in his day. In fact, Aristotle's description suggests pulley systems of some complexity. However, other sources insist that Archimedes invented the multiple pulley in the third century BC. The Roman engineer and architect Vitruvius describes a type of crane used during the construction of public buildings that may have been in use in the fifth century BC. This crane consists of two upright timbers, joined at the top with a brace and spread at the bottom, held up by adjustable guy ropes. Two pulleys were fixed at the top from which a third pulley was suspended. The power

▷ Athens seen from the bay of Phaleron. The Parthenon can be seen to the right of centre in the middle distance, with the Lycabettus Hill behind and the Pnyx–Mouseion ridge in front of it. Seamen sailing into the bay of Phaleron could see the top of the great bronze statue of Athena above the Propylaea.

▽ The Parthenon seen from the back porch of the Propylaea. This would have been the first close-up view of the temple a visitor would have. This is the back of the temple: the front is at the east end.

A One of the methods used to transport blocks of marble from the quarry to the site.

B A frame could be attached so the block could be pulled.

C–E Various methods used to lift blocks of marble; they may all have been used in the construction of the Parthenon.

was supplied by a windlass attached to the back of the frame. The reconstruction below is based on this description. A base has been added for support. The guy ropes with pulleys, and a small amount of lateral movement in the base, would allow heavy blocks to be manoeuvred into position.

Architectural refinements

The overall design of the Parthenon was in the hands of the great sculptor Phidias, but three architects, of whom the chief was Ictinus, were also employed. The Parthenon was a traditional Doric temple taken to the highest level of architectural sophistication. The basic foundations of the temple already existed, as the south side of the Acropolis, which fell away very steeply, had been terraced for the earlier temple. The artificial platform, which needed only to be extended a little to the west and north, was approached by a broad flight of steps at the west end.

The base of the temple (stylobate), measuring 69.51 by 30.86 metres (228 by 101¼ feet), was constructed in the normal Greek fashion with three steps stretching the whole length of all four sides. It was built on the south edge of the platform so that the whole temple could be seen from

△ A device used to key in column drums. It consists of two blocks of wood joined with a metal rod. Several of these have been found.

▽ A crane lifting column drums into position. Simple pulleys and windlasses were in use at this time. The reconstruction is based on a simple crane described by the Roman engineer Vitruvius.

▷ The south-east corner of the Propylaea. In the rush to finish the Propylaea before the onset of the Peloponnesian War the workmen failed to finish off this wall, and the *ancones*, the projections for handling, survive on the blocks to this day.

▽ The east end of the Parthenon, showing the curve in the steps, which were raised slightly in the middle to give the visual illusion of being straight.

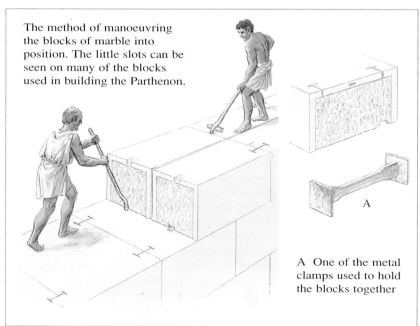

The method of manoeuvring the blocks of marble into position. The little slots can be seen on many of the blocks used in building the Parthenon.

A One of the metal clamps used to hold the blocks together

the south, towering above the walls of the Acropolis. Even the stylobate was built with minute visual compensations, known technically as refinements, in its design. A long platform appears visually to sag in the middle. To correct this illusion, the stylobate was designed to rise slightly towards the centre of each edge, by 11 centimetres (4⅓ inches) on the sides and 6 centimetres (2⅓ inches) at the front and back. The illusion was taken even further, for the west end is some 44 centimetres (17 inches) higher than the east end, and the north-west corner 17 centimetres (6⅔ inches) higher than the south-west corner. Some observers have claimed that these variations from true are errors or caused by subsidence, but the compensating angles of the columns makes it clear that they were deliberate.

The colonnade

The temple was constructed from the outside inwards. The outer colonnade consisted of 46 Doric columns. These had a diameter of about 1.9 metres (6¼ feet) at the base, and stood about 10.4 metres (34 feet) high. They were each composed of eleven drums. In order to make the blocks fit together tightly, the central part of the upper and lower surfaces were cut back very slightly, to create a vacuum effect. This technique is called anathyrosis. As the surface of the stylobate was not actually flat, minute adjustments were required in cutting the column drums so that they stood upright. The difference in height between the shorter and longer sides of these drums varied by as little as 1 millimetre. Again for visual effect, the columns were neither straight-sided nor upright. The columns bulged by 2 centimetres (about an inch) about one third of the way up (*entasis*), and the corner columns were 2½ per cent wider than the other columns, and leaned inwards. These corner columns are the only ones that would ever be seen silhouetted in isolation against the sky, and the extra width compensates for the visual slimming effect of this silhouetting. An immense amount of labour is involved in realising such refinements.

Assembling the columns

The column drums were lifted into position by cranes using the projections (*ancones*) on the sides. The drums were secured in position by small metal bars in wooden sockets set in the centre of the column drum. The top section of the column, which included the abacus and echinus of the capital, was finished complete with its twenty flutes before being put in place. It seems likely that the fluting was also cut around the bottom of the lowest drum to avoid damaging the paving of the stylobate while carving it. The *ancones* were chipped away and the rest of the fluting carved after the column had been assembled.

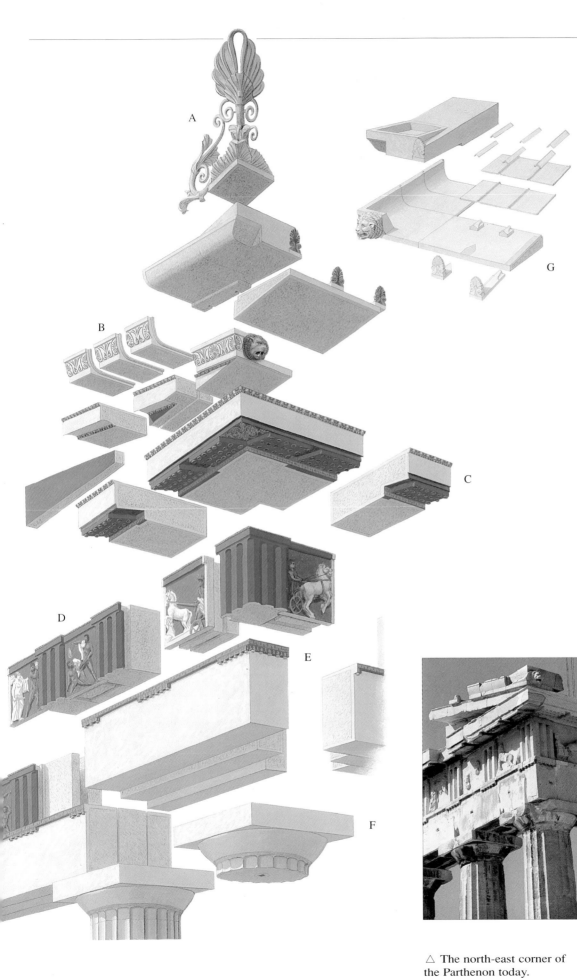

◁ An exploded drawing of the north-east corner of the Parthenon.

A The *acroterion* – small fragments of floral *acroteria* presumed to have come from the Parthenon have been found; these have no trace of colouring. But it has been suggested recently that there may have been Winged Victories at the corners of the pediment.

B The guttering. This vestige of earlier wooden temples was unnecessary on a stone temple. Traces of painted decoration have been found in several places.

C The cornice. Traces of the colouring appear on several of these blocks. The *mutuli*, the Lego-like decorations, were painted blue with red gutters between them.

D The triglyphs and *metopes*. Traces of blue paint appear on many of the triglyphs. The background of the *metopes* appears to have been either red, sometimes applied in wavy stripes, or blue.

E The architrave. Traces of painted patterns have been found on the carved decorations of the upper edge.

F The capital. The abacus, echinus and top section of the fluted column were carved in one piece.

G The white marble tiling of the roof. Both the Parthenon and the Propylaea were tiled with white Pentelic marble.

△ The north-east corner of the Parthenon today.

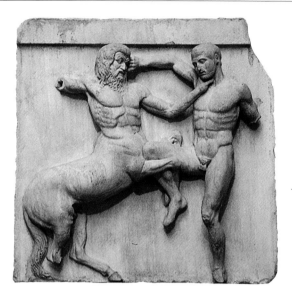

▷ A *metope* from the Parthenon, part of the Elgin Marbles in the British Museum. No trace of paint remains.

The core of the Temple

Within the colonnade the walls of the cella were built. These are mainly composed of finely cut ashlar blocks, 1.22 by 0.52 metres (4 feet by 1 foot 8½ inches) in dimension, laid in header and stretcher fashion (that is, alternating long and short sides visible), with alternate courses of single blocks the whole thickness of the wall (1.4 metres/4 feet 7 inches) and double blocks half the thickness (0.7 metres/2 feet 3 inches). The final positioning of the blocks was done with levers, the holes for which can be seen on the blocks. The Greeks did not use mortar; the blocks were held together with metal clamps.

The cella was divided in two. The main room, at the east end, would house the statue of Athena. A smaller chamber at the west end was to be a treasury for the funds transferred from Delos.

The sculptures

Providing the sculptures for the exterior decoration of the Parthenon was too great a task for one artist. Phidias had to put together a team of sculptors, which made consistency of quality impossible.

The 92 spaces between the triglyphs (*metopes*) were filled with small high-relief sculptures, 1.2 metres (4 feet) high and averaging 1.25 metres (4 feet 1 inch) wide. Most of these had two figures, but a few had more. These had to be produced to a very tight schedule because they could not be carved in position. The also had to be in position before the cornice and the roof were put on.

Each side had a different theme. The front (east) showed the mythological battle between the gods and the giants who had tried to overthrow them. The west end showed Greeks fighting Amazons. The north side showed scenes from the Trojan war, and the scenes on the south side showed a battle between men and centaurs.

The architrave round the outside of the cella (that is, inside the colonnade) was decorated with a frieze carved in low relief, showing the annual procession in honour of Athena, the Panathenaic procession. This is a continuous frieze, 160 metres (525 feet) long and about 1 metre (3 feet 3 inches) high. It shows an extremely high standard of workmanship and consistency of style. It seems odd that such fine work should be designed to be largely hidden in its position high up under the colonnade.

The subject of the sculptures of the east pediment was the birth of Athena, and that of the west pediment was the contest between Poseidon and Athena for possession of Attica.

▷ Partially restored sections of the Panathenaic frieze in the British Museum. Traces of painted decoration above the figural frieze makes a fairly certain reconstruction possible. Although traces of blue have survived on the background, no trace of colouring remains on the figures.

Colouring

Although the columns were left in the natural white colour of the Pentelic marble, all the sculptures and the other elements of the entablature were painted. Minute traces of red, blue and yellow paint have survived, enabling a fairly accurate reconstruction of the decoration of the cornice to be made. The background of the *metopes* appears to have been blue or red,

△ A sketch made by Jacques Carrey in 1674 of the right end of the east pediment of the Parthenon. At this date some of the figures still had heads and lower arms (Bibliothèque Nationale, Paris).

△ The three female figures shown in Carrey's drawing and now in the British Museum. Although it is known that these figures would have been painted, no trace of the colouring remains.

▽ A reconstruction of the three figures above, based on fragments of sixth-century sculptures found on the Acropolis.

▷ A fragment of a sixth-century painted statue found on the Acropolis (Acropolis Museum).

partly in wavy lines. The background of the Panathenaic frieze was blue, and so probably was the background of the pediments. No trace of the colour remains on the figures, but numerous fragments of earlier sculptures were found buried under the temple platform. Much of the painted decoration on these has survived, giving a reasonable idea of what Phidias' painted sculptures may have looked like. A dark ruddy brown was commonly used for men's skin, but women's skin was left white.

Completion

By 437 BC the interior of the temple was complete and the great ivory and gold statue installed. The statue had probably taken far longer to make than Phidias had planned. The temple was dedicated in that year and most of the work-force was moved to the Propylaea. It was to take Phidias and his team another five years to complete the magnificent sculptures that were to fill the 27-metre (88-foot) pediments at the front and back of the temple. Even then someone had miscalculated, and some of the figures had to be juggled to get them in.

The great statue of Athena

The interior of the temple consisted of a broad central aisle which was divided off from a narrow outer aisle running down the sides and across the back by rows of columns on two levels. The great statue stood at the west end of the central aisle. The statue was something entirely new. It was about 12 metres (39 feet) high and made of wood faced with ivory and gold. Our only knowledge of it comes from

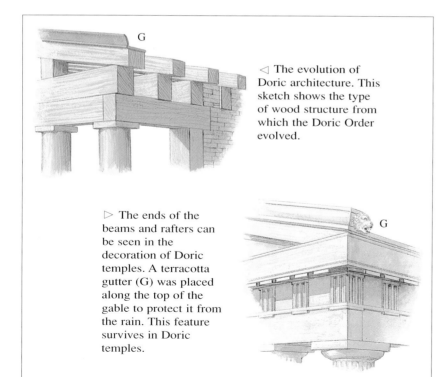

◁ The evolution of Doric architecture. This sketch shows the type of wood structure from which the Doric Order evolved.

▷ The ends of the beams and rafters can be seen in the decoration of Doric temples. A terracotta gutter (G) was placed along the top of the gable to protect it from the rain. This feature survives in Doric temples.

small copies, from coins and from the description of the Greek travel writer Pausanias. The figure wore a triple-crested helmet. It had a coiled snake and decorated shield on its left side. A winged victory about 2 metres (6½ feet) high rested on its right hand. The face, neck, arms and feet were covered with a thin layer of

◁ A view of the Parthenon as it may have appeared at the end of the fifth century BC. Holes for the metal grilles can be seen on the interior line of columns across the front of the cella. The figures in the centre of the pediment have disappeared entirely, and it is impossible to reconstruct them with any accuracy.

◁ A cutaway drawing of the Parthenon. The building has been studied so comprehensively over the past two centuries that it is possible to reconstruct it with almost total accuracy. Only such elements as the doors remain conjectural. In the background on the right is the great altar of Athena, of which nothing remains.

73

ivory and the clothing was plated with gold. According to the contemporary historian Thucydides, the gold covering the statue weighed 40 talents, about 100 kilograms (220 pounds). Pausanias tells us that there was a shallow pool of water in front of the statue intended to reflect light from the doorway up on to the statue.

Phidias' workshop

Some years later, Phidias constructed a similar statue of Zeus at Olympia, which came to be considered one of the Seven Wonders of the World. What may be the remains of his workshop at Olympia have been identified beneath an early Byzantine church. The workshop was constructed to exactly the same height and width as the central aisle of the temple, and included the two-storey colonnades, so that the artist could imagine how the statue would appear in the temple. A similar workshop must have been built on the Acropolis. Fragments of ivory and broken clay moulds for the gold elements were found in the ruins of the workshop at Olympia. These give us some idea of how the statue was made.

Phidias produced two other statues of Athena for the Acropolis, the colossal bronze statue which stood behind the Propylaea and another life-size bronze statue, the Lemnian Athena, which was considered to be the most beautiful of the three.

We are fortunate that the Parthenon was converted into a mosque after the Turkish conquest of Greece in the fifteenth century, for this ensured its survival. In 1687 the Venetians besieged Athens, a gunpowder magazine in the building was hit and the centre of the temple

blown out. Early in the nineteenth century the English Lord Elgin bought much of Phidias' sculpture from the Turks and brought it to London. It is now a prime exhibit in the British Museum.

The Erechtheum

All work on the Acropolis had ceased when the war with Sparta broke out in 431 BC. The Propylaea had been hastily tidied up and the work-force dismissed. But with the peace of Nicias work started again, and in 420 BC the building of the Erechtheum began. This was a shrine to all those gods and heroes traditionally associated with the Acropolis and not worshipped elsewhere. In particular, it was the sanctuary of the sacred wooden cult statue of Athena, so important for the Panathenaea. Work stopped when the war began again, but recommenced in 409 BC and by 405 BC the Erechtheum was at last complete.

The temple was named after the legendary hero Erechtheus, who was regarded as the first king of Athens. He was believed to have been born of the Earth, and to have been reared by Athena herself. He was closely associated with the goddess and was possibly worshipped as a demi-god in the Mycenaean palace which had occupied the spot where the Erechtheum was built.

A multiple temple

In designing the Erechtheum the architects had even greater difficulty incorporating all the cults that had existed on the site than they had encountered in the Propylaea. No fewer than ten different gods, heroes and heroines had to be accommodated within the complex. The three primary deities were Athena, Poseidon and Erechtheus, who each had their own cult

◁ The 'Varvakeion' Athena, a small copy of the Athena Parthenos made in the 2nd century AD. Hundreds of such souvenirs must have been made.

▷ Part of a gold earring found in a Scythian grave in southern Russia. It shows what appears to be a very accurate and detailed picture of the head of Phidias' Athena Parthenos.

▷▷ A reconstruction of the massive statue of Athena Parthenos made by Phidias. The statue was made of wood, plated with ivory and gold.

room. The result was a somewhat awkward building, but one not without a certain harmony. It was a multiple temple, visually unified by consistent use of the Ionic style.

In essence, the Erechtheum consisted of two semi-detached temples, one facing east and the other, the larger, facing north. Owing to the steep slope of the ground, the east-facing temple was over 3 metres (10 feet) higher than the other. Each temple had a porch supported on elaborately decorated Ionic columns. The entablature was decorated with a frieze of low-relief figures in white marble on a darker background of Eleusinian stone. The frieze extended right round the double temple like a belt holding it together.

Builders' wages

A unique find amongst the building inscriptions from the temple reveals that a large number of different sculptors were responsible for the figures in this frieze. The sculptors were paid 60 drachmae per figure.

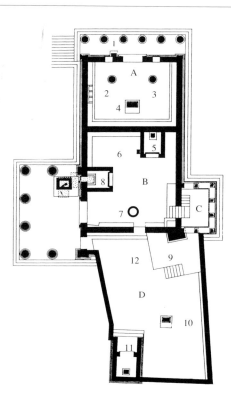

▷ A plan of the Erechtheum.

A **The east temple**
1 Altar of Zeus Hypatus
2 Altar of Hephaestus
3 Altar of Boutes
4 Altar of Poseidon and Erechtheus

B **The north-facing temple**
5 Sanctuary of Athena Polias
6 Statue of Hermes
7 Saltwater spring and trident marks
8 Tomb of Erechtheus

C **The caryatid porch**

D **The Pandroseum**
9 The tomb of Cecrops
10 Altar of Zeus Herceius
11 Temple of Pandrosos
12 Sacred olive tree

◁ The Erechtheum seen from the west, as it might have appeared at the beginning of the fourth century BC. A sacrificial procession with a lamb for sacrifice is approaching the sanctuary of Athena Polias.

The inscription lists the artists, their place of origin, the figures supplied and the fee. For example:

To Phyromachus of Kephisia for the youth beside the cuirass: 60dr.

To Praxias, resident at Melite, for the horse and the man seen behind it who is turning it: 120dr.

To Antiphanes of Kerameis, for the chariot and the youth and the pair of horses being yoked: 240dr.

To Mynnion, resident of Agryle, for the horse and the man striking it. He afterwards added the pillar (for which he was paid a little more): 127dr.

A home for Athena the Protectress

The eastern temple was primarily dedicated to Zeus the Highest, whose altar was in the porch. Inside were altars to Hephaestus, Boutes, Poseidon and Erechtheus, the last two sharing an altar.

The north-facing temple was the sanctuary of Athena Polias, the patroness of the city. Her ancient wooden statue was enshrined here, and the perpetually burning golden lamp with its chimney in the form of a bronze palm tree. The room also housed a wooden statue of Hermes, a salt-water spring and the tomb of Erechtheus. The spoils taken from the Persians during the great war, including the sword of Mardonius, were also kept here.

An annexe was built at the south end of the room in the form of a porch supported by caryatids (columns in the form of women).

△ The Erechtheum as it appears today. The interior of the building was torn out when it was converted into a church.

▷ The back of a caryatid.

▽ The caryatid porch on the south side of the Erechtheum.

A sacred enclosure

At the west end of the temple there was a sacred enclosure, the Pandroseum, containing the tomb of Cecrops, another legendary hero, and a tiny temple to his daughter Pandrosos. The enclosure also contained the sacred olive tree of Athena shading an altar to Zeus Herceius. This olive was believed miraculously to have sprouted new wood immediately after being burned by the Persians.

The Erechtheum completed the Periclean building programme on the Acropolis. Later generations were to add embellishments, but substantially the Acropolis remained as it was at the end of the fifth century BC. Most of our knowledge comes from the description provided by Pausanias in the second century AD.

The Temple to Olympian Zeus

Amongst the great temples raised to the glory of the gods in the second half of the fifth century, there appears to be one great omission: Zeus himself, king of the gods.

There were other shrines in Athens where he was worshipped, as Zeus Soter (the Saviour) and Zeus Eleutherius (the Deliverer). But somehow the great temple to Zeus was never built.

The tyrant Pisistratus or his sons began building a great temple, the Olympeion, in honour of Olympian Zeus in the sacred area to the east of the Acropolis. We do not know how far the building had advanced by the time the tyrants were overthrown, but part of the Doric colonnade must have existed for Aristotle to point to it as an example of a massive building project erected by a tyrant to keep the population occupied. The building was probably abandoned because of its association with the tyranny. The temple was still only partly built when the Persians sacked the city in 479 BC, and they may have contented themselves with knocking down some of the columns before withdrawing. Whatever the truth, many of the column drums were broken up and used to build the city wall in that area.

In the years that followed there were always more urgent or more economic projects, and the sheer scale of the project was daunting. The Athenians probably erected an altar on the site and offered sacrifice to the father of the gods there. It was more than 300 years before an attempt was made to complete the building, under the patronage of the Hellenistic king Antiochus of Syria. But he too failed to complete it. It remained for the Roman emperor Hadrian to complete the temple in the second century AD, nearly seven centuries after it was begun.

△ The east end of the Erechtheum, seen from the position of the Great Altar to Athena, with the caryatid porch on the left.

◁ The remains of the Olympeion, the great temple to Zeus, finally completed by the Roman emperor Hadrian in the second century AD.

A FESTIVAL FOR ATHENA

The great religious festival of Athens was the Panathenaea, the birthday festival of Athena, the city's patron goddess. The Panathenaic Games were part of the four-yearly Great Panathenaea, the most prestigious of all the Athenian festivals.

The Panathenaea was held every year at the height of the summer, on the 28th day of the month of Hecatombaion. A Great Panathenaea, preceded by games, had been held every fourth year since 566 BC. With democracy re-established, the Athenians had much to celebrate in 402 BC, and much for which to thank Athena, the virgin protector of the city. The Great Panathenaea of that year was special because the Acropolis was finally complete: the sacred wooden statue of Athena at last had a proper sanctuary.

Games for the gods
The Panathenaic Games was only one of several great religious sporting events held in Greece. Others were the Pythian Games held at Delphi, the Isthmian Games held at Isthmia (near Corinth), the Nemean Games held at Nemea, and the most famous, the Olympic Games held at Olympia: all these were Panhellenic games, open to all Greeks, whereas the Panathenaic Games were Athenian only. The main events were the same, though each Games had its special event, such as the contest of hymns to Apollo held in the Pythian Games. All these games were for men only. Married women were forbidden even to watch – at Olympia under pain of death. There was, however, a special games held for women at Olympia, the Heraea, held in honour of Hera, queen of the gods.

△ Front and back of a Panathenaic prize amphora.

▷ A vase painting showing a Victory carrying a *kithara* (lyre).

▽ Post holes for the wooden spectators' stands and, behind them, small stone sockets for the starting device of the race track in the Agora.

Poetry and music
In Athens, the competitions began five days before the Panathenaic feast, starting with the swearing-in ceremony for both contestants and judges, followed by the poetry and music contests. The poetic contests were judged on the recitation or singing of an extract from the works of Homer. Other poets began to be included at the end of the fifth century BC.

The musical contests were held in the Odeon, the covered theatre next to the Theatre of Dionysus, which Pericles had built specially for these contests. The two main musical instruments, the double flute (*diaulos*) and the lyre (*kithara*) had existed for a thousand years or more: they are shown being used to accompany a sacrifice on a sarcophagus from Hagia Triada in Crete from about 1400 BC. Both instruments continued to be used for this purpose, and can be seen on the Panathenaic frieze on the Parthenon.

There appear to have been at least six musical events, four for men and two or more for boys. Boys played the lyre and solo flute (*aulos*), while for the men there were singing to one's own accompaniment on the lyre, singing to the flute, playing the *kithara* and playing the solo flute. The *kithara* was the more prestigious instrument, and attracted far higher cash prizes than did the flute.

The athletic events
The athletic events were originally intended as a form of training for war. The contestants were divided into three age groups: boys aged 12 to 16, youths aged 16 to 20 and men over the age of 20. Boys and youths competed on the second

day of the festival, but probably performed only five events – the sprint, the pentathlon, the boxing, the wrestling and the 'all-in' wrestling.

The following morning there was a procession to the Agora of all the contestants for the men's sporting events. Sacrifices and prayers, both public and private, were offered, followed by the first event.

The athletic contests were held in the Agora until 330 BC, when the stadium just beyond the Ilissus river, south-east of Athens, was opened. Wooden stands were erected for the spectators alongside the 38-metre by 184-metre race track (42 yards by 200 yards) which passed down the centre of the Agora from the Altar of the Twelve Gods to the South Stoa. Excavations carried out along the Panathenaic Way at the north end of the Agora in 1971 uncovered post holes for these stands and stone sockets for the starting device, similar to that used at Delphi.

Track events

The adult games started with the *stadion*, the 184-metre (200-yard) sprint. (This was the most prestigious of all the events at Olympia: the winner gave his name to the Olympiad, the four-year dating system.) This was followed by the long distance race of twenty or twenty-four lengths of the track (3680 metres/4024 yards or 4416 metres/4829 yards).

The third track event, the *hippios*, was a middle distance race of six lengths, a little over 1000 metres (1093 yards). It was probably called the *hippios*, horse race, because the distance was the same as that run by horses.

Athletes performed naked. There were four heats for each event, the winners of the heats going through to a final. The winners of the finals received amphorae of the expensive olive oil produced in the Academy, which they were expected to sell. It could be exported free of duty. It is not known exactly how much oil was given for the men's races, but the winner of the boys' *stadion* received fifty amphorae. The oil was contained in special decorated containers called Panathenaic amphorae.

The pentathlon

The pentathlon was a combined event consisting of discus, long jump, javelin, sprinting (*stadion*) and wrestling. Since two of these were also individual events only the discus, long jump and javelin will be discussed here.

The Greek discus varied greatly in weight and size but this did not matter, for all the

contestants at a particular festival used the same one. The surviving examples, made of bronze, marble or lead, vary from 17 to 35 centimetres (6½ to 14 inches) in diameter and weigh between 1.5 and 6.5 kilograms (3¼ and 14¼ pounds).

The long jump was the only jumping contest in Greek athletics and was quite different from the modern long jump. It is depicted in a number of vase paintings. The contestant carried special weights (*halteres*) which he swung forward to give himself greater forward motion.

△ A red-figure bowl illustrating four events from the pentathlon – discus, javelin, wrestling and long jump.

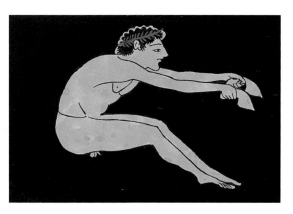

◁ A long-jumper holding weights.

▽ A pair of stone jumping weights.

△ A red-figure vase painting showing wrestlers and a judge.

One of these weights found at Olympia weighs over 4.5 kilograms (10 pounds). Evidence for how the jump was executed is confusing, but it is almost certain that the athlete did not make a long run-up. The recorded distances jumped (up to 16.66 metres/54½ feet), which are far in excess of the modern long jump record, suggest that it was almost certainly some kind of multiple jump.

The Greeks used a very light elder-wood javelin for athletics, with a throwing loop which made the javelin spin in flight, keeping it on course. Greek sources suggest that throws of 90 to 100 metres (295 to 328 feet) were possible. The decoration on a Panathenaic prize amphora shows that javelin throwing was also sometimes done from horseback, as a test of accuracy, rather than range.

△ A bronze statue of a boxer by the Athenian sculptor Apollonius, with a detail of his hands.

Wrestling

Wrestling (*pale*) was upright, where one had to throw one's opponent to the ground. There were no rounds; the contest continued until one of the contestants had gained three falls.

All-in wrestling (*pankration*) was decided by a submission, which the beaten contestant signalled by raising his hand with the index finger extended. Almost anything was allowed, including punching, kicking and strangle-holds; only biting and gouging were banned.

The contestants for both styles of wrestling rubbed themselves down with oil and sprinkled fine sand over their bodies before a fight. The ground had to be carefully prepared for wrestling. There are innumerable vase paintings showing athletes with the picks they used to break up the ground. For the *pankration* the ground was sometimes watered too, making the contest akin to mud wrestling.

Contestants for the heats were paired off by casting lots marked with letters of the alphabet, which were drawn from a helmet or bronze bowl. The *pankration* was by far the most popular event with the crowd. Many of the top contestants became professional wrestlers.

△ An armed runner with helmet and shield.

Milo of Croton

Occasionally, when a contestant completely outclassed all the others, his opponents would withdraw from the competition: he was said to have won *aknoite*, without touching the dust. Milo, from the Greek colony at Croton in southern Italy, was just such a champion. He won five times at Olympia and his reputation was so terrifying that all other contestants withdrew. On one occasion he tripped and fell on his way to receive his prize and the crowd jokingly objected to his winning because he had 'touched the dust'. Milo was considered the greatest wrestler of all time, and when he was finally defeated by a younger man at his sixth Olympics the crowd carried him shoulder high from the stadium.

Boxing

Terrifying though the *pankration* might seem, boxing was far more dangerous. Greek boxing

had fewer restrictions than modern boxing. The contestants, their hands bound with leather thongs, could hit with their hands in any way they chose; rabbit punches and blows using the butt of the hand are shown on vase paintings. Only gouging with the thumb seems to have been forbidden. The contests, which were decided by a knockout, often lasted for hours and sometimes resulted in the death of one of the contestants. In such cases, the prize was awarded to the dead man and his opponent was banned for life from those particular games. Boxers received such damage to their faces that their profession became a byword for ugliness.

The race in armour

As Greek athletics were devised primarily to keep the male citizens fit for war, it is not surprising that a race in armour (*hoplitodromos*) was introduced in 520 BC at Olympia. The contestants had to run wearing helmets and leg guards (greaves) and carrying a shield, but otherwise naked. This race, which must have produced some very humorous incidents, was the final athletic event.

The equestrian events

On the fourth day of the Panathenaic festival the venue was moved outside the walls to a suitable field towards the coast. Several horse racing contests took place here. There were chariot races with two and four horses, and horseback races. The races were divided into two categories according to the age of the horses. A fragmentary inscription tells us that the winner of the two-horse chariot race received 140 amphorae of oil, while the winner of the chariot race for foals received only 40 amphorae.

Appalling accidents

Electra, by the Athenian playwright Sophocles, includes a vivid description of a chariot race in the Pythian games at Delphi:

> They took up the positions which the umpires had selected by the casting of lots and then, at the sound of the bronze trumpet, they started off, all shouting to their horses and urging them on with their reins. The clatter of the rattling chariots filled the whole arena, and the dust flew up as they sped along in a dense mass, each driver goading his team unmercifully in his efforts to draw clear of the rival axles and panting steeds, whose steaming breath and sweat drenched every bending back and flying wheel with foam...
>
> At every turn of the lap, Orestes reined in his inner trace horse and gave his right horse its head so skilfully that his hub just cleared the turning post by a hair's breadth every time; and so the poor fellow had safely rounded every lap but one, without mishap to himself or his chariot. But at the last bend he misjudged it, slackening his left rein before the horse was safely round, and so struck the post. The hub was smashed across, and he was hurled over the rail, entangled in the reins; and as he fell his horses ran wild across the course... [he was] whirled along the ground... tossing up his limbs to heaven, until the other charioteers stopped his horses and released him, all covered with blood.

This is clearly a first-hand description. Besides the excitement and danger that Sophocles captures, he also gives us the interesting information that chariot races were run in an anti-clockwise direction. These races are shown in innumerable vase paintings which clearly depict the very light chariots in which the contestants raced.

△ Pelops, the legendary chariot racer, and his wife Hippodameia in a four-horse chariot. This late fourth-century vase painting shows a typical light racing chariot of the period. The Athenians used four-horse chariots for both ordinary chariot racing and the chariot race of the *apobates* (see p. 87).

The Parthenon frieze, depicting the Panathenaic procession. It begins at the back (west end) of the temple with horsemen preparing for the procession, which runs down each side of the temple to meet at the front. The top strip shows part of the north frieze with the Athenian cavalry galloping along at the back of the procession.

The second strip shows (right to left) the first of the eleven *apobates* charioteers, preceded by sixteen elders and a group of musicians, double flute (*diaulos*) and lyre (*kithara*) players.

The third strip begins (right) with the leading *diaulos* player, preceded by four men carrying water jars. In front of these are three *metoikoi*, foreigners living in Athens, carrying honeycombs and cakes in metal trays. They are preceded by the sacrificial animals, three sheep and four bulls.

The fourth strip shows the north end of the east frieze. A group of girls (right) carry the bowls (*phialai*) or jugs used for libations (one carries an incense burner). The two girls at the front hand an offering basket to one of the marshals. The three men ahead of the girls are marshals. The group ahead of these are five of the ten eponymous heroes of Athens. Beyond them are the gods, Aphrodite and Eros first, then Artemis, Apollo and the bearded Poseidon. Next (bottom strip, right) are Hephaestus and Athena.

Beyond these two is a young girl (some say a boy), handing the *peplos* for Athena to the king archon. To the left of these is the priestess of Athena Polias receiving a cushioned stool from a girl carrying it on her head. A second girl behind her carries another cushioned stool and a footstool. These five figures are in the centre of the east frieze, immediately over the door of the temple, the focal point of the frieze. Beyond this the figures face the other way and are connected with the procession coming along the south wall of the temple. The next three figures are Zeus, Hera and Iris, messenger of the gods. The remaining four figures from right to left are Ares, Demeter, possibly Dionysus and Hermes. Beyond these are the other five eponymous heroes.

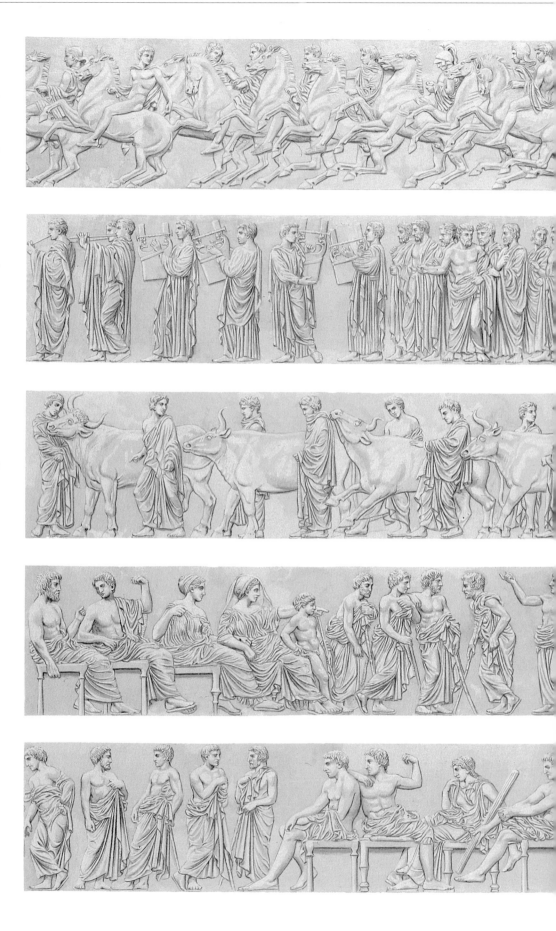

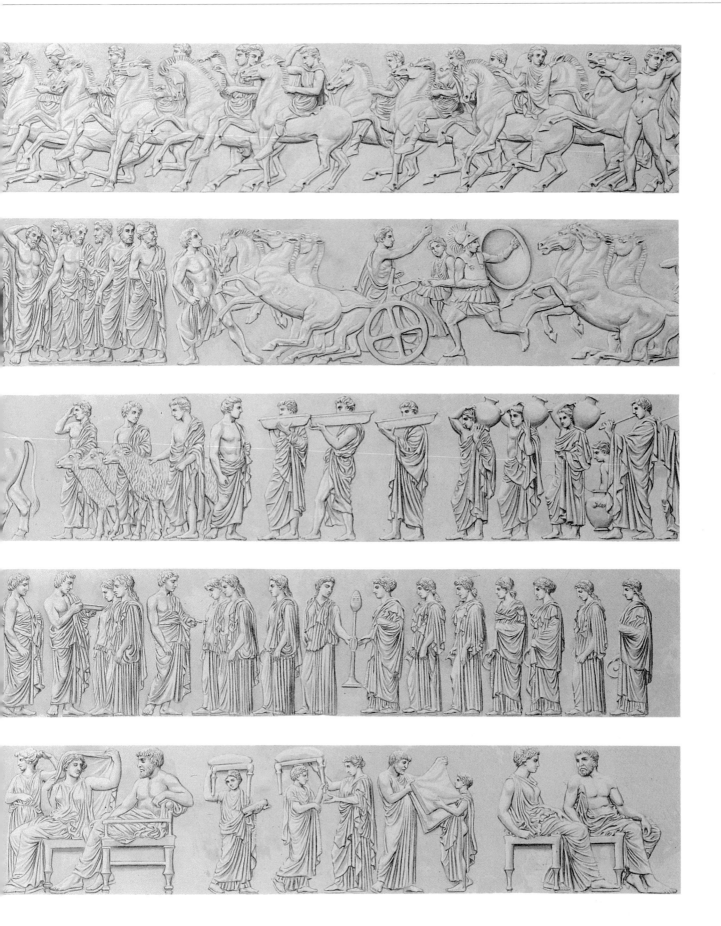

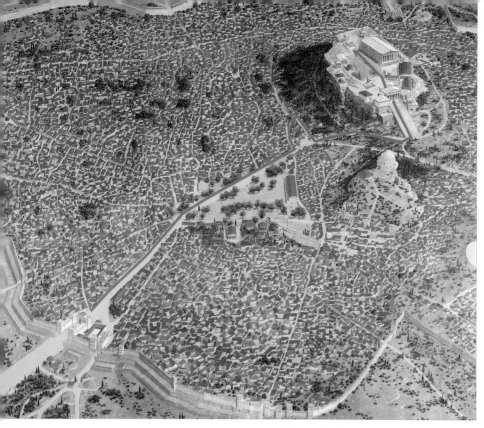

fire was carried in a torch race, a relay race by teams of forty runners from the ten tribes along the broad road from the Academy, through the Dipylon Gate, across the Agora and up to the great altar of Athena on the Acropolis, a little over 2500 metres (2735 yards). The first to reach the altar with his torch still alight was the winner. Again the prize was a bull and 100 drachmae.

The *peplos*

Preparations for the festival itself had begun nine months earlier, at the festival of the Chalcaea. The priestesses of Athena and the *arrhephoroi*, four little girls of noble family selected annually by the king archon, had set up a loom on which the new tunic (*peplos*) for Athena would be woven. This tunic, decorated with the *aristeia* of Athena, in particular her victory over Ecceladus and the Giants, was made by the little girls, the priestesses and a group of women known as the *ergastinai*. A *peplos* was a simple rectangular piece of cloth, about 2 by 1½ metres (6½ by 5 feet), which was wrapped round the wearer and pinned at the shoulders. The tunic was to clothe the statue of Athena Polias, the protector of the city, and was replaced every year. This life-size wooden statue was so ancient that no one knew where it came from or how old it was. We now do not know whether the statue was seated or standing.

There appears to have been another *peplos* for Athena, which was huge. It was made by the professional weavers of Athens and according to legend was large enough to be hoisted as a sail on a full-size ship. The poet Strattis, writing in about 400 BC, refers to countless men hauling on the ropes to raise the *peplos* to the top of the mast. This *peplos* may have been draped over the Athena Parthenos for the festival, or simply have been hung in the temple.

The tribal contests

The events of the first four days of the Panathenaic festival had been open to outsiders, but the fifth day was taken up with team events which were restricted to the ten Athenian tribes. Among the events was a male strength and beauty contest, the *euandria*, and the Pyrrhic dance, a war dance performed by teams from the ten tribes each accompanied by a *diaulos* player. Armed with spear and shield they performed a dance based on fighting – dodging, striking, crouching and other defensive and offensive movements. Teams were selected from the three age levels, but all received the same prize, 100 drachmae and a bull.

A nocturnal festival

A nocturnal festival was held on the fifth night of the Panathenaea, with music, singing and dancing. Sacrifice was offered to Athena and Eros at the Academy at dawn, and the sacred

A ritual from a forgotten past

One night, about a month before the Panathenaic festival, the priestess of Athena had given two of the *arrhephoroi* covered baskets, which they carried on their heads down the steep steps towards the old Mycenaean cistern. At the bottom of the second flight they emerged through a cave in the north face of the Acropolis and followed a narrow path eastwards towards the shrine of Aphrodite. Here they exchanged their baskets for two similarly covered baskets, which they took back through the darkness to the priestess of Athena. Pausanias himself was unaware of the significance of the ritual, and implied that nobody knew what was in the baskets. The ritual was probably connected with the myth of Aglaurus, daughter of king Cecrops, who had carried a basket in which a foster-child of Athena herself was hidden.

The great procession

The crowds began to assemble at the Dipylon Gate before dawn on the day of the feast. The procession set out at first light. The new *peplos* for Athena Polias was carried by the *arrhephoroi* at the head of the procession, with the priestesses of Athena and a long train of women bearing gifts. The leaders of the sacrifices followed with the sacrificial animals, a hundred cows and some sheep, and all those connected with the ritual. Then came the resident foreigners (metics, or *metoikoi*) in their purple cloaks and carrying trays of offerings of cakes and honey. The holy water carriers and musicians playing the *aulos* and *kithara* followed. The large *peplos*, suspended from the yards of a ship on wheels, was dragged along with the procession. Behind the musicians came the bearded old men and the commanders of the army, all carrying olive branches, hustled along by the *apobates*, armed warriors who rode in and ran beside chariots (they would race around the Agora the following day). The chariots were followed by the cavalry, walking, trotting, cantering. The victors of the various games were there too. The mass of the population followed, *deme* by *deme*. A long frieze on the Parthenon shows part of this procession in detail.

The sacrifices

The procession moved along the broad Panathenaic Way through the Agora, singing hymns to Athena, and headed up the hill towards the Acropolis. They turned left just before they reached the Eleusinium, rounded the eastern end of the block and returned to the Panathenaic Way, pressing on up the steep slope to the saddle between the Acropolis and the Areopagus.

The procession stopped in front of the Propylaea while sacrifices were offered on the Areopagus and at the altar of Athena Hygiaea. The most perfect of the heifers was sacrificed to Athena Nike (the Victorious) and Athena Polias (the protector of the city) in front of the tiny temple of Victory. The sacrifices were accompanied by prayers, including special prayers for the Plataeans who had suffered so much in the war with Sparta.

Forbidden to foreigners

Only native-born Athenians were permitted to enter the Acropolis. The many foreigners who had followed the procession, even the *metoikoi*, those foreigners who had settled in Athens, could go no further. Reaching the summit of the hill, the procession passed along the north side of the Parthenon and crowded round the great altar to Athena in front of the recently completed Erechtheum. The little girls handed the *peplos* to the *ergastinai*, the women who had helped to weave it and who once a year ceremonially carried the wooden statue down to the sea and washed both it and the *peplos*.

The animals were now sacrificed. The *ergastinai* entered the chamber of Athena in the Erechtheum and changed her *peplos*. The ceremony ended with a feast at which a set number of people from each *deme*, selected by lot, ate the cooked meat of the sacrificial animals with bread and cakes.

After the feast

The next day was devoted to two events, the chariot race of the *apobates* and the boat race. The Athenians believed that this chariot race had been introduced by the first king, Erechtheus, and it may indeed have recalled chariot warfare of the Bronze Age. Each chariot was occupied by a driver and a warrior in full armour who had to jump down and re-board the chariot while it moved at speed. The Panathenaic Way may have formed part of the circuit, as the chariots finished up by the Eleusinium, halfway up the hill to the Acropolis.

The boat race was the last of the competitions. Very little is known about this event except that it was contested by teams of rowers from the ten tribes and that it probably involved rowing ten triremes round Piraeus from the Kantharos harbour to the Munichia harbour. The following day, the last day of the festival, was devoted to prize-giving.

△ A statuette of a seated goddess, one of several found on the Acropolis. Some scholars contend that this is a representation of the famous olive-wood statue of Athena Polias, which was so old that it was believed to have fallen from the sky. But the wooden statue is known to have been adorned with a gold diadem, several gold necklaces, a gold aegis and a gold owl, none of which is depicted on this statuette, and it is hard to see how the *peplos* could be draped on such a statue.

◁ Traditional picture of Athena on Panathenaic prize vases. It would have been much easier to drape the *peplos* on such a figure.

Athens in the mid-fourth
century BC.

N4 Dromos, leading
    through the
    Kerameikos (the
    graveyard) to the
    Academy
L6 Dipylon Gate
N12 Piraeus Gate
H11 Agora
G16 Areopagus
C15 Acropolis
I19 Pnyx
G   Olympeion
B19 Kynosarges
B10 Lyceum

THE THEATRE

The theatre was among the greatest of the Athenian contributions to world culture. Athenian playwrights were long acknowledged to be the best in the world, and their plays are performed to this day.

△ The obverse and reverse of a theatre entry token found at Athens.

▽ A painting on the Pronomos vase from southern Italy showing actors in a satyr play. The god of the theatre, Dionysus, and his wife Ariadne are shown in the centre with the musicians, a *diaulos* and *kithara* player below.

The month of Elaphobolion (March) was the month of the Dionysia. It seems strange that one of the two greatest festivals of Athens should be honouring a god who was included comparatively recently among the Greek deities. According to legend Dionysus came from Thrace or from Lydia in Asia Minor, but his supposed foreign origin probably has more to do with the outlandish behaviour associated with his cult than with history. His name is found in Linear B tablets from Mycenaean Greece, so he cannot have been unknown to the early Greeks.

Although he is normally associated with wine, he is also important as the god of emotion or the release of emotion. His worship was very popular with women, though not exclusively so. The secret rites (*orgia*) of the Dionysia were associated with sexual immorality by the early Christians – hence the meaning of the English word 'orgy'.

Source material for the early theatre is very late and probably corrupt, but the development of the theatre and this festival in Athens seems to have occurred as follows. About the middle of the sixth century BC the people of Eleutherae on the border between Attica and Boeotia, constantly harassed by the Boeotians, had applied to be included in Attica. As part of the absorption, their particular cult of Dionysus was trans-ferred to Athens. The ancient wood statue of the god was carried in procession the 45 kilo-metres (28 miles) to Athens and installed in a tiny temple below the southern slope of the Acropolis. This procession was partially re-enacted each year when the wooden statue was escorted from the Academy (on the road to Eleutherae) to its temple at the foot of the Acropolis.

The great Dionysia

The main procession, escorting the sacrificial animals, probably took place on the 10th of the month. Young men dressed as satyrs, the myth-ical half-human, half-animal companions of Dionysus. Wearing masks, they danced along as a choir sang. The animals were sacrificed, the people feasted on the meat, the wine flowed and the night was spent in dancing and singing drunkenly in the streets to the music of harps and flutes. This temporary opportunity for ecstatic freedom from a normally confined life was particularly favoured by Greek women. But in about 534 BC a new element was added. The festival had previously included ritualised dramatic scenes played out in public by a chorus, but in that year a man called Thespis held a dialogue with the chorus, possibly using various masks and playing several different parts. It was the beginning of Greek drama.

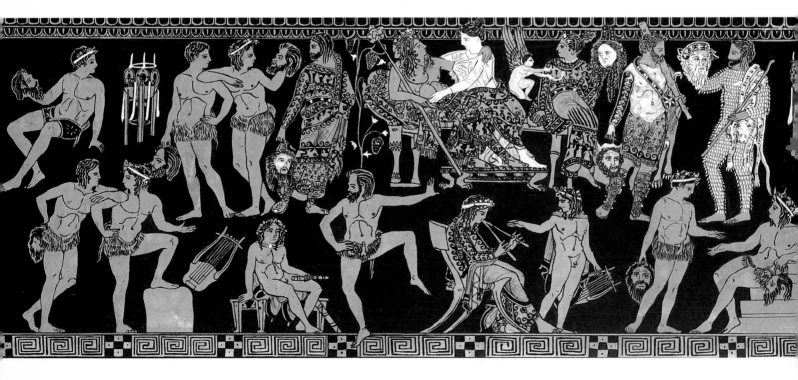

containing walls of the auditorium are almost certainly contemporary with the mid-fourth century theatre, the foundations of both being built of breccia, which did not come into use until after the Peloponnesian war. The alignment of the western side of the auditorium, G–G, appears to have been altered with the rebuilding at the end of the fourth century BC.

In the earlier fifth century there may have been only a few wooden benches at the front with the rest of the audience sitting on the hillside. Later a more sophisticated arrangement may have existed, but still with wooden benches supported on an artificial ramp resting against the lower slope of the Acropolis. Stone seating may not have existed before the fourth century BC.

The tragic poets

Early Athenian tragedies were mainly based on well-known legends. This allowed the poet to develop details of the story without complicated explanations. The audience knew in outline what was going to happen, though the playwright did sometimes produce surprises. The skill was in the dialogue, the music and the presentation. These tragedies have much in common with the modern musical, mainly spoken but accompanied by the chorus singing and dancing.

The three greatest tragic poets, Aeschylus, Sophocles and Euripides, all lived in Athens in the fifth century BC. Aeschylus was born at Eleusis in about 525 BC. He fought against the Persians in both wars. He had his first drama victory in 484 and his last in 458 BC.

The *Oresteia*

Each poet had to put on four plays, three tragedies and a satyr play. Aeschylus' *Oresteia*, first staged in 458 BC, is the only trilogy to survive intact. It is a powerful tragedy of betrayal and retribution, with an inevitability that reflected Greek ideas of the relationship between gods and humans. The fifth-century Athenians considered it the finest tragedy ever written.

The Agamemnon, the first of the *Oresteia* trilogy, is the story of Clytemnestra, the wife of Agamemnon, king of Argos, leader of the Greek armies in the Trojan War. The play begins with the news that Troy has fallen and that Agamemnon is on his way home after ten

years. The chorus in song and dance tell the background story. Their song reaches a climax as they describe how Agamemnon, faced with unending storms which prevented the Greek fleet sailing, was compelled to sacrifice his daughter Iphigenia to the goddess Artemis:

> Heedless of her tears, her cries of 'Father!' and her maiden years, her judges valued more their glory and their war. A prayer was said. Her father gave the word. Limp in her flowing dress the priests attendants held her high above the altar, as men hold a kid. Her father spoke again to bid one bring a gag and close her sweet mouth tightly with a cord for fear his house be cursed by some ill-omened cry.

Embittered by the sacrifice of her daughter, Clytemnestra falls in love with her husband's avowed enemy, Aegisthus. Together they murder Agamemnon when he returns from Troy. Their action sets in train a cycle of retribution which is worked out through the remainder of the trilogy.

Vengeance

The second play, *The Libation Bearers*, tells of the vengeance of Orestes, Agamemnon's son. Orestes returns to Argos after many years in exile and tells his sister Electra that the oracle at Delphi has ordered him to kill his mother and her lover in retribution for their father's death. Electra agrees to help him, and Orestes murders them.

The third play, *The Eumenides*, tells of the trial of Orestes on the charge of matricide. Pursued by the Furies, the terrifying and remorseless agents of divine retribution, Orestes flees to Apollo's temple at Delphi where he begs the god to justify the act he has been ordered to perform. Apollo agrees to defend him before the murder court of the

△ A fourth-century BC south Italian vase painting showing part of a wooden *skene*.

◁ Stone post sockets uncovered in the theatre at Pergamum. Similar post sockets must have been used in the theatre at Athens.

▷ A fourth-century BC south Italian vase painting showing a scene from *The Eumenides*, the third play of Aeschylus's *Oresteia* trilogy. Two of the Furies can be seen, one on the right and the other behind the tripod. Orestes is in the middle, kneeling at the *omphalos* at Delphi. He is flanked by Athena and Apollo.

Areopagus at Athens. The Furies, played by the chorus, act as the prosecution and Athena as the judge. The jury of twelve Athenians reaches a split decision and Athena casts her deciding vote in favour of Orestes.

A political message

The *Oresteia* includes many political and moral references, some possibly aimed at non-Athenians visiting Athens for the festival. Staged shortly after the breaking of the power of the aristocratic Council of the Areopagus, the play divinely sanctions its 'true' role as a murder court. The end of the play is a glorification of Athens and a plea for an end to civil strife. The old order, personified by the Furies (transformed at the end into the Eumenides or 'Kindly Ones'), is given an honourable role. The play ends with a torchlight procession. Apollo and Athena lead off the primeval goddesses, dressed in the scarlet ceremonial robes of Athens' resident aliens, to their new home in a cave in the Acropolis from which they will watch over the fortunes of Athens. The scene is packed with political significance. It celebrates the end of the old order of violence and oppression and the beginning of a new era of justice and democracy.

It is interesting to note that Aeschylus makes

Agamemnon king of Argos, rather than the Homeric Mycenae. In *The Eumenides* mention is made of the everlasting friendship between Athens and Argos. Argos was, of course, Athens' great ally in the Peloponnese.

The performers

The whole trilogy may have required only three male actors (one mute), paid by the state, who played all the speaking roles using changes of costumes and masks. There are seventeen parts, the main ones being Orestes and Clytemnestra. The system occasionally requires lightning changes, such as the point in *The Libation Bearers* where Clytemnestra, Orestes and his companion Pylades share a scene. The servant who has been speaking to Clytemnestra leaves at line 889, Orestes enters and speaks line 892 and Pylades, played by the mute actor, comes on and captures the audience's attention by unexpectedly delivering line 900. The lightning changes needed suggest that costumes may not have been elaborate.

The chorus

The chorus of twelve or fifteen men play the elders of Argos in the first play, Clytemnestra's maids in the second and the Furies in the third. They set the scene, comment on situations, and hold dialogues with the actors, cross-examining and judging them.

The trilogy also required about twenty non-speaking extras, to play Agamemnon's soldiers in the first play and the twelve Athenian jurors plus some women and girls in the third.

Despite his extraordinary dramatic achievements, Aeschylus seems to have fallen out of favour and retired to Gela in Sicily, where he died in 456 BC. He wrote his own epitaph, recording merely that he had served as a foot-soldier at Marathon.

Sophocles and Euripides

Sophocles, born about 496 BC, was reportedly an accomplished dancer and musician. He was regarded by Aristotle to have raised tragedy to the greatest heights of refinement. He won his first victory in 468 and dominated the theatre until his death in 406, winning his last victory after his death. His main innovation was the introduction of a third speaking actor into his plays, probably shortly after Aeschylus staged the *Oresteia*.

Euripides, who was about ten years younger than Sophocles, probably died in the same year. He won his first victory in 441 BC, but always worked in the shadow of Sophocles. He tried to break with the refined Sophoclean style and to get away from the traditional formula of using a well-known story by developing more light-hearted variants within the established framework. For his *Iphigenia in Tauris* he used a less familiar variant of the Iphigenia story, in which Agamemnon did not finally sacrifice his daughter and she survived to become a priestess of Artemis. Similarly in his *Helen*, the famous beauty was carried off not to Troy but to Egypt, and remained faithful to her husband Menelaus. This introduced a story-line which kept the audience guessing and paved the way for Agathon to write his *Antheus* in about 414 BC, with its entirely fictional plot.

Later tragedians never achieved the same success, and in the fourth century revivals of fifth-century plays became popular.

The satyr play

The satyr play which formed the finale to the *Oresteia* has been lost. Only its name, *Proteus*, is known. A few satyr plays have survived, but apart from the common feature of the satyrs their lack of similarity makes it impossible to define a typical satyr play. At the time of the *Oresteia*, 558 BC, satyr plays may have featured a chorus of satyrs with their fat, drunken and lecherous father, Silenus. Satyr plays probably combined tragic, comic, religious and obscene elements, and were intended to provide contrast and light relief after the tragedies.

Silenus and his satyrs are the reverse face of the Furies. One can imagine what *Proteus* might have been like. Proteus, the old man of the sea,

could change shape: one minute a man, the next a lion, a snake, a tree or even running water. Combined with a chorus of satyrs, this character would fit well into a knockabout farce.

The beginning of comedy

Comedy was widespread in southern Greece and among the Greek colonies of southern Italy, where it was associated with religious ritual. Comedy was introduced into the Great Dionysia in about 486 BC and into the less prestigious Country Dionysia (which was held in January) in 442 BC. Three tragedies, a satyr play and a comedy, were performed on the second, third, fourth and fifth days of the Great Dionysia. The length of the festival was reduced to four days during the Peloponnesian War, with a comedy after the satyr play on the second, third and fourth day. If the purpose of the satyr play was indeed to relax the audience after the tragedies the placing of the comedies after the satyr plays may account for an apparent change in the content of the satyr plays, whose original purpose was now superfluous.

An actor holding his mask, shown on a fourth-century BC south Italian vase.

Attic old comedy

The fifth-century Athenian comedies (Attic Old Comedy) relied heavily on jibes aimed mainly at politicians, parodies of other playwrights and well-known personalities, and basic vulgar humour. Until recent years, it was impossible, because of censorship, to translate properly the plays of Aristophanes, the undisputed king of Attic Old Comedy, for his humour relied heavily on a near-obsession with bodily functions of all kinds.

Aristophanes, like many fifth-century poets, may have been something of an idealist. He and Euripides both offer characters who make anti-war statements, and both make women characters a focus of interest. Aristophanes attacked the mob orator and warmonger Cleon in his second play, *The Babylonians*, written before he was twenty. Cleon hit back by indicting him for impiety, but could not make the charge stick. The poet continued to attack the demagogue until his death in 421 BC.

A dancing satyr shown on the back of the Pronomos vase.

The Clouds

Not all of Aristophanes' attacks were vindictive. He was possibly a friend of the great Athenian philosopher Socrates and shared many of the philosopher's views. One can imagine Socrates' discomfiture when watching *The Clouds* at seeing himself float on to the stage in a basket from which he was supposed to be studying the sun. Aristophanes made the philosopher one of the main characters in the play, representing Socrates as an eccentric and

▷ (Far right) A fragment of a south Italian vase showing actors in elaborate costumes.

irreligious crank. But Socrates saw the funny side of it and is supposed to have stood up so that the audience could appreciate how good the characterisation was.

△ A fragment of a fifth-century BC Athenian vase found in the Agora, showing an early female mask with the face painted white.

New Comedy

Comedy began to change during the fourth century BC. The change reflected the reduced status of Athens after the Peloponnesian war and the ultimate defeat of the Athenians by Philip of Macedon in 338 BC. One can see the change already beginning in Aristophanes' later plays. Gradually the chorus became less important, obscenity and attacks on individuals largely disappeared, to be replaced by the ridiculing of caricature parasites, gluttons and drunks. Stock characters such as old men, young men and slaves began to appear, and themes were increasingly drawn from daily life.

The greatest single influence on the new style was Euripides, who died long before the change started. Menander (342-290 BC) was the king of New Comedy. His plays were adapted in Latin by Terence and Plautus, and continued to be produced for hundreds of years after his death. It is said that every type of joke can be found in Aristophanes, but that all modern comedy is based on the New Comedy.

Costume

Actors' costumes were generally based on everyday dress, the tunic (*chiton*) and cloak (*himation*). Sleeves were added, perhaps because the weather was inclined to be cold at the Dionysiac festivals. The Lenaia, a less important Dionysiac drama festival, was held in January, and even at the Great Dionysia, held in March, it could be very chilly.

The Pronomos vase gives a good impression of theatre costume around 400 BC. Satyrs generally wear only a hairy loin cloth with phallus and tail plus a bearded mask with pointed ears. Silenus, the father of the satyrs, wears a similar mask and a hairy body stocking. Other characters wear decorated cloaks and tunics, often coming down to their ankles, and soft calf-length boots.

The most luxuriously dressed person was the *aulos* player who accompanied the chorus. The lyre player who accompanied the actors when they sang solo did not appear on stage. The producers (*choregoi*), who paid for the costumes, masks, scenery and props, were usually wealthy men trying to impress the audience.

Grotesque costumes with pot bellies and huge buttocks were used in comedy. These consisted of a waist-length tunic worn over padded tights, often with a huge phallus. These went out of fashion in Athens in the fourth century BC, but remained in use in southern Italy.

Masks

All the performers including the chorus wore masks. In the fifth century BC these were fairly accurate representations of the characters, with slightly open mouths. Masks were made of strips of glued linen moulded on the actor's face, producing a light stiff mask that could then be painted. Satyr masks may have been painted red, and female masks generally white.

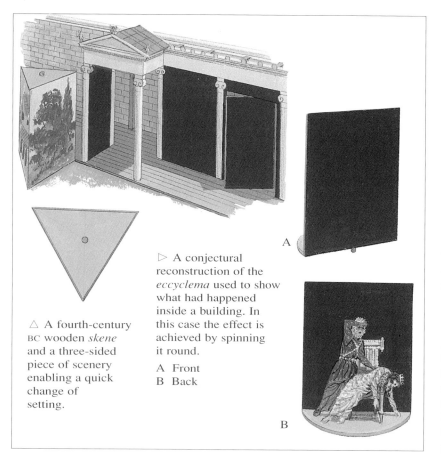

△ A fourth-century BC wooden *skene* and a three-sided piece of scenery enabling a quick change of setting.

▷ A conjectural reconstruction of the *eccyclema* used to show what had happened inside a building. In this case the effect is achieved by spinning it round.

A Front
B Back

A

B

Aristophanes always required caricature masks for the people he was ridiculing, such as a Cleon mask for *The Knights* and a Socrates mask for *The Clouds*. There must also have been shock masks, such as those used for the chorus of Furies in Aeschylus' *The Eumenides*, or for Oedipus who appears blinded and bleeding in Sophocles' *Oedipus the King*. The chorus appeared as different types of bird in Aristophanes' *The Birds* and perhaps with white masks in *The Clouds*.

Masks became more formalised in the fourth century as stock characters began to appear.

Scenery

Fifth-century Athenian drama certainly used scenery, and Sophocles is said to have introduced it, but little more than this is known. There is reason to believe that scenery in early drama was minimal. Later, there may also have been free-standing scenery, sometimes double or even three-sided, which could be rotated for changes of scene. The *Oresteia* is mainly set outside the palace at Argos, but the scene changes to outside the temple of Apollo at Delphi for the third play, and then changes again to outside the temple of Athena at Athens. The last change could be done simply by changing the cult statue, but there was probably some way of indicating a temple as opposed to a palace. Some form of back-cloth may have been used. Two columns and a pediment could have denoted a temple.

Deus ex machina

Early in the fifth century a crane was introduced to bring gods down and carry them off stage again. This sometimes had to be a very robust affair, as in Euripides' *Medea* where the heroine had to fly in a chariot, possibly drawn by winged serpents, accompanied by the bodies of her dead children.

This piece of equipment (*deus ex machina*), designed for the tragedies, presented a great opportunity to the comedy writers, who used it to whip characters off the stage. Aristophanes must have used it to bring on Socrates in his basket.

A platform on wheels (the *eccyclema*) was used to show what was going on within a building. Clytemnestra kills Agamemnon and Cassandra the prophetess inside the palace in the *Oresteia*. She and the two bodies were then wheeled out onto the stage through the central door so that the audience could see what had happened.

The first stone theatre

In the second half of the fourth century BC the first fully integrated stone theatre was erected on the site of the Theatre of Dianglos. This development, oddly enough, seems to have been accompanied by a loss of freshness and

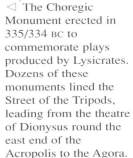

◁ The Choregic Monument erected in 335/334 BC to commemorate plays produced by Lysicrates. Dozens of these monuments lined the Street of the Tripods, leading from the theatre of Dionysus round the east end of the Acropolis to the Agora.

▽ A plan of the theatre and sanctuary of Dionysus. The mid-fourth-century buildings are shown in red.

A   The great altar of Dionysus
D–D Drainage channel
M   Choregic monuments
O   Odeon of Pericles
S   Long stoa
T1   Early temple
T2   Later temple

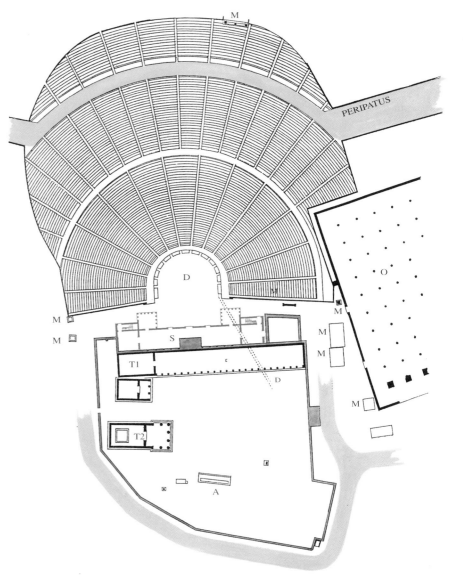

originality in the plays. The Athenians realised that something had been lost, and revivals of fifth-century plays became very popular.

The new *skene* was moved forward 7 metres (23 feet) so that the old wall H–H formed the rear wall of the backstage area. The new *skene*, which had three doorways in it, was fronted by a closed colonnade. It also had two wings projecting forward 5 metres (16½ feet), which were fronted with an open colonnade. Entries could now be made at five different points. The new stage was raised above the *orchestra*, as it is in the modern theatre, which made direct contact between the actors on stage and the chorus difficult. This reflected the much reduced importance of the chorus. The platform D was now almost certainly used as the base of the crane. This new theatre may not be so very different from its predecessor and may reflect the state to which the old wooden *skene* had developed.

The seating capacity seems to have been greatly increased, with stone seating extended right up to the cliff face of the Acropolis (which was cut back to accommodate it). The *orchestra* assumed the semi-circular shape it retained through the rest of antiquity, with the drainage channel (*canopus*), which carried off rainwater from the hillside, running round the edge of the orchestra.

The autumn of Athens

Spartan domination did not last long. The Thirty Tyrants were quickly overthrown. A general anti-Spartan feeling was rising. Corinth, Argos and Thebes revolted and Athens joined them. The Long Walls to the Piraeus were rebuilt and Athens began to build up a new maritime confederacy. But the days of Athenian supremacy were over. The new Greek power was Thebes, which defeated Sparta in two classic battles. The myth of Spartan invincibility was destroyed.

Athens had by now totally recovered from defeat. Although the Athenians never again achieved the cultural standards of the Periclean age, they gradually rebuilt their city's trade, and the prosperity of fourth-century Athens was as high as any state in Greece. Athens had stable government and artistic and intellectual achievements renowned throughout the world. Athenian plays were performed in every theatre in the Greek world and the great thinkers of the age again headed for Athens.

The followers of Socrates had fled from the city after his execution. Plato returned in about 387 BC and set up a school of philosophy in the Academy, about 3 kilometres to the north of Athens.

The supremacy of Thebes was short lived. Already a new power was rising. By 350 BC Philip II of Macedon had absorbed the states in Chalcidice which had been allied to Athens, invaded Thessaly and reached Thermopylae. Athens and Thebes formed an alliance against the Macedonians, but were defeated at Chaeronea in 338 BC. Thebes was totally destroyed by Philip's son Alexander, but Athens survived as a centre of learning. But even as Alexander was conquering Persia an even greater power was establishing its supremacy in central Italy. Macedon and the rest of Greece were to come under Roman control from about 148 BC, and for the next 650 years Rome was to dominate the Mediterranean.

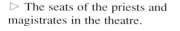

▷ The seats of the priests and magistrates in the theatre.

△ A reconstruction of the late fourth-century theatre. It is only at this late date that we can be reasonably certain what the theatre was like. The Sanctuary of Asclepius is at the bottom left.

◁ The stone seating for the audience and the stepped gangway with rutted steps to prevent people slipping. Spectators sat on the raised part of the bench, and put their feet on the sunken part of the bench below.

101

GALLIA NARBONENSIS

Comum

Bellunum

Aquileia

PO VALLEY

Po

Cremona

Sarsina

Orange

Carrara

SENONES

Ancona

Salonae

ILLYRIA

Marseilles

UMBRIA

APENNINES

Clusium

ETRURIA

Adriatic Se

CORSICA

APULIA

Rome

Cann

Tyrrhenian
Sea

Capua

SARDINIA

SICILY

Syracuse

Zama

Carthage

MEDITERRANEAN

ROME

Rome at the height of her power in the early second century AD was very different from Athens more than half a millennium earlier. In the first century BC, Dionysius of Halicarnassus said the three most significant works of Rome were its aqueducts, paved roads, and sewers. The Roman geographer Strabo agreed, saying that the Romans 'had the best foresight in those matters which the Greeks made little account of,' and this was a view also shared by other ancient writers. Perhaps the best-known acclamation of the aqueducts of Rome was given by Frontinus, Rome's Water Commissioner at the end of the first century AD. He said, 'With such an array of indispensable structures carrying so many waters, compare, if you will, the Pyramids or the useless, though famous, works of the Greeks!'

Rome had developed from a collection of small hill settlements on the banks of the Tiber into a formidable political and military power. By the early second century AD Rome was *caput mundi*, 'head of the world', and as such was a model for the cities of her vast empire.

The city's development was shaped by many factors. One of the most significant was its location on the Tiber, which provided a gateway to the Mediterranean via the port at Ostia. Another factor was the important technical development of Roman concrete and the use of large-scale vaulting. This was shown to greatest effect after the great fire of AD 64. Much of the city centre had to be rebuilt, and some of Rome's greatest public buildings – the Colosseum, the Baths of Trajan, and the Temple of Venus and Rome – were built over the next 60 years.

In the late Republic, the city's history was dominated by the activities of the famous: Cato, who demanded the destruction of Carthage; Cicero, the great orator; and Pompey the Great and Julius Caesar, both prominent figures in the politics of Rome in the first century BC, who were responsible for major building programmes within the city.

By the early fourth century AD, Rome was no longer the political centre of the Empire. After the disintegration of the Empire in the West in the fifth century, Rome's importance continued as the centre of Christendom. Today, it is still a major centre of pilgrimage.

THE SITE OF ROME

From its origins as a town at the lowest bridging point of the River Tiber, Rome grew steadily as the power of its people expanded. As the early monarchy gave way to the Republic, and the Republic to the Empire of Augustus, the city acquired its first great monuments and civil engineering projects.

△ A hut urn for a cremation burial of about the ninth century BC, found in the area which was later developed into the Forum Romanum.

△ Plan and elevation of a ninth or eighth-century BC hut on the Palatine

▷ The site of Rome, showing the Tiber crossing, the Via Salaria and other roads.

▷ The site of Rome, showing the Palatine and Capitoline hills, and Campus Martius.

The city of Rome developed on the banks of the River Tiber at a point where the flood plain of the river becomes quite narrow. This provided good defensive positions for the early settlements on the hills. Most importantly, however, Rome grew at the lowest bridging point of the Tiber. The city was positioned where overland trade routes from the south or east to the Etruscan territories would cross the river. The first bridge across the river was the Pons Sublicius. This was the famous bridge which, according to the Roman historian Livy, was held by Horatio against the forces of the Etruscan king, Lars Porsenna of Clusium, in 509 BC. It was traditionally built in about 600 BC, on wooden piles driven into the river bed. It is significant that the title of Rome's chief priest was Pontifex Maximus,

'bridge-builder in chief', a title still carried by the pope today.

The Tiber was navigable for shallow-draft vessels at least as far as Rome. Along the south bank of the river was an ancient trade route, the Via Salaria, the 'Salt Road', which ran from the salt-pans at the mouth of the Tiber high up into the Appenines.

The great temple to Jupiter

Towards the end of the sixth century BC the first great temple to Jupiter Optimus Maximus was built on the Capitoline Hill. Only part of the podium of this first temple remains today, but the plan is known. It was an Etruscan-style temple built on a high stone podium; the walls were probably mudbrick faced with stucco. At the back of the podium were the three *cellae*, or

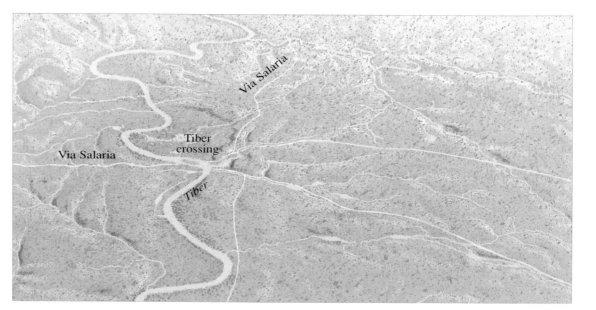

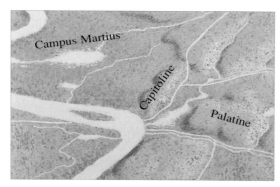

shrines, the central position being occupied by the cult statue of Jupiter with his wife, Juno, to the left and Minerva (Athena) to the right. Three rows of six columns stood at the front, forming a deep porch; a row of seven columns ran down either side.

The republic

At the end of the sixth century BC the kings were overthrown, and soon after a republican government was in place. This was essentially an oligarchy, with two chief magistrates (who came to be known as consuls) chosen from the aristocracy and elected annually. In the early republic power in all areas of public and religious life was concentrated in the hands of the patricians. These were a small privileged aristocratic group who were considered to be of noble birth. They were the great landowners. This monopoly on all aspects of the state caused great resentment among the plebeians (everyone who was not a patrician), and for 200 years the 'Struggle of the Orders' was fought as the plebeians, some of whom were as rich as the patricians, gradually gained greater access to the administration of the state. From the early fifth century BC tribunes of the plebeians were elected to defend their rights. The tribunes had the right of veto in any situation where the interests of plebeians were threatened. In about 450 BC the Law of the Twelve Tables was published, which ensured the same legal treatment for all.

By the early fourth century the plebeians had gained the right to be elected to all junior magistracies, and in 367 BC the first plebeian became a consul. However, these events did not mean that there was democracy in Rome; power still depended on wealth. To commemorate the agreement between patricians and plebeians, a temple of Concord was built at the foot of the Capitoline Hill overlooking the Forum.

The place of assembly
The Forum was the focus of public and political life. Its site was originally a marshy valley between the Palatine and Capitoline hills and the lower slopes of the Esquiline and Quirinal. The Forum was crossed by the Cloaca Maxima, which drained the area between the Quirinal and Esquiline hills and emptied into the Tiber near the old bridge. This may have originally been developed as a drainage ditch and storm drain during the sixth century BC; it became Rome's main sewer and eventually had to be covered over in the second century BC. There was a marshy pond (the Lacus Curtius) in the Forum itself and another (Lacus Iuturnae) near the south corner.

Shops with private houses behind them lined the north-east and south-west sides of the Forum. The people assembled to vote in the Comitium, a rectangular enclosure oriented to the four points of the compass at the north-east corner of the Forum. The senate house (Curia) was built into the north end of the Comitium, with a speaker's platform (the *rostra*) in front of it. From here the magistrates could address the assembly.

The house of the king
Traditionally at the south-east end of the forum stood the palace (Regia) of the kings (*reges*). During the Republic this area was occupied by the residence of the chief priest, the Pontifex Maximus. Also residing in this area were the Vestal Virgins, responsible for the sacred fire at the shrine of Vesta, the goddess of the hearth (the temple also acted as a sacred records office). The Vestals were young girls of aristocratic family, chosen by the chief priest. They were bound to celibacy for 30 years, under pain of death.

The long road to empire
In the fourth century BC Roman political influence expanded to the north and south in Italy. A great effort by the Latins and the Greek colony at Cumae had overthrown Etruscan power south of the Tiber, and Rome became first a member, then leader, of a league of Latin towns fighting the hill peoples to the east and the Etruscans to the north. For more than a hundred years the Latins were in conflict with the peoples further north, until at the beginning of the fourth century BC they began at last to get the upper hand. Rome's nearest Etruscan neighbour, Veii, 15 kilometres north of Rome, fell after a long siege in 396 BC.

The Gallic sack
But then disaster struck. For a century Gallic tribes from central Europe had been infiltrating northern Italy, gradually supplanting the Etruscans in the Po Valley. One particular people, the Senones, who had established themselves on the Adriatic coast near Ancona, crossed the Appenines in 390 BC and invaded central Italy. They overwhelmed the Latin army and sacked Rome, before withdrawing back to the north. According to legend, only the fortified Capitol held out. Rome did not suffer another similar sack for almost 800 years, until Alaric the Goth sacked the city in AD 476.

The conquest of Italy
Rome recovered quickly. Within fifty years it had taken over the Latin League and begun the conquest of Italy. One by one

▽ Terracotta temple decorations from early Rome (seventh and sixth centuries BC).

△ The Forum Romanum and Capitol with the Temple of Jupiter, at the end of the second century BC.

the Etruscan cities fell. The hill peoples followed. The Samnites, occupying the hills further south in Italy, put up the greatest resistance, but by 290 the whole of central Italy was under Roman control. The Gauls continued to raid central Italy and in 283 BC the exasperated Romans launched an all-out attack on the Senones, and drove them out of Italy. Roman attention now turned to the Greek states of southern Italy, and despite the intervention of Pyrrhus, the king of Epirus, Rome had gained control of all Italy south of the Po valley by 275 BC.

Carthage

Rome now became involved in its two most costly wars, both against Carthage. The first Carthaginian (or Punic) war was for the possession of Sicily (264–241 BC). In the second war (218–201 BC), the Carthaginians were led by their general, Hannibal. Hannibal invaded Italy from a Carthaginian power base in Spain in 218, and after three great victories, including one at Cannae in Apulia in 216 BC, managed to detach much of southern Italy from Rome's influence. But the Romans then took the war to the Carthaginians. They campaigned in Spain and then in North Africa under the Scipios. Finally, in 202 BC, Hannibal was defeated at the Battle of Zama, outside Carthage itself.

Ruler of the Mediterranean

Rome emerged from the war as the greatest power in the whole Mediterranean. Philip V of Macedon, who had supported Hannibal, was defeated in 197 BC, and Antiochus the Great, king of Syria, in 189 BC. The war with Hannibal had given Rome a foothold in Spain, which came under Roman control during the second century BC, although the north-western part

was not subjugated until the time of Augustus. The Celts of northern Italy were taken over early in the second century, and Roman colonies were established in the Po valley. The Roman province of Gallia Narbonensis was organised beyond the Alps in 121 BC. In the Eastern Mediterranean Achaea, Macedonia and Asia were all Roman provinces by 129 BC.

The city on the seven hills

The city had expanded as Rome's power had grown. Massive walls had been constructed after the sack of the city by the Gauls in 390 BC. These walls, traditionally thought to have been built by king Servius Tullius in the sixth century BC, are now generally accepted as belonging to the period immediately following the sack by the Gauls. They are built mainly of yellow-grey tufa from the Grotta Oscura quarries near Veii, which would not have been available until after the conquest of that town in 396 BC. The walls, 11 kilometres (7 miles) in circuit, enclosed the traditional seven hills, the Capitoline, Quirinal, Viminal, Esquiline, Caelian, Aventine and Palatine, an area of 400 hectares (1000 acres). The buildings destroyed by the Gauls were rebuilt.

At the end of the fourth century BC several great civil engineering projects were undertaken. One of the first and most famous of the Roman roads, the Via Appia from Rome to Capua in Campania, and the first aqueduct, the Aqua Appia, bringing fresh water from springs 12 kilometres (7½ miles) east of Rome, were both built in 312 BC.

Civic buildings

The Roman hills, and in particular the Palatine, became the home of the wealthy. The poor huddled into the valleys, particularly the Subura, the low-lying area to the north-east of the Forum. The valley between the Palatine and the Aventine had been used for chariot racing from the earliest times, and by the end of the fourth century BC it had been formalised as the Circus Maximus.

Several important temples were constructed in the republican period. A temple to Juno Moneta was built at the north end of the Capitoline in the middle of the fourth century, and a temple to Magna Mater, the Great Mother, had been established on the Palatine hill at the beginning of the second century BC. Rome's conquests in southern Italy and Sicily during the third century had a great effect on architecture and culture, as the Roman armies brought Greek artefacts, tastes and practices back with them. By 241 BC Latin adaptations of Greek plays were being shown in Rome.

The Forum was monumentalised with the addition of two basilical buildings, one next to the Temple of Castor and Pollux in 170 BC, and another of about the same date on the opposite side of the Forum.

The social war

The early 1st century BC was a time of great political instability. A struggle for power developed between the Opitmates, the extremely conservative, power-monopolizing clique of the upper classes, and the Populares, other ambitious politicians from less distinguished families, whose only route to power was to appeal for popular support. The Gracchi had fought successfully on their behalf in the later second century, as tribunes of the plebeians. Now, however, ambitious politicians, unable to get their way with the Senate, appealed directly to the people. Marius, who held the consulship an unconstitutional five times in a row (104–100 BC), was followed by the dictator Sulla, who marched on Rome.

The sack of Athens

Rome became involved in wars in the East against Mithradates, king of Pontus. Sulla set out for the east and laid siege to Athens, an ally of Mithradates. The city fell early in 86 BC and Sulla defeated the armies of Mithradates in two battles in Boeotia. In 85 BC peace terms were agreed and Sulla turned to Italy.

Bloody civil war

In Rome Sulla's power had been usurped first by Marius and then by Cinna. Having landed in Italy, Sulla marched on Rome, his army swelled by Pompey's three legions. He defeated the opposition in several battles. Marius's supporters in Rome fled the city. Sulla is said to have massacred many others who had supported his enemies. Sulla then revised the constitution, strengthening the Senate and restricting the power of the tribunes.

At this time major work was carried out in the Forum. The ground level was raised by nearly a metre and the area was paved with marble. The borders of the Forum were regularised. Along the northern side of the Forum the Curia was rebuilt, and rising up on the slopes of the Capitoline was an impressive new records office, the Tabularium.

A new temple to Jupiter

Sulla ordered the rebuilding of the great temple to Jupiter on the Capitoline. He had seen the unfinished temple to Olympian Zeus in Athens and ordered the marble columns to be shipped to Rome to be used in the new temple. The temple kept its sixth-century plan and podium; only sections of the podium still survive.

Gaius Julius Caesar

Sulla died in 78 BC after an astonishing career. He had been adored by thousands of soldiers and certainly by some of the more conservative senators. But his efforts to re-establish traditional aristocratic dominance had done nothing to solve the causes of political unrest. Within a few years the same tensions had resurfaced – but this time the Populares had a leader who, though unscrupulous, was an astute politician.

Gaius Julius Caesar was in his early twenties when Sulla died, and only his youth had saved him from being punished as a supporter of Marius. He became governor of Illyria, the Po Valley and southern Gaul in 58 BC. In the next nine years he conquered all of Gaul west of the Rhine, and built up a veteran army that would follow him whatever he did. The Senate, fearing his power, tried to remove him. When this failed they called upon Pompey, his only rival as a great general, to defend Rome. This resulted in more civil war. Caesar was victorious. Although he did not carry out massacres and confiscate the property of the defeated, his apparently insatiable desire for power brought him enemies, and he was assassinated in 44 BC. This was followed by yet another civil war. Peace returned only with the defeat of Mark Anthony and Cleopatra by Caesar's nephew, Octavian, in 31 BC at the Battle of Actium.

Octavian gained all the power that Caesar had sought, but presented himself to the people only as the leading citizen (*princeps*). On 16 January in 27 BC the Senate conferred upon him the title of Augustus, and he also accepted the title *imperator*, which was given to victorious generals.

With Augustus came the passing of the Republic and the establishment of the Principate, an institution which was to change the face of Rome.

THE IMPERIAL CAPITAL

The physical appearance of the city was transformed in the reign of Augustus, as new and imposing monuments were built in marble and countless older buildings restored. But the changes made by some of his successors were less well received by the citizens of Rome.

◁ The Forum Romanum at the time of Augustus.

A Tabularium
B Temple of Concord
C Temple of Saturn
D Basilica Julia
E *rostra*
F Temple of Castor and Pollux
G Temple of the Deified Julius Caesar
H Temple of Vesta
I Regia
J Basilica Aemilia
K Curia Julia
L Forum of Julius Caesar
M Temple of Venus Genetrix
N Forum of Augustus
P Temple of Mars Ultor

While claiming to be restoring the republic, with himself as *princeps*, Augustus was creating an autocratic system of government. He put great effort into concealing the true implications of his political changes. He could make a pretence of consulting the Senate because all its members were his nominees.

Changing the face of Rome

Caesar and Pompey had both erected monumental buildings in Rome. Pompey had built a massive theatre on the Campus Martius. Caesar had built a basilica stretching along the south-west side of the Forum Romanum, and to the north he had started a new forum. Under Augustus there was a massive programme of refurbishment of existing monuments. He completed Caesar's projects, and claimed to have

restored eighty-two temples in one year (28 BC). Pompey's theatre was restored and two new theatres built, the Theatre of Balbus and the Theatre of Marcellus. The old aqueducts were repaired and two new ones built – the Aqua Virgo by Agrippa, Augustus' son-in-law in 21–19 BC, and the Aqua Alsietina, which was built by Augustus to supply a great artificial lake for aquatic displays.

According to Suetonius, the emperor claimed that he had found Rome a city of brick and left it a city of marble. This is only partly true: much of the ordinary housing of Rome continued to be built of mud-brick, timber and rubble-work. However, for the construction and decoration of public and religious monuments, Augustus exploited a new source of white marble in Northern Italy at Luna (Carrara); until this time most of the white marble used in Rome had been brought from Greece. He also imported coloured marbles from North Africa, Greece and Asia Minor. This was the first time such decorative stones had been used on a large scale – for columns, paving and veneers.

The Forum Romanum

The Forum had undergone considerable rearrangement at the west end as a result of Caesar's plans. Under Augustus its redesign was completed, and remained virtually unchanged thereafter. He enlarged and completed the Basilica Julia on the south-west side and the new senate house, the Curia Julia, begun by Caesar on the north-east side next to the Basilica Aemilia. The *rostra* was moved across to the foot of the Capitol to provide an axial focus. At the opposite end stood the Temple of the Deified Caesar in front of the Regia, with Augustus' own triumphal arch alongside.

The Forum Augustum

Augustus' Forum was constructed to the north of the Forum Romanum. It was vowed during the Battle of Philippi in 42 BC and begun five years later, to celebrate the victory over Caesar's assassins. The Forum and Temple of Mars Ultor, the Avenger, were dedicated in 2 BC. The whole complex was very large and employed a number of Greek features, including caryatids to support the entablature of the porticoes. Behind the porticoes were exedrae, which housed statues of the Julian family and illustrious men of the Republic, alongside mythical figures such as Romulus and Aeneas.

▽ A view from the Palatine hill of the Forum Romanum today.

◁ The Ara Pacis, the great Altar of Peace erected between 13 and 9 BC by order of the Senate, to commemorate the return of the emperor Augustus from campaigning in Gaul. The reliefs which decorate the structure depict scenes of abundance, peace and prosperity.

△ A detail of the imperial procession on the Ara Pacis, showing Agrippa (with head covered, on the left) followed by members of the imperial house.

The Ara Pacis

In 13 BC the Senate decreed that an altar should be erected on the Campus Martius, beside the Via Flaminia, to commemorate the victories of the emperor in Spain and Gaul. This large rectangular structure, known as the Ara Pacis (Altar of Peace) and now standing by the Tiber, carried a variety of sculpted reliefs celebrating the blessings of peace brought to Italy by Augustus. On three sides of the exterior of the structure ran reliefs depicting the emperor, senators and their families in procession at the dedication of the altar. Beyond it to the west the Horologium Augusti was oriented to the Ara

Pacis; the pointer of this immense sundial was an obelisk brought by Augustus from Egypt.

A modest house on the Palatine

According to the literary sources, Augustus lived in an elegant but modest house on the Palatine, adapted from a number of first-century BC houses. Today this residence appears to be divided into several living areas. The House of Livia to the north-east consists of a large peristyle with a suite of family rooms to the west. The House of Augustus comprised several state reception rooms which were open to the south and paved with marble alongside the portico of the Temple of Apollo. These houses have some of the best-preserved wall paintings yet discovered in Rome.

Wall decoration

The styles of decoration used in these houses were like those found in Pompeii. These were derived from Hellenistic sources and have been divided up into four historical groups, known as the four Pompeian styles.

The First, or Masonry, style was used until about 80 BC and imitated slabs of coloured marble. The Second, or Architectural, style added architectural motifs and landscapes to give an illusion of depth.

The Third style developed towards the end of the first century BC, and was characterized by the use of large panels of colour with candelabra supporting pictures.

From about AD 35 until the end of the first century AD, the tendency to use scenery and false architecture became even more accentuated, and this is known as the Fourth style.

◁ The House of Augustus on the Palatine: a reconstruction of ceiling decoration in upper bedroom 15.

▷ The House of Augustus: a reconstruction of decoration in upper bedroom 15.

◁ The House of Augustus: wall decoration of upper bedroom 15, shown in its actual condition.

Wall painting

△ **A** The masonry style, the Hellenistic forerunner of the First Pompeian style, from the Hieron at Samothrace, dating from the later fourth century BC. The plaster work (*stucco*) is moulded to look like stone masonry. This style lasted to the beginning of the first century BC.

△ **B** A fourth-century BC example of the masonry style from the 'François' Tomb at Vulci in Etruria. Several colours have been used for the imitation stone masonry.

△ **C** The First Pompeian style: an example from a bedroom in a house in Pompeii.

◁ **D** The late First style, from the Temple of Jupiter in the Forum at Pompeii. The three-dimensional effect is achieved by the use of light and shade. Narrow upright blocks have been introduced and panels are often framed.

△ **E** The early Second style, from the Villa of the Mysteries outside Pompeii. Many of the elements of the First style have been kept, but columns standing on a plinth create the illusion that the panels between the columns are set back. The illusion is further enhanced by the coffered arches at the top.

△ **F** The fully developed Second style from the Villa of Poppaea at Oplontis (Torre Annunziata) on the Bay of Naples. A true perspective effect is achieved, with trees and buildings in the background helping to create the illusion of depth.

◁ **G** The early Third style from the Villa of Poppaea at Oplontis (Torre Annunziata) on the Bay of Naples.

△ **H** The developed Third style, from the house of L. Ceius Secundus at Pompeii. The black and red panels focus the eye on the central picture. The columns and architrave of previous styles have now become a white frame for the picture and a narrow panel above it. The architectural designs across the top are characteristic of the Third and Fourth styles.

△ **I** The Fourth style from the house of Octavius Quartio at Pompeii. The fourth style is very varied; this example illustrates the development from the Third style. This style is characterized by fantasy architectural schemes. Pictures are often reduced in size on the larger plain panels.

▽ **J** A reconstruction of second-century AD wall decoration from Ostia. This illustrates a development from the Fourth Pompeian style, but the style is not as fine as those of the first century.

Hypocrite, madman, fool and knave

These are the words that the Roman historian Tacitus uses to describe Augustus' successors, all relatives from his Julio-Claudian family. Tiberius, the first, was less bothered about keeping up republican pretences. Augustus had kept his bodyguard, the Praetorian Guard, some miles outside Rome. Tiberius built a new camp for them on the outskirts of the city, the Castra Praetoria. He built himself a large palace on the north corner of the Palatine (the Domus Tiberiana). Very little of this survives today, but it is known that it was built around an enormous peristyle.

The madman

Caligula came to power in AD 37, at the age of 25, with the help of the Praetorian Guard. The early months of his rule seemed the dawn of a new era. Political offenders were pardoned and taxes reduced. Lavish entertainments increased the emperor's early popularity. But within a few months he fell seriously ill. He recovered in body but never in mind, and his undisciplined character succumbed completely to the temptations of power.

In the Hellenistic kingdoms of the East it had been common practice to worship their rulers even before their death as gods. Augustus had seen this as a useful way of securing the loyalty of his eastern subjects, and allowed cults to be established for the worship of the emperor and his family, but forbade such honours in Rome until after his death.

Caligula became obsessed with the belief that he really was a god. Far from merely allowing his worship in the east, he insisted on it and nearly caused a rebellion in Judaea by demanding that his statue be set up in the Temple at Jerusalem.

According to historical sources he extended Tiberius' palace towards the Forum, incorporating the Temple of Castor and Pollux as a kind of vestibule. According to Suetonius he also built a large viaduct across to the Capitoline so that he could commune more easily with Jupiter.

The blade of the assassin

Caligula apparently obtained funds by forced legacies, extraordinary taxes and judicial murders. The fear awakened by his capricious violence soon resulted in a conspiracy against his life. Early in AD 41 he was cornered in the palace garden by a tribune of the Guard and dispatched, after a reign of only four years. His wife and baby daughter shared his fate.

The fool

Caligula was succeeded by his uncle Claudius, whose physical ailments led his opponents to assume that he was also stupid. Their assessment was seriously wrong. Claudius gave Rome a short period of judicious and stable government. He began the great harbour at Portus to the north of Ostia to facilitate imports of food to Rome, and finished the construction of two new aqueducts (the Aqua Claudia and the Aqua Anio Novus).

The knave

Nero came to the throne in AD 54 at the age of 16. His character, his passions, and his susceptibility to flattery all made him unfit to rule a powerful empire.

Nero loved the arts, gymnastics and chariot-racing and believed himself exceptionally gifted. He provided a large set of public baths and built a new bridge across the Tiber and a large market place, but his name will always be associated with his brutality and his determination to build a colossal country estate in the centre of Rome.

The gardens of Maecenas on the Esquiline had become part of the imperial estate under Tiberius. These sumptuous gardens were more than half a kilometre from the palace on the Palatine, and Nero was determined to gain direct access from one to the other. The construction began of a palace – the Domus Transitoria – which stretched across the valley to the Esquiline.

The great fire

On 18 June AD 64 a fire broke out in the Circus Maximus. According to Tacitus it was the worst fire Rome ever experienced. It raged for six days and gutted the centre of the city. There was talk of arson, especially when Nero seized the opportunity to build his large country estate in the damaged area. Witnesses claimed to have

▽ A plan of the area of the Domus Aurea

A Domus Tiberiana

B The Palatine

C Temple of the Deified Claudius

D Site of the Colosseum

E Esquiline wing of the Domus Aurea

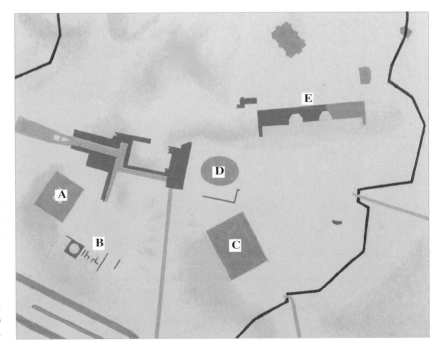

▷ A map showing the
fourteen regions of
Rome, instituted by
Augustus in 7 BC.

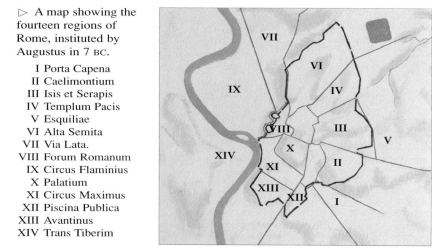

    I Porta Capena
   II Caelimontium
  III Isis et Serapis
  IV Templum Pacis
   V Esquiliae
  VI Alta Semita
 VII Via Lata.
VIII Forum Romanum
  IX Circus Flaminius
   X Palatium
  XI Circus Maximus
 XII Piscina Publica
XIII Avantinus
XIV Trans Tiberim

▽ A reconstruction of the Domus Aurea, built by Nero after the great fire in
AD 64. At the bottom left is the Palatine. The great palace of Domitian has yet
to be constructed.

seen people heaping fuel on the fire. Inevitably
the finger of suspicion pointed at the emperor.
It was claimed that he sang an aria on the burning of Troy, accompanying himself on the lyre,
while the fire raged. On the other hand he was
said to have given shelter to the homeless and
to have reduced the price of grain to feed them.

A fire break finally brought the blaze under
control, but it broke out again in another part
of the city. In the end ten of the fourteen areas
of the city were damaged; three were totally
destroyed.

The police and fire brigade

Augustus was the first Roman ruler to
approach systematically the problem of civil
law and order. In order to check non-political
disorder and suppress crime, and carry on

other police functions, he organized three *cohortes urbanae*, urban cohorts. Each was made up originally of 1500 men, who were regarded as soldiers. They served for 20 years.

During the Republic the task of protecting the city from fire was assigned to a small number of public slaves under one of the aediles. In AD 6 Augustus created a corps of 7000 *vigiles* (watchmen), organised in seven cohorts, one for every two of the fourteen regions. They served as both fire brigade and night police and were commanded by the *praefectus vigilum*, who was second in authority only to the Praetorian Prefect.

Persecution of the Christians

Popular opinion demanded a scapegoat for the great fire, and Nero's advisers blamed the

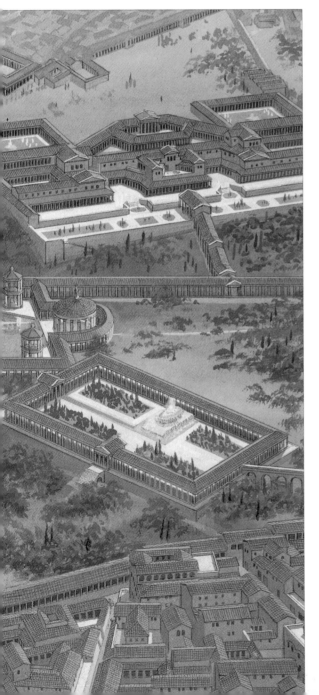

Christians in Rome. Several Christian communities existed in the city. The obscurity of their practices, incendiary talk in some of their writings and the popular belief that they ate human flesh made them a prime target for public vengeance. The fact that so many temples had been destroyed seemed to support the accusation. Many Christians were tried and condemned on charges of anarchistic tendencies and suffered terrible deaths. Some were crucified; others were covered with inflammable material and lighted as torches in Nero's gardens. This was the first persecution of the Christians conducted by the Roman government.

△ An aerial view of the centre of Rome today.

The Golden House

Between AD 64 and 68 Nero's new palace, the Domus Aurea ('Golden House'), was constructed. It was a villa covering a ground area of 125 acres, stretching from the Palatine across the valley to the gardens on the Esquiline Hill. It was laid out as a country estate with a lake, fields and woodland. The entrance, which incorporated two of Rome's roads, the Sacra Via and the Nova Via, was in the valley between the two hills.

Suetonius' description

The Roman historian Suetonius describes the Golden House in some detail:

> Its vestibule was large enough to contain a colossal statue of the emperor 120 feet (36 metres) high. It was so extensive that it had a triple colonnade a mile (1500 metres) long. There was a pond too, like a sea, surrounded with buildings to represent cities beside tracts of country, varied by tilled fields, vineyards, pastures and

▷ The Domus Aurea: Third style wall paintings with architectural motifs and painted landscapes.

woods, with great numbers of wild and domestic animals. In the rest of the house all parts were overlaid with gold and adorned with gems and mother-of-pearl. There were dining rooms with fretted ceilings of ivory, whose panels could turn and shower down flowers and were fitted with pipes for sprinkling the guests with perfumes. The main banquet hall was circular and [the ceiling] constantly revolved day and night, like the heavens. He had baths supplied with sea water and sulphur water. When the building was finished he deigned to say nothing more in way of approval than that at last he was beginning to be accommodated like a human being.

Remains of the Golden House have been found at several points. Substantial remains of the west wing have been discovered beneath the Baths of Trajan. In these rooms are wall-paintings of the Third style. Architecturally the most important room is an octagonal room covered by a dome with an oculus.

An enemy of the state

It was not the scale or the extravagance of the building that offended the people. It was the fact that Nero had built his villa in the centre of Rome.

▽ The Domus Aurea: structures on the same alignment and assumed to be part of the same building.

▷ The Domus Aurea: a plan of the surviving west wing, on the Esquiline Hill. The grey area on the right shows the probable extent of the east wing.

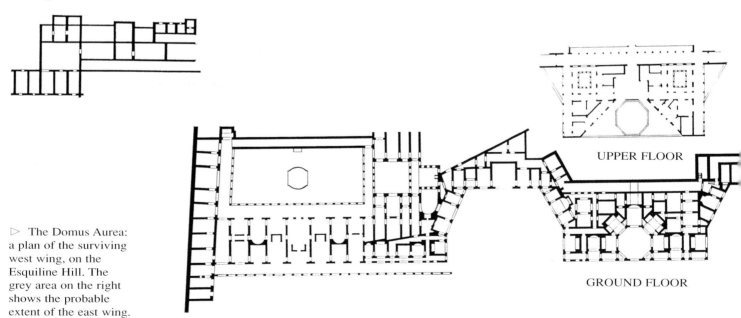

UPPER FLOOR

GROUND FLOOR

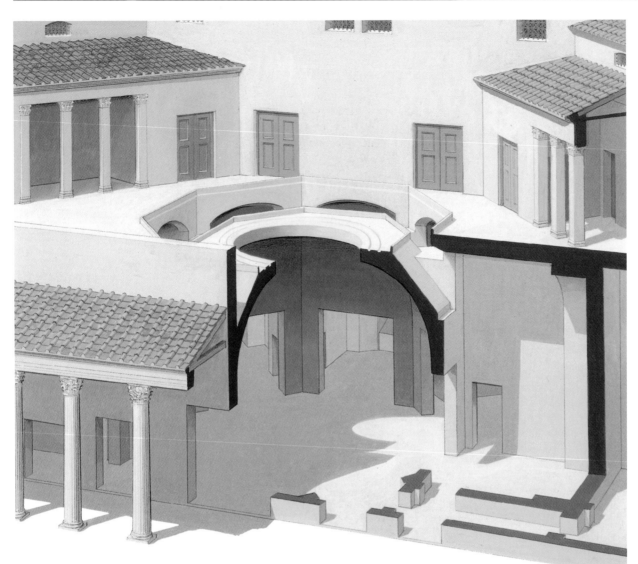

△ The Domus Aurea: a reconstruction and cut-away of the octagonal room.

In pursuit of artistic fulfilment Nero went to Greece. He ordered the postponement of the Olympic Games from AD 65 to AD 67 in order that he might compete himself, and was awarded 1800 prizes, including the crown of

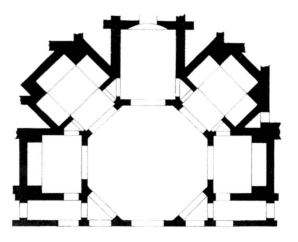

▷ The Domus Aurea: enlarged plan of the octagonal room.

victory for the chariot race in spite of the fact
that he had fallen out of his chariot and not
completed the course. The farce came to an end
in AD 68 when the Praetorian Guard mutinied,
offered the throne to Galba, the governor of
Spain, and declared Nero a public enemy. With
the help of a one-time concubine the deposed
emperor managed to summon up the courage to
kill himself, with the words 'What an artist dies
in me.'

The death of Nero ended the Julio-Claudian
imperial line. Within a year Rome saw four
emperors. Galba tried to secure his position by
assassinating likely opponents, but the
Praetorian Guard turned against him and nom-
inated another emperor, Otho. Galba was murdered by the Guard.

The return of civil war

Meanwhile, events on the frontiers had already
overtaken those in Rome. The legions on the
Rhine had refused to swear the oath of alle-
giance to Galba and declared the governor
Vitellius emperor. The Danube legions
declared their support for Otho. Civil war had
returned. The two sides met at Cremona in the
Po valley. Otho was defeated and committed
suicide. Vitellius tried to consolidate his position by executing many of the centurions from
the Danube legions, but only hastened his own
end: already another army was on the march.
Vespasian, the governor of Syria, with the
backing of all the troops in the East, declared
himself emperor. The humiliated Danubian
legions took up his cause and advanced into the
Po Valley. A second battle was fought at
Cremona. The victorious Danubian legions
marched on Rome. There was fighting in the
streets. Vespasian's elder brother, in command
of the urban cohorts, was killed before the
Danube legions arrived and the great temple of
Jupiter was again burned. The Danubian
legions seized Vitellius and lynched him. Rome
itself now lay at their mercy, and the city
awaited a blood bath. Fortunately Vespasian's
own legions, under the command of Mucianus,
were not far behind and arrived in time to prevent any more blood-letting. Vespasian himself
arrived in Rome in the spring of AD 70.

The triumph of Vespasian and Titus

Vespasian had made his reputation as leader of
the Roman forces against the Jewish insurgents
in Palestine. When he set off for Rome, he
entrusted the conclusion of the Jewish war to
his elder son Titus, who at once laid siege to
Jerusalem. The city fell to the Roman forces
and the Temple was destroyed.

Titus was voted a triumph by the Senate and
spoils from the war were carried through the
streets of Rome.

▷ The Arch of Titus.
The reliefs on the arch
depict the triumphal
procession of Titus
through Rome after the
sack of Jerusalem in
AD 70.

▷ The Triumph of
Titus. A reconstruction
of the procession
through Rome of the
spoils of war from the
sack of Jerusalem in
AD 70.

Vespasian and the Colosseum

Vespasian was responsible for a number of building projects in Rome. He rebuilt the Capitoline temple, and near Augustus' Forum he built the Forum Pacis, celebrating the return of peace to Italy. It was also used as a museum for the spoils brought back by Titus from the sack of Jerusalem.

His greatest project, however, was the construction of the Colosseum, a huge amphitheatre built on the site of the lake of Nero's Domus Aureus.

Domitian

Vespasian died in AD 79. His son Titus succeeded him as emperor, but reigned for only two years. His younger brother Domitian succeeded him. Domitian carried out a series of major building projects in Rome, the most important of which was the construction of a new imperial palace on the Palatine.

Domitian was never a popular emperor, and the later years of his reign are marked by a series of treason trials. In AD 96, after several years of suspecting plots against him, he fell victim to the dagger of the assassin. His memory was cursed and his name erased from public monuments (*damnatio memoriae*).

The Golden Age

A leading senator, Marcus Cocceius Nerva, was the Senate's choice as emperor. He was 60 years old and was unable to win the support of the soldiery, especially the Praetorian Guard. Nerva therefore adopted as his son and heir Marcus Ulpius Traianus (Trajan), commander of the troops in Upper Germany. When Trajan succeeded Nerva in AD 98, he was the first emperor of provincial origin; his successor, Hadrian, was also a native of Italica.

Under these two emperors the city of Rome entered a Golden Age.

GOVERNMENT

Roman society was based on clearly-defined social classes, with distinct career opportunities in public service open to each. Even under the Empire, the administration of law was one of the main tasks for senior civil servants, and there were many courts and magistrates in the city.

▽ The *cursus honorum*. This was the career structure followed by any Roman politician. The structure changed and developed over time, but the consulship was always the highest magistracy for any politician to hold.

The stratification of Roman society into senatorial, equestrian and lower classes became more sharply defined in the imperial period. For each class a distinct field of career opportunity and public service was provided, conforming as far as possible to tradition: for senators, the magistracies and the chief military posts; for the *equites*, a new career in civil and military service of the emperor; and for the

lower classes, service as privates or junior ranks in the professional army. The classes were not closed and it was possible for successful men to advance from the lower to higher grades.

The Senate and the senatorial order

During the Republic the Senate had been the centre of administration. By the third century BC it had a fixed membership of 300. Augustus fixed the number at 600. Senators held their seats for life unless guilty of grave public or private misconduct. Consuls and ex-consuls were automatically members of the senate and by the time of Sulla membership was open to the junior magistrates. Senators wore a toga with a broad purple stripe; their sons received this by right of birth. The possession of property valued at 1,000,000 sesterces was a requirement for admission to the Senate. The Senate met in the Curia building in the Forum Romanum.

Senatorial careers

The prospective senator had to follow a set career plan, the *cursus honorum*, which involved both military and civilian posts. Through these he would gain experience in administration, finance and diplomacy. At the age of 25 he might hold the quaestorship and at 39 the praetorship. The pinnacle of his career would be election to the consulship, but he could not hold this position before he was 42.

The *equites*

The equestrian order developed in the third and second centuries BC, although it is only in the time of Gaius Gracchus that the *equites* really emerge as a class. The class consisted of the more prosperous businessmen. Their name indicates that these were men wealthy enough to provide themselves with a horse, and the censors regularly assigned them to cavalry service in the army. Under Augustus, the *equites* were drawn into the financial administration of the provinces.

The equestrian order was open to all Roman citizens of 18 years and over, of free birth and with a census rating of 400,000 sesterces. Admission to the order was controlled by the emperor and carried the right to wear a narrow purple stripe on the tunic and to receive a horse

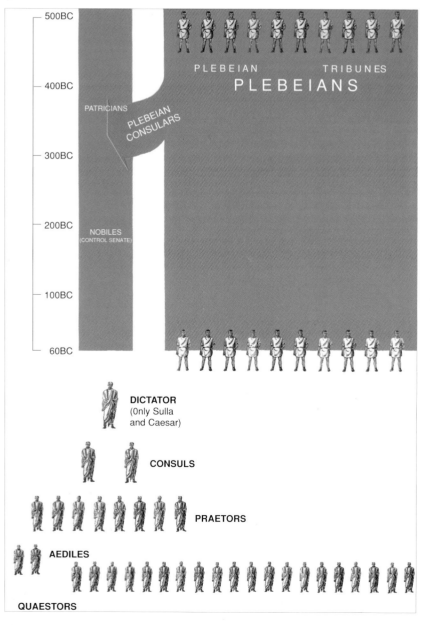

PLEBEIAN TRIBUNES
PLEBEIANS

PATRICIANS

PLEBEIAN CONSULARS

NOBILES
(CONTROL SENATE)

DICTATOR
(Only Sulla and Caesar)

CONSULS

PRAETORS

AEDILES

QUAESTORS

The emperor

When Augustus came to power he claimed that he was only *primus inter pares*, the first amongst equals. Nonetheless, he systematically acquired all the political powers necessary to rule as sole emperor and autocrat. Officially, one of the consulships could be held by the emperor or a member of the imperial family.

As a result of the assumption of administrative control by the emperor, an imperial civil service developed whose officials were appointed by the emperor himself.

The law

Roman law developed over many centuries. The legal codes were added to as necessary. The first important piece of legislation was put together in the mid-fifth century BC. This is known as the Law of the Twelve Tables. The original text is not preserved. According to Livy the Twelve Tables were inscribed on bronze. Pomponius claimed they were of ivory, and some modern scholars say they were on wood and were displayed in the Forum.

From the fragments of the Twelve Tables which have been preserved, it is clear that their provisions related to all areas of legal order at the time. They remained relevant well into the imperial period. During the Republic, although the state provided courts, conducted trials and provided magistrates to pass judgements, it was the responsibility of the victim and his or her family to apprehend and prosecute the offender. There was no public prosecutor's office, and to get redress in the courts a person had to initiate proceedings himself.

The law courts

Legal cases were heard in a variety of places around Rome's monumental centre. The literary sources are full of references to the massive increase from the time of Augustus in the work of the public courts.

The Forum Romanum was one of the major venues for court cases, but because of the increase Augustus apparently allowed the use of his forum also for the hearing of certain court cases. The *praefectus urbi*, who was responsible for maintaining public order in Rome, heard cases here. The *praetor urbanus* heard cases concerning Roman citizens in the Forum Romanum near the Temple of Castor; cases between Roman citizens and foreigners, and cases between foreigners, were put to the *praetor peregrinus* and were also held in the Forum Romanum.

The *centumviri* (literally one hundred men) met in the Basilica Iulia. This court was established at the end of the third century BC and it

△ The Curia was constructed of concrete faced with fired brick. The lower part of the exterior walls were veneered with marble. The upper sections were covered in a layer of plaster or stucco decoration, which was moulded to represent fine ashlar masonry.

△ The Curia Julia, where the Roman Senate met. It was originally built by Julius Caesar in 44 BC and finished by Augustus, who dedicated a statue of Victory inside. The present building dates from the time of Domitian (restored after a fire under Diocletian in 283). Its survival is due to its conversion into the church of Sant'Adriano in 638.

▽ A detail of the procession of senators on the Ara Pacis.

is thought that from the time of Augustus the *centumviri* dealt with claims concerning inheritances of a minimum of 100,000 sesterces. They probably also judged disputes over land ownership and guardianship. The cases presented to the *centumviri* attracted a great deal of public attention. It was not only the brilliant speeches which might be heard, but also the juicy pieces of scandal which might be revealed.

From the second century BC separate tribunals were set up to judge crimes against the state. These eventually covered treason, electoral bribery, embezzlement of state property, adultery and murder by violence or poison.

Trial and punishment

The evidence for the detailed procedures of some of these courts is very scanty. The magistrate would sit on an elevated tribunal and in the Forum Romanum the jury would sit on benches set up on the forum paving.

Criminal trials were heard before the appropriate magistrate, and at the end of the lawsuit, the presiding magistrate gave his judgement and this was binding on all parties.

Punishments were administered according to social rank. Men and women of the upper classes might suffer exile, loss of status, or a private execution, usually by beheading. Under some emperors there was great fear of attracting his suspicion and displeasure; according to Seneca the punishments could be particularly horrible: the rack, the impaling stake, the cross, wild beasts, chariots to tear a victim apart.

The lower classes were subject to beatings and public executions. They might be condemned to die in the arena for public entertainment, or might suffer their punishment in the public streets. It was possible to hire the services of *carnifices* to execute slaves for their masters. The Roman poet Martial describes their whips, which were knotted around sharp pieces of bone or metal to inflict greater pain.

The place of public execution and flogging was on the Via Tiburtina outside the Porta Esquilina near the public burial ground.

The prison

The *carcer* (prison) is mentioned by Pliny the Elder, who says that it was situated west of the Curia building. It has been identified as a chamber beneath the church of Giuseppe dei Falegnami in modern Rome. An inscription dates the travertine facade to the early first century AD, and the chamber behind was probably originally a cistern. It is also known as the Tullianum or Mamertine Prison.

△ A section through the prison or Tullianum. This is thought originally to have been a cistern. On the lower level is a round structure, dating perhaps from as early as the sixth century BC. A spring still exists in the floor. In the Roman period, prisoners were kept here to await execution.

The Curia Julia

The Senate met in the Curia or Senate House. This was situated at the west end of the Forum Romanum, near the Comitium. The original senate house was the Curia Hostilia, said to have been built by Tullus Hostilius, one of the Etruscan kings. It was rebuilt several times and was replaced by the existing building, known as the Curia Julia, which was begun by Sulla in 80 BC. Julius Caesar began a rebuilding programme in 44 BC after a fire. It was completed by Augustus. Domitian restored the Curia, and the building was rebuilt by Diocletian after a fire in 283, according to the original design.

The building stands 21 metres high. Wooden seats for the senators were placed on steps running down the full length of the sides. A raised platform opposite the door provided seating accommodation for the presiding magistrates. Augustus presented a statue of Victory, which presumably stood by the tribunal. Two doors at the rear of the building opened into the Forum of Julius Caesar.

The most distinguished senators sat on the front benches. By the time of Augustus the Senate had nearly 1,000 members, and there was not enough seating if all senators attended. As a result, the youngest and least prominent had to stand at the back on the top step. During meetings the doors of the Curia were kept open so that sons of senators could observe the way that business was conducted.

▷ The Curia Julia: a reconstruction of the interior.

FOOD AND WATER

As Rome's population grew, the provision of food and water became increasingly important. By the imperial period the bureaucracy was in place to manage and maintain the supply of water via aqueducts, and to import large quantities of grain, wine and olive oil from the empire.

Population

There are many problems with trying to estimate the size of the population of Rome. What figures we have relate to the number of male adult citizens, and then only a proportion of them. They take no account of women, children under the age of ten or slaves. From the second century BC the population certainly increased, as Rome's power and influence grew. Estimates vary from 250,000 in the late Republic to 2 million in the later first and early second centuries AD. Most scholars now believe that a figure of 1,200,000 for the city in the second century AD is probable. Such a population posed enormous problems for the supply of basic foodstuffs and water.

Food supply

Supplying food to the ever-growing city was a constant challenge to Roman organisational skills. At first, the hinterland of the city could meet most of its needs. From the late Republic, however, more and more food, especially grain, wine and olive oil, was imported from other parts of the Mediterranean.

Grain, the staple of the Roman diet, came from Egypt and North Africa. Wine was imported from Campania, Gaul and Spain in large quantities, and olive oil came from southern Spain and North Africa. The wine and olive oil were transported in amphorae – pottery jars – which varied in shape according to their contents and where they were made. The amphorae were transported up the Tiber to Rome by river barge, and unloaded at the major port area below the Aventine hill; this was known as the Marmorata (there were also port facilities further upstream near the Forum Boarium).

The amphorae were unloaded and emptied at the wharves, and their contents were stored in huge warehouses. Most of the amphorae were then thrown away. Beside the Tiber, there is a huge man-made hill of pieces of broken olive oil amphorae, mainly from Spain and North Africa. This is known as Monte Testaccio, and is 34 metres (112 feet) high and has a circumference of 1 kilometre (920 yards). It is thought to contain the fragments of at least 53 million amphorae.

Grain was distributed free to poorer citizens (that is, males over the age of ten). This practice started in the late Republic, but it was Augustus who organised the distribution into the *annona* (dole), under the control of an equestrian prefect. In 5 BC Augustus distributed free grain to 320,000 adult males, but no details of qualifications for this dole or its actual distribution are known.

△ Different kinds of amphorae, all of which were in use in the early Empire. These jars varied considerably in shape and size. They were used to transport mainly liquids (wine, olive oil and fish sauce), but some have been found on shipwrecks which contained whole olives or dried fruit. In the foreground is the round type of amphora which was used to transport olive oil from southern Spain, mainly to Rome and Gaul.

◁ A reconstruction of the villa at Settefinestre near Cosa to the north of Rome. This large and rather grand villa was at the centre of an estate from the early first century BC and is typical of the type of large slave-run estates which developed in the late Republic. Various additions were made about AD 100, including what is thought to have been a piggery.

Puteoli and the grain fleet

The shipment of grain from Egypt may have been partly by a special fleet sailing from Alexandria to Puteoli (modern Pozzuoli) on the Bay of Naples. But the organization of this fleet is now unknown, and its actual existence is doubtful. Private contractors, however, were certainly involved in the grain transport. Once the ships arrived at Puteoli, the grain was loaded into smaller boats that then sailed up the coast to Ostia. In 37 BC Agrippa and Octavian built a second port at Puteoli, called the Portus Julius.

Ostia and Portus

Ostia is situated at the mouth of the Tiber, and served as the river port of Rome, but it could not easily handle large sea-going vessels like those that might have made up the grain fleet. Claudius built a new all-weather harbour much closer to Rome at Portus, 3 kilometres (about 2 miles) to the north of Ostia. This was a huge project, involving the construction of two great moles jutting out into the sea. A lighthouse was built at the end of one of these moles: a large ship that Caligula had used to transport an obelisk from Egypt was filled with concrete and sunk to form its foundations.

Claudius's harbour was very exposed to the weather, and Trajan built a new land-locked inner basin, linked to the Tiber by a canal, the Fossa Traiana. Trajan's new basin was hexagonal and measured 200 metres (656 feet) across. Warehouses and other facilities were also provided. Large numbers of sea-going vessels could thus be handled very efficiently, much closer to Rome.

▷ A detail of the northern part of the Bay of Naples, showing the location of the harbours at Puteoli.

▷▷ A map showing the west coast of Italy from the Bay of Naples in the south up to Rome in the north.

◁ An aerial view of the Tiber from Ostia up to Rome, showing the location of Portus to the north. The Tiber had a particularly meandering course between Rome and Ostia.

In the early imperial period, Ostia was a bustling, commercial town, full of warehouses for storing grain and other goods. As Portus grew in importance, so Ostia declined.

The aqueducts

Until the later fourth century BC, Rome was supplied with water from wells, springs and rainwater collected in cisterns. But in 312 BC the first of Rome's aqueducts was built, the Aqua Appia, by the censor Appius Claudius Caecus; by the time of Trajan, Rome was supplied by ten major aqueducts.

Many of the city's aqueducts drew water from sources in the Anio valley to the east of Rome. In 272 BC the Anio Vetus was built with funding from the spoils taken from the defeated Pyrrhus, King of Epirus. As its name implies, the intake for the aqueduct was from the Anio river, above Tivoli.

In 144 BC the Aqua Marcia was constructed, and quickly became renowned for the purity of the water it carried. This water was drawn from springs in the Anio valley. For the upper part of its course the channel of the Aqua Marcia was mainly subterranean, but once it left the hills at Tivoli it was carried across the flat plain to the city on an elevated, arcaded structure. This was the first such structure, and was an astonishing engineering achievement; it cost more than 180,000,000 sesterces. As the construction of these arcades was so expensive, the channels for the Aqua Tepula (built in 125 BC) and the Aqua Julia (33 BC) were built on top of the Marcia on the approach to Rome, to form a triple-decker in the arcaded section.

The Aqua Virgo was constructed in 19 BC. This aqueduct was the only one to enter Rome from the north, though it was also fed by springs in the Anio valley. The Virgo was constructed by Agrippa to supply his large public baths on the Campus Martius, the first time that an aqueduct had been constructed for this specific purpose.

The Aqua Alsietina was built by Augustus in 2 BC, to supply his Naumachia on the west bank

▽ The wharves on the Tiber in the Marmorata quarter after excavation at the end of the 19th century. Note the ramps and mooring dogs.

▷ A map showing the course of the ten great aqueducts of Rome. The first, the Aqua Appia, was built in 312 BC. The last major aqueduct was the Aqua Traiana, although one further aqueduct, the Aqua Alexandrina, was built in AD 226.

Aqua Appia

Aqua Anio Vetus

Aqua Marcia

Aqua Tepula

Aqua Julia

Aqua Virgo

Aqua Alsietina

Aqua Claudia

Aqua Anio Novus

Aqua Traiana

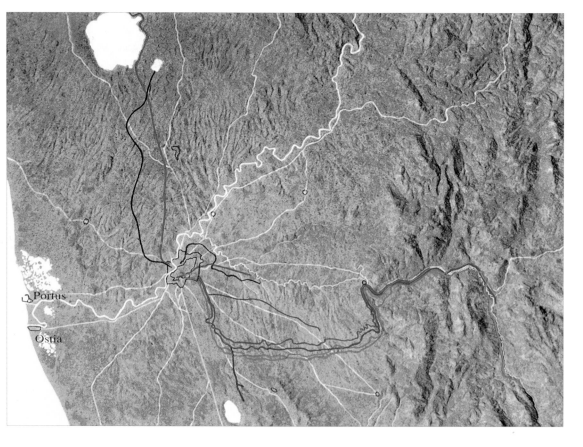

Portus

Ostia

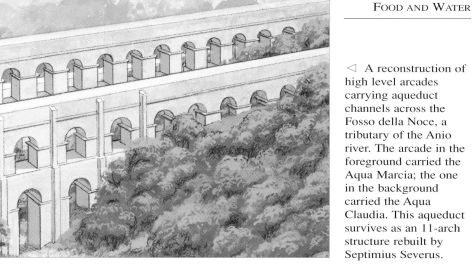

◁ A reconstruction of high level arcades carrying aqueduct channels across the Fosso della Noce, a tributary of the Anio river. The arcade in the foreground carried the Aqua Marcia; the one in the background carried the Aqua Claudia. This aqueduct survives as an 11-arch structure rebuilt by Septimius Severus.

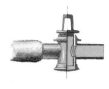

A valve which enabled domestic supplies to be turned off or diverted. Taps and valves of this kind were rare in Roman water systems and the water usually ran 24 hours a day.

This bronze nozzle, or *calix*, was made in several standard sizes and was used to connect domestic houses to the mains water supply.

▷ A reconstruction cross-section of the arcade and channels of the Aqua Claudia, with the channel of the Aqua Anio Novus on top.

▽ A view of the arcade carrying the Aqua Claudia and Aqua Anio Novus as it approaches Rome from the south-east.

△ A reconstructed view of the water system beneath a street. The drain ran under the middle of the street. The lead pipes carrying the freshwater supply ran under both the road and the pavement. Branch pipes were taken off the main line at intervals to supply public and private buildings.

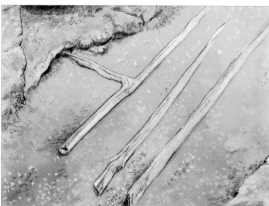

△ A view of lead pipes still in place at Pompeii.

△ An interior view of the Cloaca Maxima. It was covered with a vault in about 100 BC.

▷ The outlet of the Cloaca Maxima into the Tiber, pictured before the construction of the modern embankment.

of the Tiber: this was a great artificial lake used for the staging of mock sea-battles and other large-scale aquatic entertainments.

The two greatest aqueducts in terms of volume of water carried were the Aqua Claudia and the Aqua Anio Novus, both completed by AD 52. The Claudia was fed by springs in the Anio valley upstream from those serving the Marcia. The Anio Novus, like the Anio Vetus before it, was fed by the Anio river itself.

The last of the great aqueducts to supply Rome was constructed under Trajan: the Aqua Traiana. This entered the city at the Janiculum hill, safeguarding the water supply to inhabitants of the west bank if supplies from across the river were cut. A large *castellum*, or receiving tank, was found on the Via Aurelia, and the channels radiating from it seem to have served every quarter of the city, especially the Baths of Trajan on the Esquiline hill. From the third century its waters also powered grain mills just below the crest of the Janiculum; these apparently produced much of Rome's flour.

Frontinus and the Cura Aquarum

Under Augustus, Agrippa had headed a government department overseeing the maintenance and general running of the city's aqueduct system, the Cura Aquarum. The most famous holder of this post was Frontinus. Frontinus was in charge of Rome's water supply under the emperor Nerva, and wrote a book on the subject, *De Aquis Urbis Romae*. This gives historical details and descriptions of the aqueducts of Rome up to his day. He provides information on the problems of providing water to such a large city, and the regular maintenance that the system required. He also gives much valuable legal information relating to water supply. It is clear that corruption was a problem here as in many other aspects of Roman life.

Sewers

The sewers carried away effluent from the baths, overflow water from the streets, and sewage and waste from both houses and streets. They usually ran underneath the street and

could be flushed by the overflow from public fountains. Very few houses were attached to a mains sewer. Instead, waste was collected in internal cess-pits that could be emptied periodically and the contents sold for fertilizer. Roman drains and sewers lacked traps to prevent gases like hydrogen sulphide and methane escaping, and thus had no inbuilt protection against odour or the danger of explosions. Equally, the sewers could back up when the level of the Tiber rose during floods. Sewage and waste water which normally drained into the Tiber would then be forced back into the network and up any domestic connections to it.

The Cloaca Maxima

The most famous Roman drain is the Cloaca Maxima, whose original construction is attributed to Tarquinius Priscus. This was originally an open ditch to help drain the marshy site of the city, particularly in the Forum Romanum area. Although it was intended to carry off surplus water, it inevitably also carried sewage. In the later Republic, the Cloaca Maxima was enclosed in a subterranean channel; in part it is still in use today. As the crow flies, its length is over 900 metres (985 yards), but its course meanders because of diversions around buildings. Its size is remarkable: in places it is 4.2 metres (13 feet 9 inches) high and 3.2 metres (10 feet 6 inches) wide, and Roman writers agree that it was large enough for a wagon load of hay to pass through. Agrippa is reported to have sailed in a boat through the underground world of Rome's drainage system on a tour of inspection.

Public toilets

Later Roman historical sources record 144 public latrines in Rome, though only a few are known from archaeological evidence. One example, dating from Hadrian's reign, is above shops in the Forum Julium, and others are in the Largo Argentina area near the Theatre of Pompey. Latrines were basic facilities in bath buildings, and were flushed with waste water from the baths themselves. Many private dwellings in Rome, particularly the high-rise dwellings, did not have latrines; they lacked the running water supply that made flush latrines practical.

A reconstructed view of the latrines which can be seen today at the back of the Largo Argentina area. They were actually attached to the Portico of Pompeii. These latrines were very big, possibly seating as many as 100 people. As can be seen they have a very open design. The inset picture shows a close-up of one of the latrine seats.

HOUSES AND APARTMENTS

The inhabitants of Rome lived in a variety of houses and apartment blocks, some of which were strikingly modern in concept and design. The wealthy enjoyed luxurious furniture and elaborate facilities at home, but all Romans faced squalor and lawlessness in the city's streets.

Rome, like Athens, developed in a haphazard way. Buildings spread along the old roads leading to the Palatine and Capitol and their side streets until the city became a network of narrow, gloomy alleys. There were almost 90 km (56 miles) of roads, mostly without pavements. In the centre only the Sacra Via and the Nova Via, both leading to the Forum, were wide enough to justify being called streets; the rest were generally too narrow for vehicles to pass each other. Some were so narrow that houses with projecting balconies or upstairs rooms almost touched each other.

The streets were filthy and unhealthy, as people dumped their rubbish and sewage there. It was not unusual for a passer-by to be hit by the contents of a pot tipped from an upper floor window. In fact, laws were passed regulating the damages one could claim for injuries sustained in this way.

Laws governing the streets

Living conditions in the city prompted Julius Caesar to pass a decree ordering householders to clear up in front of their houses, and to make the city magistrates (aediles) organize gangs of cleaners to keep the streets clean.

Filth and disease were not the only problems. Many people were killed or maimed in traffic accidents due to the narrowness of the streets and the lack of pavements. The streets became so dangerous that Caesar banned wheeled vehicles, except those on official business, from entering the city during daylight hours. This ruling created two separate worlds, the normal world of the day and the sinister city of the night. No decent citizen went out at night. At dusk everyone barred their doors and left the streets to the carts, and none of these ventured out without an armed guard, for the streets were unlit and filled with muggers. Even without wheeled vehicles the streets were crowded; further laws had to be passed forbidding traders from displaying their goods in the streets.

Early houses

Excavations on and around the Palatine Hill have uncovered evidence of houses from as early as the eighth century BC. The evidence of the very earliest houses consists only of post holes, but recently the remains of several luxurious late sixth-century BC houses were found

△ The remains of an apartment block on a street alongside the Forum of Julius Caesar.

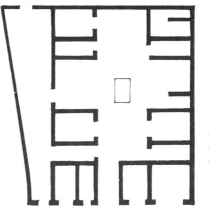

△◁ Plan and reconstruction of one of the sixth century BC houses on the south-eastern slope of the Palatine hill.

▷ Rome in the early empire. Many writers describe the city as crowded, with unstable buildings rising five or six storeys above the filthy streets.

along the north-east slope of the Palatine Hill. These consisted of rooms on one or two levels grouped round a central hall (atrium).

The homes of the rich

The. Etruscan atrium-style house gradually evolved into the typical Italic house familiar to us from Pompeii and Herculaneum. Gradually, under Greek influence, these developed into luxurious buildings with colonnaded (peristyle) gardens. The House of Augustus and the so-called House of Livia on the Palatine were clearly developments of this type of house. We know that atrium/peristyle houses still existed in Rome as late as the end of the second century AD because a group of them are shown on a marble plan of Rome drawn up at this time.

This type of house, normally built on one floor, consisted of a series of bedrooms grouped round three sides of the hall, with an entrance corridor entering the hall (atrium) between the front bedrooms. The main rooms of the house, the dining-room (triclinium) and office (tablinum), usually occupied the fourth side of the hall, opposite the entrance. The peristyle gardens and any utility rooms were usually at the back.

The owner usually received his clients and conducted his business in the atrium first thing in the morning.

The homes of the poor

The atrium/peristyle house was always the domain of the rich. From the earliest times, poorer working people had lived in rooms behind or above their places of work, just as they did in Athens. In Pompeii and Herculaneum, many house owners rented out street-facing downstairs rooms, particularly the bedrooms on either side of the entrance, for conversion into shops, workrooms or restaurants, often with living space included. Several houses were completely converted into workshops. Other house owners rented out rooms or converted parts of their houses into flats. Rooms and apartments built on and jutting out over the streets at first- and even second-storey level, with access by an outside stairway, are a common feature at Herculaneum. Both the House of the Wooden Partition and the adjoining house have rooms built on to the front at first- and second-floor levels (see page 138).

Plan of a typical
Roman house
A Atrium
B Bedrooms
T Tablinum
D Dining-room
G Garden
S Shop

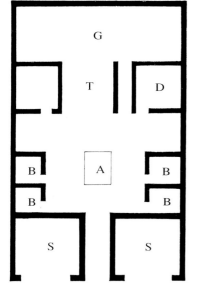

△ Part of the marble plan of Rome, showing three atrium/peristyle houses.

▷ A reconstructed bedroom, with an alcove for the bed and a walk-in wardrobe, from the House of the Centaur at Pompeii. This style of wall decoration, known as the Pompeian First Style, had developed in Greece between the fifth and second centuries BC.

▽ A late second-century BC house based on examples from Pompeii. The court (atrium) is entered by a passageway (*fauces*) from the street. The atrium has bedrooms on either side. The office (tablinum) is opposite the entrance, with the dining-room to the right.

▷ Most early houses collected rain-water. The water from the roof fell into the pool or *impluvium* (I) in the centre of the atrium, and drained into a cistern below the floor. C is the well-head at the top of the cistern shaft.

C

I

cistern

A concrete jungle

The main building materials used at Rome were limestone (in particular travertine, quarried at Tivoli, which was formed through the deposition of calcium carbonate in water), volcanic tufa (a very light stone), fired brick and concrete.

The development of concrete and the use of the vault made possible robust buildings of vast size. Concrete (*opus caementicium*) was developed in Campania during the third century BC. It was not like modern concrete, but was a mixture of stone and/or brick forming an aggregate, which was laid in alternating courses with mortar. The mortar was made with pozzolana, a volcanic sand which gave extra strength and cohesiveness to the material and allowed it to set even under water. The materials used for the aggregate depended on what was being constructed: heavy limestone would be appropriate for foundations, but light volcanic pumice was often used in vaults (see pages 226–7).

Brick and other materials

Fired bricks were manufactured in several standard sizes: *bipedalis* 2 Roman feet (59 cm) square, *sesquipedalis* 1.5 Roman feet (44 cm) square, *pedalis* 1 Roman foot (29.5 cm) square and bessalis 8 inches (20 cm) square. Marble, granite and porphyry were also important materials for building and decoration. From the mid-second century BC until about 35 BC, all white marble used in Rome was imported from Greece. Coloured marble from North Africa and the Aegean was used in the private houses of the rich, and was much criticized for its gaudiness by the writers of the day. From the time of Augustus, coloured marble and other decorative stones were used more and more in public buildings for veneer and for columns, which were often monolithic rather than made up of drums. From the later first century BC, white marble was quarried at Carrara in northern Italy and was used extensively at Rome.

△ The House of the Wooden Partition and the adjoining house at Herculaneum. Both have rooms built on at upper levels. Such additions were usually built of timber-framed rubble and mortar (see below).

▽ *Opus craticum*: a timber framework filled with rubble and mortar. It was cheap but a notorious fire hazard.

Apartment blocks

The conversion of houses into flats undoubtedly took place at Rome too, where the pressure on space was far greater than at Herculaneum. However, there is a type of building found at Rome which is completely absent from Pompeii and Herculaneum: the multi-storey apartment block (*insula*). These had existed in Rome at least as early as the third century BC. They were originally built of *opus craticum* (see below), and could be exceedingly dangerous, liable to catch fire or collapse unexpectedly. With no legal building restrictions, owners built them higher and higher. Life in these buildings was not easy. With no water and no toilets above the first floor, they could be squalid and unhealthy.

Augustus imposed a height limit of 18 metres or 60 feet (five storeys) on insulae. Clearly this order was ignored, for after the fire of AD 64, laws were passed restricting the height to 21 metres (70 feet) and ordering a 3-metre (10-foot) space between buildings. The law also ordered that a flat-roofed portico be built across the facade of adjacent buildings so that firefighters could manoeuvre more easily. Brick-faced concrete replaced the less durable and less stable mudbrick for the construction of these high-rise blocks (see below). But the abuses continued, forcing Trajan to restrict the height of *insulae* again to 18 metres (60 feet).

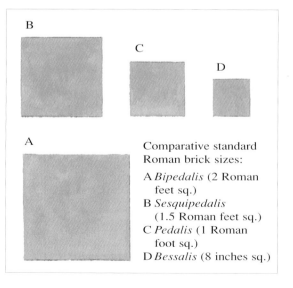

Comparative standard Roman brick sizes:

A *Bipedalis* (2 Roman feet sq.)
B *Sesquipedalis* (1.5 Roman feet sq.)
C *Pedalis* (1 Roman foot sq.)
D *Bessalis* (8 inches sq.)

Walls

For foundations, concrete was built in layers between wooden shuttering, which was usually left in place. For walls above ground, concrete could be faced in a number of ways. The earliest facing used in Rome was *opus incertum*, made of small, irregularly shaped but roughly uniform-sized stones. From the later second century BC *opus reticulatum* was used. This facing was made up of small pyramid-shaped blocks, laid so that their bases formed a net pattern. Modern scholars have invented the term *opus quasi-reticulatum* to describe a less neat form of the same facing, but the distinction depends more on the type of stone used; tufa was the most common in Rome.

Opus testaceum, a facing using fired bricks, was common in Rome from the time of Nero. Sometimes the larger bricks were cut down to triangles so that the point could 'bite' into the concrete core.

Opus mixtum was a facing made up of panels of *opus reticulatum* and fired brick, and was particularly common under Augustus, though it enjoyed a revival under Trajan and Hadrian.

Scaffolding and roofing

As in modern times, scaffolding was used to give access to a building during its constuction. Sometimes putlog holes survive in the facing of a wall where a wooden beam rested to stabilize the scaffolding.

Roofs were made of wood covered with flat terracotta tiles (*tegulae*). These were rectangular, usually 45 cm by 60 cm. The junction between two tiles was covered by a semi-cylindrical tile (*imbrex*).

△ A wall painting from the tomb of *Trebius Justus* at Rome, showing a brick-faced concrete building under construction.

◁ *Opus incertum*: a facing for concrete made of small, roughly shaped stones.

◁ *Opus testaceum*: a facing for concrete made of fired bricks. In the earlier period, the bricks were often cut into triangles.

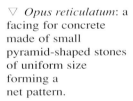

▽ *Opus reticulatum*: a facing for concrete made of small pyramid-shaped stones of uniform size forming a net pattern.

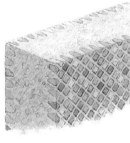

◁ A foundation trench lined with planks nailed to uprights to form shuttering. The aggregate and mortar were laid in courses between the planking.

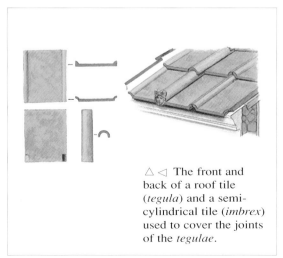

△ ◁ The front and back of a roof tile (*tegula*) and a semi-cylindrical tile (*imbrex*) used to cover the joints of the *tegulae*.

▷ A mosaic from Pompeii, showing an architect's set square and plumb-bob.

◁ Three types of set square with plumb-bobs used for levelling.

▷ A selection of architect's instruments, including various dividers and a plumb-bob, found at Pompeii.

Architects

A Roman architect was required to have a much broader education than architects of today. According to the architect Vitruvius, who wrote in about 25 BC, they had to be well versed in geometry, history and music, have some knowledge of medicine, and be well-acquainted with astronomy and cosmology. The architect had to draw up plans for the building project, and often also to act as supervisor of the work in progress. An architect was usually engaged by a patron, but Vitruvius condemned unscrupulous and money-grabbing architects who vied for contracts. He praised wealthy householders who built for themselves, ensuring that their money was well spent. A number of examples of architects' instruments have survived, including plumb-bobs, foot rules and set squares; they are remarkably like their modern equivalents.

Apartment blocks at Ostia

In the reign of Trajan, AD 98–117, a huge development project took place at the port of Ostia, at the mouth of the Tiber. The greatly increased population was housed in high-rise apartment blocks, no doubt based on the type common in Rome. A large portion of the town was excavated in the first half of this century, revealing numerous apartment blocks built of brick-faced concrete, sometimes with upper floors still standing. Where it faced a main street, the ground floor usually consisted of shops, mostly with a mezzanine floor for storage or accommodation.

▷ An apartment building known as the House of Diana at Ostia, showing the shop fronts with their mezzanines above.

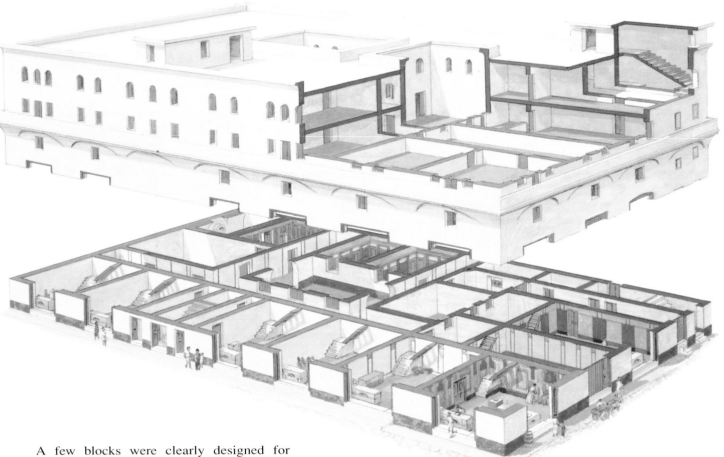

A few blocks were clearly designed for wealthy occupants. These apartments echoed traditional house design, with main hall, dining-room and office in the conventional positions, and their own toilet and kitchen. But most of the buildings were designed to house the less wealthy.

The so-called House of Diana, shown reconstructed above, is such a building. It has shops on two sides at ground-floor level with mezzanines above, and some also with back rooms. There are apartments on the other two sides, some of which are elaborately decorated. There was a communal toilet, with space for nine or ten persons.

The first floor, of which only the foundations survive, consisted of apartments of two, four and five rooms, and possibly some single rooms. There was probably a communal toilet immediately above the toilet on the ground floor. The rooms in the centre of the block were lit by light wells.

Apartment blocks in Rome

The remains of a few apartment blocks have been identified in Rome and several more are shown on the marble plan (see page 137). The remains of a block similar to the Ostian House of Diana was discovered beneath the Galleria Colonna shopping precinct. This block had shops, some with back rooms, on all four sides on the ground floor. There was an arcade on the west side, facing the ancient Via Lata, which extended to the adjoining buildings in accordance with the fire regulations of Nero. The upper floors were composed of separate apartments reached by a stairway at the north-east corner of the building.

A block on the Capitoline

Between 1928 and 1930, a unique apartment block was uncovered along the north-west side of the Capitoline next to, and partially beneath, the steps up to the church of Santa Maria in Aracoeli.

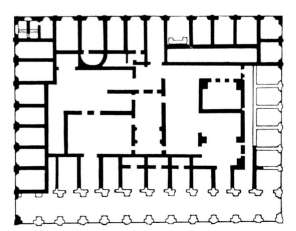

△ A reconstruction of the House of Diana at Ostia. This apartment block had shops along two sides, some of which (if not all) were decorated. The rest of the building was composed of apartments. The remains of the stairs show that the building was at least three storeys high. It is not known whether the outside of the building was plastered.

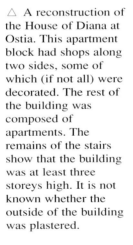

◁ A plan of the apartment block discovered at Rome beneath the Galleria Colonna shopping complex. It had shops on all four sides and an arcade running along the front. It was built in the early second century AD under Hadrian.

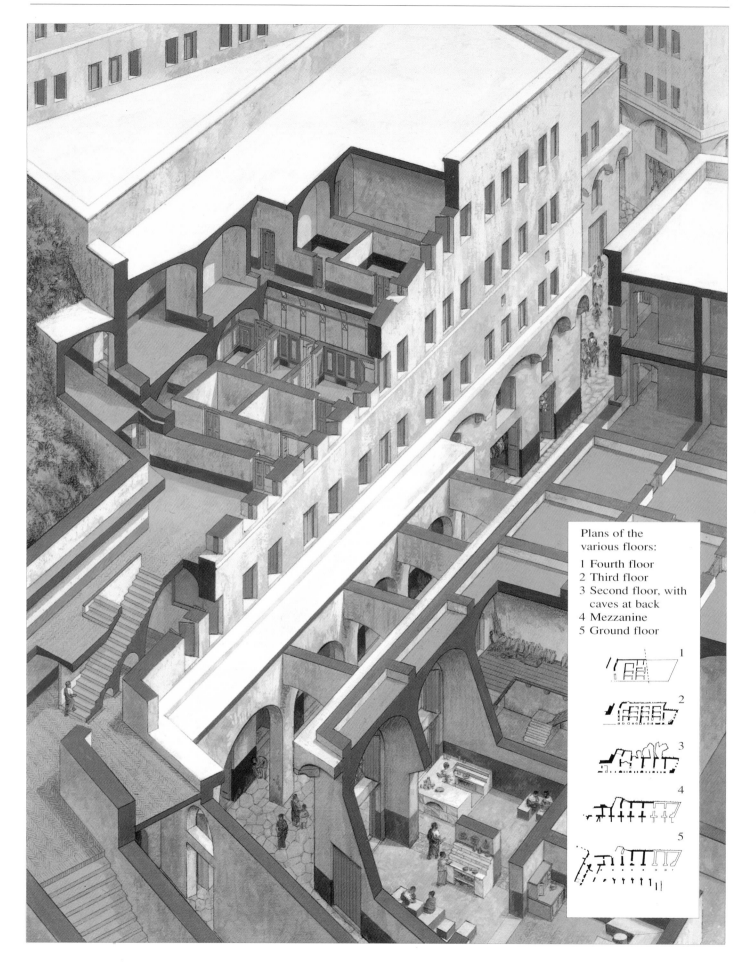

Plans of the
various floors:

1 Fourth floor
2 Third floor
3 Second floor, with
  caves at back
4 Mezzanine
5 Ground floor

▷ The remains of a second-century AD Roman apartment block, rising to the fifth storey, built against the north side of the Capitoline at Rome. The shops with their mezzanines are below the level of the modern pavement.

This block, built against the side of the hill, survives up to sixth-floor level and is connected to another block which continued up the hillside. Unfortunately the bulk of the latter building remains beneath the Capitoline Museum. The first block is built of brick-faced concrete, and many of the interior rooms were covered by concrete vaults. The ground floor consists entirely of shops, with a Neronian fire regulation arcade in front and mezzanines above. The third level, which is only partially excavated, is divided into three apartments. The fourth floor has rows of single rooms, poorly lit from the corridor by tiny windows. The partial remains of a fifth floor suggest that it had a similar arrangement of single rooms. The stairs to the upper floors have not survived, but were probably at the east end of the building.

▷ A wooden lattice-work window shutter preserved at Herculaneum. More conventional shutters made of wooden planks have also been found.

▽ An iron window grille discovered at Pompeii. Grilles made of terracotta have also been found.

Windows

Unlike Roman houses, which are characterized by their tiny windows, apartment blocks had large windows. The block on the side of the Capitoline hill had exceedingly large windows (2 metres high by 1.3 metres wide) in the facade, serving as the only source of light for the whole building. Glass was used only in the wealthier apartment blocks. The evidence from Pompeii and Herculaneum suggests that such windows were barred with grilles of iron or terracotta and closed with wooden shutters.

Numbers of occupants

James Packer, in his survey of the apartment blocks of Ostia, estimates that an average apartment block housed 40 people. In the mid-fourth century AD, Rome had 46,602 such multiple dwellings, which must have housed more than a million people. One of these buildings, the

◁ A cutaway reconstruction of the apartment block built against the side of the Capitoline at Rome. The rooms at all levels are vaulted to support the floor above. The stairs to the upper floors have not survived. The building has an arcade running along the front, as demanded by the Neronian fire laws, to allow fire fighters to get from building to building.

insula of Felicula, built in the second century AD, was so high that it was listed among the sights of Rome.

Despite the regulations, unsafe buildings continued to exist. Juvenal, writing during the reign of Trajan, ridiculed Rome for its buildings supported on beams 'as long and thin as flutes':

▷ The third-floor corridor of the Capitol apartment block, with doors to two back rooms. There are small windows above the doors to allow light from the corridor into the rooms.

▽ The rooms off the corridor above. The foundations of the dividing walls can just be seen. The rooms and the corridor would have been plastered and painted.

'Here we inhabit a city supported for the most part by slender props; for that is how the bailiff patches up cracks in the old wall, telling the residents to sleep at ease under a roof ready to tumble about their ears. No, no, I must live where there are no fires, no nightly alarms. [The resident] below is already shouting for water and moving his belongings; smoke is pouring out of your third-floor attic above, but you know nothing about it; for if the alarm begins on the ground floor the last man to burn will be he who has nothing to shelter him from the rain but the tiles, where the gentle doves lay their eggs.'

The household gods

Each household had its shrine (*lararium*) to the household gods (lares and penates), to whom an offering was made each morning. The lares were the spirits of the family's ancestors. The penates were the guardians of the family larder. In a conventional house the *lararium* was usually in the atrium. It may have been no more than a niche in a wall with a painting or little statuettes of the spirits, much as one might find a little shrine in a Catholic home today. Sometimes they were quite elaborate shrines in the form of a miniature temple.

A strongbox containing the family documents and valuables was also usually found in the lararium. Several fine examples have been found at Pompeii, made of wood sheathed with iron and bronze. They sometimes had a special stand built of masonry, to which the strongbox was secured by an iron rod. It is likely that both the lararium and the strongbox were located in the main reception room of an apartment.

Furniture and fittings

Much of the furniture of the late Republic and early imperial period followed Greek fashions, with ornate decoration. Wood, bronze and stone, particularly marble, were used. Compared with today, furniture was sparse, and chairs and tables were often moved from room to room as needed.

A large amount of furniture has been recovered from Pompeii and the other sites destroyed by the eruption of Vesuvius in AD 79. Stone and bronze tables and benches have been recovered from Pompeii, but at Herculaneum, many examples of wooden furniture and fittings are preserved in a carbonized form.

Tables

The Romans used five types of table, all of Greek origin. There were rectangular tables with three or four legs, round tables with three zoomorphic legs, square tables with a single central support, and square tables supported by a single upright slab at either end. Examples of most of these have been found at Pompeii and Herculaneum. The three-legged table was particularly popular, having the great advantage of being steady on an uneven floor. The upright slab type, of which many stone examples have been found at Pompeii, was often used in the atrium or outside. The upright slab supports at either end were usually carved in the form of animals.

Cupboards and chests

Several cupboards have been found at Pompeii and other sites around Vesuvius. Roman cupboards were very similar to those of today: a rectangular case, often with shelves inside, usually mounted on feet, with full-length panel doors.

The very elaborate cupboard shown on page 146 was found at Herculaneum in 1935. The upper part was flanked by columns and probably was once adorned with a pediment. Bronze, terracotta and glass vessels and statuettes were found inside it. This was clearly a dual-purpose wardrobe and *lararium*.

Chests of various sizes and shapes, from linen chests of Greek type to jewel boxes, are also known to have existed. Shelves were commonly used and have been found in both shops and homes at Herculaneum.

Seating

The Romans used a great variety of seating, ranging from heavy chairs and armchairs to folding stools and benches.

Elaborate chairs with turned legs are often shown in Roman paintings and sculptures. A carbonized leg from such a chair, sheathed with bronze, was found at Herculaneum. These chairs are often depicted with rectangular legs, and sometimes with arms and back supports. Another type of chair was a heavy, majestic seat with solid sides, used for official occasions. Two famous sculptures from Germany depict high-backed armchairs made of wicker, very similar to examples from the earlier part of this century. Thrones are often shown with footstools.

Stools

Several different types of stool are shown in Roman paintings and sculptures. These varied from chairs without sides or a back to folding stools. A form of folding stool (*sella curulis*) was used by Roman magistrates for official occasions. It had curving crossed legs, often terminating in animal feet. In fact, it had a wider use than just its official one: a relief from Ostia shows a woman seated under a tree on just such a stool. A fine example with bronze legs was found at Pompeii.

Benches

Benches were common, and were generally regarded as the seating of the poor. Some excellently preserved bronze examples have been

△ A painting showing the Lares and Penates from Pompeii.

▷ A *lararium* with the remains of a lattice-work screen from the House of Menander at Pompeii.

△ A strongbox made of wood bound with bronze and iron, found at Pompeii.

△ A stand for a strongbox discovered in the House of the Vettii at Pompeii. It has a metal rod to secure the strongbox against theft.

▷ A round-topped, three-legged wooden table from Herculaneum.

△ A bronze, marble-topped table with a single leg from Pompeii.

◁ A marble table with decorated 'upright slab' supports from Pompeii.

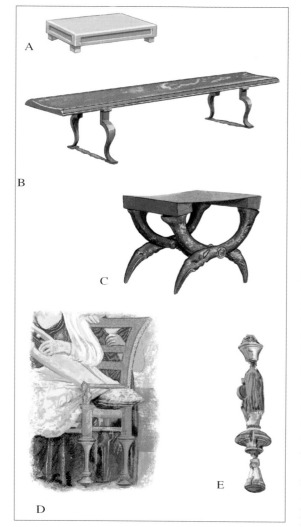

A. A wooden floor stool reconstructed from a Pompeian painting.
B. A bronze bench from the baths at Pompeii.
C. A folding bronze stool (*sella curulis*) from Pompeii.
D. Part of a painting from Pompeii showing a woman sitting on a throne with arms and a high back.
E. A bronze-sheathed wooden chair leg found at Herculaneum.

△ A wooden cupboard cum *lararium* found at Herculaneum.

examples are known. They were commonly used in the waiting rooms of public places, as they are today. No doubt the majority of benches were made of wood.

Beds and couches

It is impossible to differentiate between Roman beds and couches. Virtually the same piece of furniture appears to have been used for both dining and sleeping. Many fragments of couches have been recovered from the excavations at Pompeii and Herculaneum. There are also many paintings and sculptures showing Roman couches. The most popular form, which has turned legs, had a rectangular wooden frame on which the mattress must have been supported by leather straps, webbing, cord or wooden slats. It had a wooden headboard supported by an often highly decorated metal fulcrum. This type appears to have been introduced into Rome early in the second century BC, when Roman armies were operating in Greece and Asia Minor.

Several other couches, more similar to the modern couch, have been found at Herculaneum. These have a wooden framework to support the mattress or cushions. The exca-

vations at Herculaneum also uncovered a carbonized wooden crib.

Bedding is often shown on wall paintings in both houses and brothels. Blankets, mattress covers and pillowcases are usually shown with a striped pattern.

Partitions and shutters

The discovery of wooden partitions at Herculaneum has added enormously to our appreciation of the internal appearance of Roman houses. Rooms could be divided by wooden partitions with doors in them, which would normally leave no trace in the archaeological record. The House of the Wooden Partition at Herculaneum has its atrium divided in this way. Another house had a folding lattice-work partition incredibly well preserved. Lattice-work was also sometimes used for window shutters, especially where the window faced on to an enclosed garden. Outside shutters, which are also preserved at Herculaneum, were of solid wood planking. Very elaborate multi-leaf shutters were discovered at a recently excavated villa at Oplontis, between Herculaneum and Pompeii. These were made of several hinged panels, and are very similar to the familiar nineteenth-century framed panel shutter. This was the basic design of all better-quality internal doors. It was also used for cupboard doors.

Although there are no archaeological remains, it is clear from literature, painting and sculpture that curtains were widely used to partition rooms, and instead of doors for both rooms and cupboards.

The kitchen

As cooks were usually slaves, the kitchen had a lower status in a Roman house than in ours. There was no set place for the kitchen. In Pompeian houses, it was usually found somewhere behind the atrium. The kitchen was normally a small room equipped with a stove, a sink and probably shelving on the wall. The stove was totally unlike a modern oven, consisting of a rectangular table-like masonry construction with an arched space beneath it for keeping the fuel, charcoal and shavings. A small fire was lit on top of the stove and the food either boiled in a pot on an iron tripod or grilled on a gridiron. As far as is known, there were no chimneys and smoke escaped through the window.

Pots and pans

A small fully-equipped kitchen was found in the laundry of Stephanus at Pompeii. Lunch was being prepared at the time of the eruption, and the cook fled leaving a pot still on the boil. When the kitchen was excavated, pots, pans and a gridiron were found hanging on the wall or resting on the edge of the stove ready for

▽ A painting of a bed with bedclothes from Boscoreale, near Pompeii.

▷ Part of the wooden partition found in the House of the Wooden Partition at Herculaneum (see page 138).

▽ A sliding lattice-work screen found at Herculaneum.

▷ The bronze support for the headrest of the bed shown below.

▽ A detail of the lattice screen.

▽ A bed restored from bronze fittings found at Pompeii.

△ An angled couch restored from bronze fittings discovered at Pompeii.

▽ A plaster cast of the multi-leaf folding shutters discovered at a villa at Oplontis, near Pompeii.

▷ A carbonized wooden couch found at Herculaneum.

▽ A couch made of wood and leather found at Herculaneum.

▽ A carbonized wooden crib for a baby, found at Herculaneum.

147

△ A typical kitchen of the first century AD, with cooking implements hung on the wall. The toilet is alongside the masonry stove.

use. Innumerable other kitchen utensils made of earthenware or bronze have been found at Pompeii and Herculaneum. Besides pots and pans, bronze buckets, ladles and strainers have also been recovered.

The toilet

Toilets were often located near or in the kitchen, so that they could share a common drainage system. A recent survey at Herculaneum has concluded that practically all houses and apartments, even those at first-floor level, had toilets. These discharged into the public sewers or, where these did not exist, into cesspits which had to be emptied regularly at the expense of the house owner. Toilets were probably flushed out with a bucket of water; only the wealthier houses would have been able to afford a running-water flushing system such as that used in the public toilets. The location of the toilet in the kitchen allowed kitchen waste water to be used to flush it.

The dining-room

The dining-room was usually in the far right-hand corner of the atrium. It did not need to be a particularly large room, for although the Romans had adopted the Greek custom of reclining to eat, they had formalized it. A normal Roman dining-room had only three couches, placed along three walls, with the fourth side left open for serving. The custom of using only three couches gave the dining-room its name (triclinium). The three couches could accommodate nine or ten people.

▷ A selection of kitchen utensils found at Pompeii.

A A bronze pot on an iron tripod.
B A bronze pot
C A gridiron
D and E Terracotta pots
F A bronze pan
G A bronze ladle
H A bronze strainer

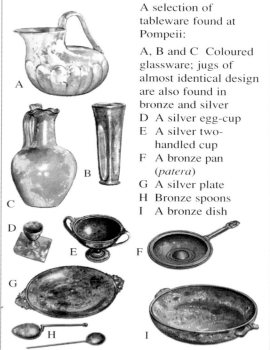

A selection of tableware found at Pompeii:

A, B and C Coloured glassware; jugs of almost identical design are also found in bronze and silver
D A silver egg-cup
E A silver two-handled cup
F A bronze pan (*patera*)
G A silver plate
H Bronze spoons
I A bronze dish

Summer dining-rooms

Wealthy houses had a winter and a summer dining-room, the latter being open to the air or even outside in the garden. Several of these summer dining-rooms have been discovered at Pompeii. Because of problems of damp, the normal wooden dining couches were sometimes replaced by permanent couches made of masonry. An excellent example in the house of Lucretius at Pompeii (see right) has furniture made completely of masonry and gives a very good insight into how the people of the house dined. The couches, which would have been covered with mattresses and cushions, sloped up towards the round table in the middle. There is a low shelf just below the level of the front of the couch, on which the diners could place their food and drink if they did not wish to hold them. There are similar shelves beyond the side couches where cold food or food ready to be served could be placed. There must have been many similar winter dining-rooms with fitted wooden furniture.

Not all people enjoyed reclining to eat all the time. There is a restaurant attached to the House of Julia Felix at Pompeii which also had furniture made of masonry, where people could either recline or sit to eat.

Guests for dinner

An inscription on the wall of another Pompeian house indicates that women were not banned from the dining-room, as they had been in Athens:

'A slave must wash and dry the feet of the guests, and spread a linen cloth over the cushions on the couches.

Do not cast lustful glances or make eyes at another man's wife.

Do not be coarse in your conversation.

Restrain yourself from getting angry or using offensive language. If you cannot do so, then go home.'

These reminders give a good idea of how bawdy some dinner parties could be.

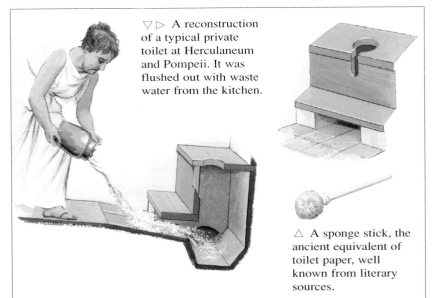

▽▷ A reconstruction of a typical private toilet at Herculaneum and Pompeii. It was flushed out with waste water from the kitchen.

△ A sponge stick, the ancient equivalent of toilet paper, well known from literary sources.

△ The summer dining-room in the House of Lucretius at Pompeii. Several such fitted-masonry dining-rooms have been discovered at Pompeii.

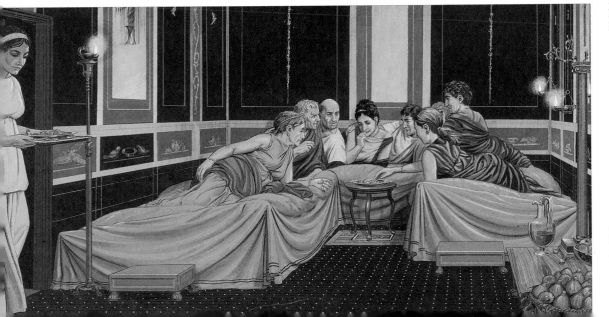

◁ A reconstruction of dinner party at the house of Lucius Ceius Secundus in Pompeii.

149

DAILY LIFE

As in fifth-century BC Athens, men in Rome in the early second century AD spent little time at home. However, Roman women of all classes had much greater freedom. Although they spent more time at home than men, they were still able to go out on their own and sit at table with their husbands and guests.

Ritual surrounded the birth of a Roman child, perhaps because miscarriage and the death of a woman in childbirth were both common. The father formally acknowledged the newborn child in the ceremony of *sublatus*, when he raised the baby in his arms. Nonetheless, a Roman father also had the right to reject his child: the exposure of unwanted babies to die was a fact of Roman life, though we do not know how common it was.

Names were given to girls on the eighth day after birth and to boys on the ninth. Men in every family had two names, and often three: the second was always the family name. Under the Republic, women had a single name, that of the family. Under the Empire, however, two names became common for women – the first her family name, the second taken from either her father or mother. Registration of the birth took place within thirty days at the Temple of Saturn.

Infancy and games

At all levels of society, the proportion of Roman children who survived infancy was small. Those that did survive enjoyed a variety of toys and games, some of which are familiar to us today. Knucklebones (*astragali*) made of bronze, glass or onyx were thrown like dice, each side having a different value. Counters and marbles in different materials have also been found.

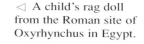

◁ A child's rag doll from the Roman site of Oxyrhynchus in Egypt.

▽ A terracotta statuette from Roman Egypt of a child learning to walk with a walking frame.

◁ A gold *bulla*. from Pompeii. The *bulla* was the symbol of free birth. It was worn by boys from infancy until manhood.

▷ A Roman bas-relief of a boy in a toy chariot pulled by a goat (now in the Louvre, Paris).

E

F

G

H

Bone and stone objects of the Roman period used to play a variety of games.

A A selection of bone counters used for different kinds of board games.

B Marbles of different sizes (British Museum).

C Five ordinary dice of varying sizes (British Museum).

D Two multi-faced dice (British Museum).

E A stone board for a board game (Trier Museum).

F, G, H Three gaming pieces; the inscriptions read MALEST (probably 'bad luck'), VICTOR ('winner') and NUGATOR ('fool').

Education

The education of children in the Republic could be a very haphazard process. In richer and better-educated families the parents sometimes played a part in the early education of their sons, but the formal education of girls was very rare. Opportunities for formal education increased steadily in Rome from the time of Augustus to the middle of the second century AD, but it remained a haphazard affair. All education of young children relied heavily on rote learning.

For those children who did receive an education, instruction was divided into three levels: primary school, grammar school and rhetoric school. Primary schools were attended by lower-class girls and boys from the ages of seven to fourteen, and taught reading and arithmetic. These schools were privately run and lessons were held in porticoes or public areas; the great exedra of Trajan's Forum, for example, was used as a school-room. The children of the rich were educated at home by a teacher

◁ A Roman bas-relief showing a classroom scene (Trier Museum).

▽ A selection of Roman writing materials:

A A terracotta inkwell.

B A reed pen with a split nib.

C A bronze pen with a remarkably modern appearance.

employed by their parents, and the sources are full of references to how little such teachers were paid.

The second level of education was taught by the *grammaticus*, who taught Greek and Latin grammar. The number of students who progressed to this level was small. At the third level, a *rhetor* taught the art of rhetoric – that is, the art of speaking and writing formally in the most effective and persuasive way. Students at this level had to study and analyse texts.

Only the sons of well-to-do families were likely to receive what was considered a full education.

Growing up

At an appropriate time between the age of fourteen and nineteen, every young Roman man celebrated his formal coming of age, usually on 17 March, the festival of Liber and Libera. His family celebrated with him. He would dedicate the clothes of his childhood to the household gods, and put on a new, white *toga virilis* (toga of manhood), which symbolised his status as a full citizen. His family escorted him to the Tabularium to be registered, then they went on to the Forum for further ceremonies. A large banquet was usually given for families and friends in the evening.

A son usually moved to his own house when he married, but he remained under the authority of his father as long as he lived.

In earlier times, boys became liable for military service at the age of seventeen, but as the early Roman army was not a professional force, they did not serve continuously. From the time of Augustus the Roman state had a professional, paid army and many younger sons of ordinary families joined the legions for a fixed period of service, often 25 years. On retirement, a soldier was given land and other privileges. By the second century AD, however, most of the

A
B
C

D
Four fragmentary wooden writing tablets. These were thin sheets of wood covered with wax, on which school pupils could write with a stylus. Several were often bound together to form a sort of book.

E
Three bronze styluses for writing on wax tablets. The flat end of the stylus was used for erasing.

152

legions were drawn from the provinces rather than from Italy. Under the Empire, the sons of equestrians and senators might serve as junior staff officers as part of a general political and administrative career.

The course of a Roman girl's life varied according to her social status. A daughter of a well-to-do family would not work outside the home, but would be involved in the general running of the household. She would visit her friends, go to the baths and generally have a much freer life than her counterpart in ancient Athens. The daughters of shopkeepers and other traders might be required to work for the family business.

Marriage

Roman girls were considered of marriageable age at twelve and boys at fourteen, though many did not marry until they were somewhat older. Augustus legislated that women of twenty and men of twenty-five who were still unmarried should be penalised.

Marriages were usually arranged, particularly amongst the upper classes. At first, the marriage of close relations was a crime, *incestum*, but by the second century BC marriage between first cousins was not unusual. Roman law did not recognise a marriage between a Roman and a foreigner, and a Roman woman could not marry a slave.

A young couple became engaged with the consent of their fathers, but engagement was an informal agreement to marry made in writing, and could easily be renounced. A betrothal ceremony was held in the presence of friends and relatives, with a banquet to follow. The girl received gifts from her fiancé and a ring. The prospective groom made a substantial gift to his fiancée, usually returnable if the engagement was broken off. The girl would have a dowry, which would be paid by her father to the groom.

The wedding ceremony

June was the favourite time of year for weddings. The wedding ceremony began in the morning, when the groom arrived with his family and friends at the home of the bride. The matron of honour performed the ceremony of linking the couple's right hands (*dextrarum iunctio*). Sacrifice was then made, usually a pig, and the marriage contract, which involved the dowry, was signed. This was followed by music, food and dancing, usually at the expense of the groom. After the time of Augustus, the cost of such festivities was not allowed to exceed 1000 sesterces.

Preparing the bride

On the day before her wedding, a girl would ritually surrender her childhood toys and clothes to the household gods. The bride's appearance at the ceremony was also ritually prescribed. She wore a tunic-type dress without a hem (*tunica recta*), secured at the waist by a girdle of wool (*cingulum herculeum*). Over this she wore a saffron-coloured *palla* or cloak. She wore an orange veil (*flammeum*), and her hair was dressed in an old-fashioned way with six strands parted using a bent iron spearhead.

The wedding procession

After the wedding banquet, all the guests accompanied the bride to her new home, in a procession similar to that in an Athenian wedding. The bride was closely escorted by three young boys: one held her left hand, another her right, and the third carried a torch in front of her. The torch had been lit from the hearth at the bride's home. As the procession neared the bridegroom's house, the torch was thrown away; whoever managed to catch it was traditionally promised a long life.

When the wedding procession arrived at the groom's house, the bride smeared the doorposts with oil and fat and wreathed them with wool. She was then carried across the threshold. Once inside the house, she symbolically touched fire and water, and then was led to the bedchamber. Here she was helped to prepare for bed by women who had been married only once, and the bridegroom was admitted. The Roman marriage contract stated explicitly that the purpose of marriage was the procreation of children.

▽ A Roman relief showing a bride, her head covered with a *flammeum*, joining her right hand with that of the groom (*dextarum iunctio*) to pledge troth.

Four reliefs from a Roman wedding altar in the Museo delle Terme:

△ Two maenads dancing around an altar.

▽ Children carrying a sunshade for a bridal procession to the groom's house and ritual offerings for the marriage sacrifice.

△ Two children carrying items connected with the marriage ceremony, including dough to make a ritual wedding cake.

▽ A bride and groom pledging their troth.

▷ A bas-relief from the Arch of Constantine. It shows (left to right) a man in a tunic and *pallium*, a boy similarly dressed, a man in a tunic and toga, a woman in a long tunic and *palla*, and a man in a tunic.

△ A typical male hairstyle of the early Empire.

Examples of men's clothing:

A A hitched up tunic, for working men.

B A tunic and *pallium*.

C A tunic and toga.

D A *paenula*, or hooded cloak.

E A hobnailed sandal, for soldiers and workmen.

F A hobnailed boot.

Men's clothing

Roman and Greek clothes were very similar. The tunic was the basic garment for everyone. Several of these have been found at desert sites. Some examples from Ein Gedi on the Dead Sea have a coloured stripe (*clavus*) descending from each shoulder, which would have indicated the status of the wearer. Tunics were generally made of two rectangular pieces of woollen cloth joined at the shoulders and hanging down to the knee. They were usually untailored, the excess width forming simple sleeves, though some were tailored with proper sleeves. Most were made of undyed wool, and thus had a colour similar to oatmeal. The tunic was tied at the waist by means of a belt. Members of the wealthier classes wore a longer tunic.

The most famous form of dress for Roman men was the toga, worn over a tunic. All free-born citizens were legally allowed to wear the toga, but because it was so cumbersome only the upper classes would have worn it for any length of time. The toga was a sign of formality; a magistrate or a senator would wear one when carrying out his state duties. Important officials wore a toga with a purple stripe.

The toga was a large piece of fine woollen cloth, roughly semi-circular in shape, and was worn draped over one shoulder (leaving the other arm free), falling to about ankle-length. In essence it was like a cloak, but was worn wrapped round the body instead of flowing free.

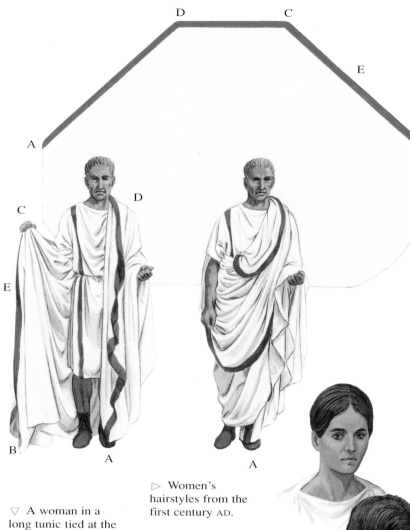

◁ A senatorial toga trimmed with purple. It was folded along line A-B and draped over the left shoulder so that A was level with the left foot; the rest of the toga passed across the back, under the right arm and back over the left shoulder, then area C-E was pulled over the front.

Another, similar garment worn by men was the *pallium*, the Roman version of the Greek *himation*.

Men's hairstyles

A typical day for a Roman man might start with a visit to the barber (*tonsor*). Roman razors were poor quality, so most men did not attempt to shave themselves. The barber's shop would be crowded and a source of the latest news and gossip. Hair was removed by several different methods. A sort of poultice called *dropax*, of various resinous waxes, were used to remove hair. It was also possible to use tweezers (*forcipes aduncae*), though this was presumably very painful. Some men practised whole body depilation.

Roman men usually kept their hair short and until the early second century were more often than not clean-shaven. The fashion for beards, an influence from the Greek East, was promoted by Hadrian, although men are shown wearing short, clipped beards in some later first century AD sculpture.

Women's clothing

Women wore a *stola*, a loose-fitting long tunic rather like the Greek *chiton*. Over this they wore a *palla*, a large rectangular shawl made of wool, draped around the shoulders and often drawn up over the head. Beneath the tunic they wore a sleeveless under-tunic and a *strophium*, a soft leather band beneath the breasts. The toga was not worn by girls or respectable women; for Roman women, wearing a toga was the sign of a conviction of adultery or of employment as a prostitute.

Women's hairstyles

Women's hairstyles changed many times from the Republic to the late Empire. Hairstyles also varied according to social status and age.

During the Republic, hairstyles were simple, with the hair drawn back from a central parting and gathered into a bun at the nape of the neck. Younger girls might wear their hair in a ponytail. Sometimes a fine fringe of curls softened the rather severe style.

Women's hairstyles became more elaborate during the reign of Augustus, with the hair often braided before it was drawn back into a bun. It was under the Flavian emperors and Trajan, however, that female hairstyles became most elaborate and ornate, with masses of curls piled high on the head.

▷ Women's hairstyles from the first century AD.

▽ A woman in a long tunic tied at the waist and below the breasts.

▽ A woman wearing a tunic and *palla*.

▽ An elaborate women's hairstyle of the late first century AD.

A *calmistrum* was used to obtain lasting curls. This was a hollow iron instrument in the shape of a rod, which was heated over glowing coals. Hairpins, ribbons, nets and tiny combs were used to hold the hair in place. Sometimes false hairpieces were also used.

Combs were used to prepare these hairstyles. These could be made of ivory, horn, bronze, tortoiseshell or even gold. The hairdresser (*ornator*) and the comber (*pectinator*) were indispensable, and in the houses of the rich there was often a permanent post for a hairdresser.

Late Roman dress

Our evidence for styles of dress in the later Roman period is, as for the earlier period, mainly artistic. However, there are also some examples of textiles which have been preserved in the very dry conditions of the Egyptian desert.

In the fourth century the toga continued to be worn by men of the upper classes. Long-sleeved tunics became much more popular and trousers, both tight and baggy, were worn more often. Military style belts with highly decorated tunics were worn by high ranking army officers and members of the militarised bureaucracy. Rectangular cloaks fastened with large fibulae (brooches) were worn over these.

In some respects women's dress displayed fewer major changes. Tunics tended to be full-length with long, wide sleeves often worn with a cloak fastened on the right shoulder with an ornate brooch.

Cosmetics

Cosmetics were also very important for a Roman woman's appearance. Creams, perfumes and unguents were traded in great quantities. They were sold in small ceramic vessels, glass phials or alabaster pots.

Make-up for the face was mixed in small plates, often using the lanolin from unwashed sheep's wool. Red for tinting the lips and cheeks was obtained from ochre, from a lichen-like plant called *ficus*, or from molluscs. Eyeliner was made from soot or a powder made from antimony; these could also be used to thicken the eyebrows.

The mirror was a basic necessity. These were made of sheet metal highly polished, and were often elaborately decorated on the reverse.

A woman's life

Roman women spent much of their time in the house, attending to household business, supervising slaves and looking after children. Nonetheless, all classes of women enjoyed a much freer lifestyle than the women of ancient Athens.

◁ △ The *palla*. A rectangular woollen mantle worn by women. It was normally draped over the left shoulder, across the back and under the right arm, with the remainder carried over the left arm.

▷ A bronze statuette of a woman wearing a *strophium*, the Roman equivalent of a bra.

◁ Women's footwear: a sandal and a soft leather shoe.

▽ Late Roman dress as depicted in a fourth-century mosaic from Piazza Armerina, Sicily.

◁ A Roman painting depicting a woman pouring perfume (Museo delle Terme, Rome).

▷ ▽ An ivory pyxis, probably used for cosmetics, and two silver spatulae for applying make-up.

◁ A bone comb, three ivory hair pins and a silver mirror from Pompeii.

▽ A Roman relief from Neumagen (now in Trier Museum) showing a woman with four female attendants. The woman sits in a wicker armchair.

A woman enjoyed prestige corresponding to her husband's social position. She was formally in charge of everything within the household, though in well-to-do households such tasks as fetching water and the preparation of food was delegated to slaves. She had formal custody of the household keys and directed the daily lives of children and household slaves. In her husband's absence, she had full control of family business. At dinner parties women ate with the guests, and from the time of Augustus they reclined on couches as did the men.

Women went out of the house to shop, to pay social calls, to attend public entertainments and to worship at temples. Upper class women would travel around the city in a sedan chair (*sella*). A woman would also visit the baths, bathing at different times of the day from men, or using separate bathing establishments.

Divorce and adultery

All laws which placed a woman under the authority of her husband were abolished very early in Roman history. Marriages could be dissolved without legal formalities or state participation, at the free will of either party, except in the case of certain marriages between aristocrats. However, since divorce required the return of the dowry to the wife's family, most Roman husbands would not have taken such a step lightly. When a divorce took place the children remained in the custody of the father.

The *Lex Julia de Adulteriis* of 18 BC made adultery a public crime, but it was not until Constantine's reign that men could be charged. If they were found guilty, the wife and her lover were banished to different locations. She forfeited half of her dowry as well as a third of her own property, and it was a criminal offence for anyone to marry her after her conviction.

Patrons and clients

There was no man in Rome who did not feel himself tied to someone more powerful than himself by bonds of respect and obligation; a network of such client-patron relationships was central to Roman society. Even an otherwise unemployed man might be the client of a wealthy patron. The patron was obliged to invite his clients to eat at his table on occasion, and to give them gifts. In return, the client might run errands or carry out business transactions for his patron. Most importantly, the client was expected to vote for his patron if he stood for office.

Work

There is evidence for a very wide variety of occupations in ancient Rome. The wealth of the upper classes was based on land owned outside the city. With the growth in trade, however, many men made a very good living from owning

△ A black and white mosaic from the headquarters of the guild of the grain-measurers at Ostia. The grain is being brought in sacks and measured in a bucket-shaped container, a *modius*. The *mensor*, the measurer, is the figure in the middle holding a measuring stick in his right hand.

◁ A relief showing a Roman banker and a customer (from the Palazzo Salviati, Rome).

◁ A Roman relief, now in the Vatican, of a cutler's shop. There is an impressive choice of sickles, pruning knives and long carving knives on display.

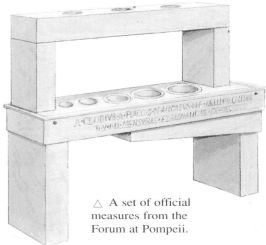

△ A set of official measures from the Forum at Pompeii.

◁ A Roman relief from Aquileia showing a blacksmith at work. The tools of his trade are depicted on the right-hand side.

businesses importing and exporting or buying and selling locally a wide range of goods, from basic foodstuffs to luxury items such as silks and perfumes.

Guilds

Guilds (*collegia*) played an important part in the organisation of small-time businessmen and craftsmen in Rome. These guilds were similar to trades unions today, organized to further the common trading or professional interests of their members; guilds were authorised by the state. Over 150 such guilds are known in ancient Rome. From Ostia we have evidence for many such guilds, ranging from guilds of barge owners to fullers, bakers and rope-sellers.

Craftsmen

There were many craftsmen active in Rome. On the Campus Martius were several workshops of *marmorarii*, marble-workers and sculptors, producing statuary and architectural elements. Goldsmiths, jewellers and bronze founders were to be found in the Saepta Julia. In the professions connected with dress, such as boot-making or cloak-making, manufacture and sale took place under the same roof.

△ Three Roman coins from the British Museum:

A *sestertius* of Caligula
B *denarius* of Julius Caesar
C *aureus* of Augustus

▽ A terracotta statuette of an actor playing a slave.

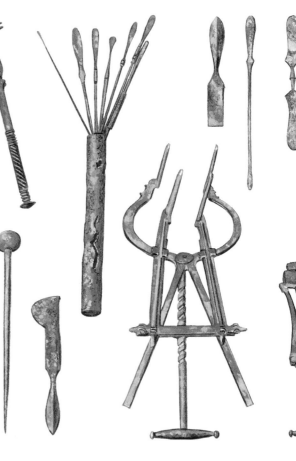

▽ A set of Roman bronze surgical instruments from Pompeii.

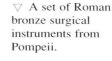

△ △ Two bronze cupping vessels for blood-letting (top). They were often used as signs of the medical profession, as in the votive plaque from Roman Athens (below). The plaque depicts two cupping vessels and a series of surgical instruments.

△ A relief from a Roman sarcophagus from L'Aquila showing a funeral procession. The deceased (shown reclining) lies on a bier. The procession is led by musicians (to the right) and the mourners follow behind (to the left).

Pastimes

A Roman man would spend most of his daily life away from the house, whether he was a shopkeeper, an artisan or a senator. Once he had finished his day's work, there were a number of entertainments on offer. He would almost certainly visit the baths, perhaps spending several hours there; the baths were very much social centres, and a good place to meet people in the hope of a dinner invitation. Otherwise, Rome offered numerous bars where people could play dice and gamble.

Slaves and freedmen

Slave ownership was very widespread in the Roman world. Slaves might be owned by private individuals; a family's slaves were considered part of the *familia*, as were its freed slaves and clients. But slaves might also be owned by public bodies to carry out various civic duties. For example, in Rome the maintenance gangs for the aqueducts under Frontinus were all publicly-owned slaves.

In the late Republic and under Augustus many slaves came on to the market as a result of wars; both slaves and their children were marketable commodities. Nonetheless, most slaves were reasonably well treated, if only in recognition of their value as property. Moreover, many slaves had specific and highly-prized skills, such as training and experience as a tutor or doctor. A special place was held by the *verna*, a slave born into a household, either from the union of two slaves, or born to a temporary favourite of the master of the house. A *verna* often provided a playmate for the children of the household and might later be entrusted with their early education.

Slavery was not necessarily for life. Slaves of the imperial household could rise to hold positions of quite considerable power and could earn enough money to buy their freedom. On occasion, manumission was given free and the slave obtained the name, status and rights of a Roman citizen.

The freedmen were an important social group, mostly concerned with trade and business. A freedman could rely on his former owner as patron. He could not himself hold public office, but his sons and descendants could.

Sickness and medicine

Roman sources are full of references to ailments and diseases. Some of these were quite clearly related to poor living conditions; a bow-legged condition very like rickets, for example, was very common amongst the young children of the poor of Rome. Stomach upsets were very common, mainly because of the problem of keeping perishable food fresh.

The importance of the doctor's place in the community is demonstrated by the fact that in 46 BC Julius Caesar granted Roman citizenship to foreign doctors working in Rome. Several Roman medical treatises survive, and they give us a general picture of medical knowledge and practice at the time. Herbs and herbal preparations were the mainstay of medical treatment, as well as blood-letting, which was believed to cure or alleviate almost every known ill.

Galen, who was at one time physician to the gladiators at Pergamum in Asia Minor, makes a number of references to surgical operations. Surgery was never undertaken lightly, and speed was essential in the absence of any effective anaesthetics. A number of sets of surgical instruments have been recovered from the Roman world; a set from Pompeii includes forceps, probes, needles, catheters, bone chisels, scalpels and drug boxes.

▽ Late first-century BC
Tomb of Eurysaces the
baker, near the Porta
Maggiore in Rome.
The circular openings
are thought to represent
ovens, and a frieze
running round the top
of the structure depicts
the different stages of
breadmaking.

Death

Life expectation in ancient Rome was much lower than that in most countries today. Deaths in childbirth were common, and babies often did not survive beyond infancy. The so-called diseases of luxury, such as gout and ulcers, commonly afflicted the wealthy male population and could cause an early death. Nonetheless, many well-to-do Romans seem to have reached respectable ages of 50 or 60. Lower class males, with a lifetime of heavy physical labour, rarely lived beyond the age of 50.

There were also times during the imperial period when severe plague epidemics affected Rome and killed thousands of people irrespective of their social standing.

Funerals

Death in ancient Rome was followed by the display of the body of the deceased so that friends and family could pay their last respects. This could last for seven days and ended with a funeral procession. If the deceased was a very prominent person, masks of the ancestors of the family were worn or carried in the procession, so that the whole family could be present. This was a show of the family's grief, but also an affirmation of its pride in its lineage.

For someone active in politics, the funeral procession wound its way to the Forum Romanum where an appropriate oration was given. In the Republic this honour was usually reserved for men, but from the early Empire it became customary to give full funerary honours to distinguished women also. In early Rome the body of the deceased was normally disposed of by cremation, but from the later first century AD inhumation became more common. If the family could afford it, the ashes or body were placed in a tomb.

Less distinguished and poorer people were given a simpler funeral, but there was still a procession accompanying the body or ashes to the burial place. The family returned to the tomb periodically during the mourning period. On special family occasions afterwards it was customary to picnic at the tomb in memory of the deceased, without any of the solemnity associated with memorial services today.

Tombs

A law of the Twelve Tables forbade cremation or burial within the city. It remained very important in Roman society to be remembered after death, however, and it became the custom, if one could afford it, to build a tomb where it could be seen easily and visited readily. Tombs were therefore built along the main roads out of the city.

Tombs could take a number of different forms, including unusual designs like the Pyramid of Cestius near the Porta Ostiensis in Rome. Often these were family tombs, but it was also possible in life to subscribe to a burial club, which would arrange and pay for funerals and provide space for deceased members in a communal tomb. Tomb interiors were often richly decorated with painted and moulded plasterwork. The exterior of the tomb was also given decorative attention as it was designed to impress the passer-by.

△ The remains of a Roman family tomb outside the Porta Romana at Ostia.

A typical style of tomb at both Rome and Ostia is the *columbarium*. Its central feature is usually a rectangular, barrel-vaulted chamber, with niches in several rows in the walls. Urns containing the ashes of the dead were placed in these niches. In front of the tomb chamber there was often an open area enclosed by a wall. Here the funerary banquet was held and subsequent family gatherings took place. A particularly good example of a *columbarium* survives at Ostia. Plasterwork survives in the niches, and the walls were built of concrete faced with *opus reticulatum* (see Chapter 5).

More modest tombs might take the form of chests or a pedimented pillar. In the Isola Sacra cemetery near Ostia, the graves of the very poor were marked by amphora necks projecting from the ground. Libations to the dead could be poured through the neck of the jar.

△ A section of the painted interior of a Roman tomb on the Via Portuensis betweeen Rome and Portus.

◁ Amphora burials of the poor in the Isola Sacra cemetery near Ostia.

SHOPS, BARS AND RESTAURANTS

Rome was well provided with major markets, but the main streets were also lined with a great variety of shops. Bars, restaurants and even fast food outlets compensated for the lack of kitchens in many houses, and provided a focus for socializing.

△ A view of the shops (*tabernae*) behind the Markets of Trajan. In the foreground is a shop with the remains of two ovens; this was probably a bakery. Steps in the corner led up to a mezzanine level.

▽ A reconstruction of the shops at the back of the Markets of Trajan.

Shopping

Although the Forum was originally the main commercial centre of Rome, by the late Republic several other commercial centres had developed. The Forum had grown into an architectural showpiece, where the more basic commercial activities were no longer appropriate. So new commercial areas were established, closer to the Tiber: the Forum Boarium, for selling cattle and livestock, and the Forum Holitorium, for dealing in fruit and vegetables. Some commercial activity remained in the Forum, however: goldsmiths and silversmiths continued to sell their wares there.

Shops (*tabernae*) lined many of the main Roman streets, fronting houses or high-rise residential blocks. They usually consisted of one ground-floor room, with a masonry or wooden counter for selling goods near the entrance, and the rear space for storage. There was usually a mezzanine floor above the shop reached by a staircase or ladder. This was where the shopkeeper lived, unless he prospered and could afford a separate residence.

A great variety of goods was sold in the shops, ranging from foodstuffs to clothing and fabrics, pans, jewellery and books. Shopkeepers often displayed their wares on the pavements, and temporary stalls were set up between the columns of porticoes. Domitian attempted to free the streets from encroachment by shopkeepers: 'Barber, taverner, cook, butcher keep to their own thresholds. Now Rome exists: of late it was a huge shop'.

A number of terracotta plaques from Ostia, once attached to tombs, depict various kinds of food shop. These show, for example, a butcher with different cuts of meat, including a pig's head, hanging from hooks above his head. Another shows a shop with a woman standing behind the counter selling poultry. Rabbits are also for sale from hutches beneath the counter.

A food shop

Bread was very important in the Roman diet, and there would have been many bakeries in Rome, though interestingly the Roman writer Pliny the Elder states that there were no bakers in Rome until after 174 BC. Until that time all bread was made at home. Behind the Markets of Trajan is a row of shops which includes a bakery. All the shops have stairs in one corner giving access to a mezzanine floor above, where the baker and his family lived. In the bakery there are two brick-built ovens. A counter was built across the front of the shop, partially blocking the doorway. The bread would have been sold here hot from the oven.

▷ A section of a baker's oven.
A The part of the oven where the fire was kindled and the bread was baked
B The passage along the front of the oven
C The chimney
D The space for storing the fuel

△ A reconstruction of a bakery at Pompeii.

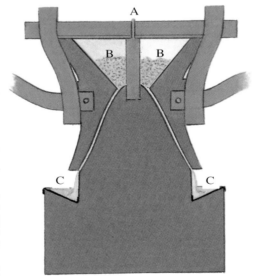

△ A section of a Pompeian flour mill. The lower half of the mill was in the form of a cone set into a round masonry base. A wooden stake (A) with a pivot at the top was inserted into the head of the cone. The wooden frame which held the upper half of the mill in position rotated on this pivot. The grain was poured into the conical space in the top half of the mill (B). Around the edge of the base was a trough lined with lead (C), where the ground flour was collected.

△ A typical Pompeian loaf of bread.

△ A wall painting from Pompeii showing a baker selling loaves of bread.

Grain was delivered to the shop and was usually ground into flour on the premises. No mills survive in the Markets of Trajan shop, but at Ostia and Pompeii many bakeries have evidence of mills towards the rear of the shop. These were made from two pieces of hard volcanic stone. The upper hour-glass shaped stone was turned against the conical lower stone either by manpower or by a horizontal beam attached to a donkey or mule. The grain was fed into the mill at the top and the flour was collected in a trough around the lower grinding stone. The flour was then made into a dough and baked in a large oven, very like the pizza ovens still used in Italy. Pliny the Elder mentions that bread varied according to the shape of the loaves and to taste.

Shops might also be arranged around a colonnaded court. These large market halls, or *macella*, are found at Ostia, Pompeii and Pozzuoli. They are often associated specifically with the buying and selling of fish or meat. In Rome a number of *macella* are recorded. In 209 BC Livy mentions a food market near the Forum Romanum; under Augustus the Macellum Liviae was constructed on the Esquiline Hill, and under Nero the Macellum Magnum on the Caelian.

A bar

Many establishments on the streets catered for a quick drink or a more leisurely refreshment. Bars varied in size from tiny rooms opening directly onto the street, to larger places with seating. Guest rooms might be provided on the upper floor. Few bars have survived in Rome, but at Herculaneum there is a good example on the ground floor of the House of Amphitrite.

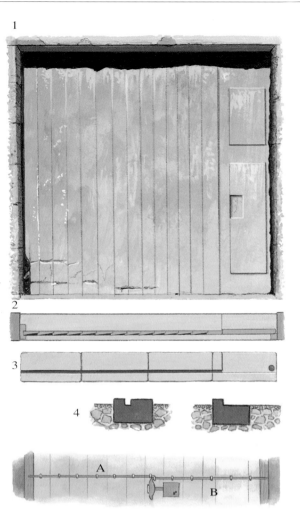

This bar has a counter with large jars set into it, from which hot food and drinks could be served. Counters with inset jars are not found at Ostia, however, and this arrangement may not

◁ 1. A plaster cast of the shutters and door of a shop from Pompeii
2. Plan of a shop entrance showing how the planks and door fit into the threshold
3. A shop threshold
4. Sections through the threshold

(Lower diagram) The locking mechanism of a shop door. Bar A is inserted through the rings riveted to the planks. Bar B is similarly inserted and the two are locked together.

▽ A terracotta plaque from Ostia depicting a poultry shop. A woman stands behind the counter. Baskets of fruit or possibly eggs are displayed on the counter. Chickens hang from hooks in the background and rabbits are kept in hutches underneath the counter.

have been common in Rome. The bar at Herculaneum had an oven, and amphorae were stored in a large wooden wall-rack, and on an upper mezzanine floor.

Bars were popular places not only to eat and drink but also to gamble, and many establishments concealed gambling dens in their back rooms where bets could be placed and games of chance could be played. Bars were frowned upon by the upper class as places of drunkenness and political intrigue.

Drinks and snacks

Many of these bars provided food. The *caupona* offered lodging as well as food and drink, and the term *popina* covered a wide range of establishments, from drinking den to respectable restaurant. Wine mixed with water and flavoured with herbs, honey or resin would be served. A great variety of food would be available, from appetizers such as olives, to soups and bread, seafood, and meat stews. Roasted meat in cubes was popular, as were sausages, pies, fish, sweets, fruit and filled buns.

Evidence from Herculaneum suggests that the Romans made a form of pizza. These were called *ofellae* and were small circular dough pieces with some kind of topping. However, although the Romans did make cheese, they did not have tomatoes!

Eating out

As many families did not have proper kitchens in their houses, the bars, inns and restaurants which served hot food were very important. But they were frequented mainly by men and women of low social standing. It was also possible to buy food to take away to eat elsewhere.

A restaurant

Ancient Rome must have had many eating places. A particularly good example was found

△ A marble veneered counter of typically 3rd century type from Ostia.

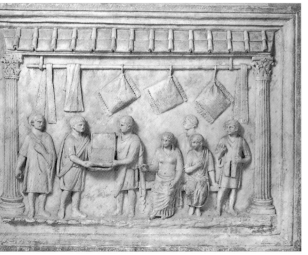

△ A relief of a cloth merchant's shop. Note the way in which the cloth is displayed hanging from a bar above the shop.

△ A reconstruction of a very small tavern in Herculaneum.

167

△ A restaurant in the Via di Diana at Ostia.

at Ostia, on the Via di Diana. At the entrance is a wide counter with wall-shelving on which glasses, dishes and food for sale were displayed. Beneath the counter were two basins for washing glasses and dishes. The counter and shelves were veneered with marble. Further inside the shop is a marble cupboard for storage, plus more shelving. Above these is a large painting, illustrating some of the food on sale: olives in brine, grapes, pomegranates. A room to one side of the main room may have been a kitchen and has a large *dolium* (jar) sunk into the ground, possibly for the cool storage of wine. Apart from paintings of food, the walls of the restaurant were decorated with frescoes made up of geometric shapes in yellow, red and blue.

Outside the front of the restaurant are benches for customers to rest while taking a cool drink or eating a quick snack. At the rear is a small open court, with a plain mosaic pavement, a small fountain and a stone bench, again providing seating for customers.

Ingredients and tastes

Roman food was often highly spiced. A favourite flavouring, particularly for casseroles and stews, was known as *garum*. This was made from fish guts, heavily salted and then allowed to ferment in large open tanks. The result was then strained and put into amphorae. Foods tended to be hot, spicy and sweet-and-sour in flavour. Pepper was used to season everything, even sweet home-baked biscuits.

The most popular dishes had a meat base. The Romans often used game meats such as partridge, hare, venison, wild boar, crane and pheasant, in addition to poultry, mutton, beef and pork. Fish was also eaten in great quantity. Red mullet was considered a great delicacy, as were shellfish, particularly oysters and mussels. A sauce was always served with fish, no matter how it was cooked.

▷ A reconstruction of a restaurant on the Via di Diana, Ostia. A counter is located at the entrance. Shelves were attached to the wall behind on which glasses, dishes and food for sale were set. The counter and shelves were lined with second-hand marble. A marble cupboard further inside the shop provided space for storage and more shelving.

MANY GODS

Roman religion was based on public and private sacrifice to a variety of deities, many adopted from the Greek pantheon and directly associated with the origins of Rome itself. The emperor was also worshipped, and cults from other parts of the empire became established.

▷ A reconstruction of the Temple of Jupiter Optimus Maximus on the Capitoline Hill.

▷ Two reliefs from the Tetrarchic Decennalian monument (early 4th century) in the Forum Romanum. Above: a *suovetaurelia* (sacrifice of a boar, ram and bull). Below: A sacrifice scene. The central figure is probably the Emperor Diocletian. He is making a libation on the altar using a dish or *patera*.

▷ A relief from the Temple of Vespasian in the Forum Romanum, depicting the equipment needed for a sacrifice

The traditional religion of Rome was based on the idea of a contract between mortals and the gods. It was important in every area of Roman life. Offerings and sacrifices had to be made to the gods in order to obtain their goodwill.

Roman religion was agricultural in origin. Roman deities were not depicted in human form until the later third century BC, when they were incorporated into the Greek pantheon. The most senior deities made up the Capitoline Triad of Jupiter, Juno his wife and Minerva his daughter. Also important were Apollo, Mars, Vesta, Venus and the goddess Roma, the personification of the Roman city and state.

The imperial cult

The origins of the imperial cult, the worship of the emperor and his family, lay in the practice of king-worship in the Hellenistic East. Augustus was the first to introduce the cult of the emperor's *genius*. The Romans believed that the *genius* or *numen* was the divine part of a person. A priesthood (the Augustales) was set up to carry out the various rituals.

Each emperor after Augustus increasingly encouraged emperor worship. Nero had a statue of himself portrayed as the Sun God set up in the Domus Aurea, and Domitian insisted on being addressed as lord (*dominus*) and god (*deus*).

△ A view of the Temple of the Deified Julius Caesar in the Forum Romanum.

△ A reconstruction of the Temple of Portunus (commonly called 'Foruna Virilis') in the Forum Boarium. The temple is of typical Republican form with a high podium and frontal staircase.

▷ An altar in the Temple of Vespasian on the east side of the forum at Pompeii. It stood in front of the temple and depicts a sacrifice scene.

Lares and *penates*

An important link with the imperial cult was the worship of the *lares compitales*. These were the deities of the crossroads, whose worship took place at a central shrine in each of the fourteen regions of Rome.

In the home, the *lares* and *penates* were worshipped. These were the guardian deities of the household, the spirits of the ancestors who watched over the fortunes of the family, its slaves and the house itself. They were worshipped in the *lararium*, a small tabernacle or shrine which was placed in a prominent position in the *atrium*. Gifts of food and flowers were given, particularly at festivals and anniversaries, to maintain the goodwill of these spirits.

Priests and priestesses

The Romans did not have a separate profession of priests for carrying out the complicated rites of public religion. Usually the major religious offices were held by people prominent in political life. In the late Republic and early Empire there were four main colleges of priests: the sixteen *pontifices* headed by the Pontifex Maximus, sixteen *auguri* in charge of divination, fifteen men designated *sacris faciendis* for conducting sacrifices, and ten *epulones* in charge of feasts. The *auguri* and *pontifices* had a more distinguished standing than the others, and the *pontifices*, literally 'bridge-builders', were the most senior college. Each priesthood, unlike a political magistracy, could be held for life. When a post became vacant an election was conducted by the Senate from a list of nominees.

Sacrifices

Animal sacrifice was a regular feature of Roman religious life. The choice of an appropriate victim was laid down in religious law, and depended partly on the god involved and partly upon the reasons for the sacrifice. Male animals were offered to gods, female to goddesses. The most usual animals offered for sacrifice were the ox, pig, sheep or chicken. A larger animal was stunned with a pole-axe, and then its throat was cut. As the blood ran out, the animal was cut open and its entrails examined. This was to ensure that the omens were favourable. It was then roasted over a fire: the best portions of meat were offered to the god, and the worshippers usually feasted on the rest in the temple precinct. More modest, private offerings might be cakes, flowers or small votive offerings.

△ The circular Temple of Vesta, which sheltered the sacred flame and was symbolic of the eternal power of Rome.

△ A Vestal Virgin.

The Temple of Vesta

The cult of Vesta was symbolic of the eternal power of Rome. The Temple where the Vestal Virgins guarded the sacred fire was a circular building with twenty Corinthian columns, on the eastern side of the Forum Romanum. The temple was burned down on several occasions, including AD 64. The building on the site today dates from the Severan period.

Inside the temple was a secret room which housed, among other things, the statue of Pallas Athena, supposedly carried off by Aeneas from Troy. No one was allowed inside this room apart from the Vestals and the Pontifex Maximus.

The Vestal Virgins

The Vestal Virgins were the only female priesthood of Rome. They kept alive the sacred fire, which burned continuously in the Temple of Vesta. There were six Vestals, chosen by the Pontifex Maximus as young girls from the old patrician families. They served for thirty years and took a vow of chastity.

It was a great honour to be a Vestal Virgin, even though they were not allowed to marry during their thirty years' service. Any misdemeanour was severely punished. During the Republic an unchaste Vestal was buried alive, a practice enforced also by the emperor Domitian.

The cult statue of Vesta was kept in a small shrine near the entrance to the House of the Vestal Virgins.

The House of the Vestal Virgins

The Vestal Virgins lived in the Atrium Vestae, next to the Temple of Vesta in the Forum Romanum. It was rebuilt by Augustus, and again after the fire of AD 64. It was a large rectangular building, with rooms arranged around a spacious courtyard. In the courtyard were three large ponds and statues of honoured Vestals. By the imperial period the building probably also provided accommodation for the office of the Pontifex Maximus.

The foreign cults

The conquest of the East brought Rome into contact with the cults and beliefs of the Hellenistic world, including Judaism and early Christianity. The first of these to be established in Rome was the cult of the Great Mother, Magna Mater or Cybele. She was an Anatolian

◁ A statue of a Vestal Virgin, now in the Capitoline Museum.

◁ A statue of a Vestal Virgin, from the Atrium Vestae.

▷ A reconstruction of the House of the Vestal Virgins, or Atrium Vestae, in its mid-late imperial form, located next to the Temple of Vesta in the Forum Romanum. It is a large rectangular building with rooms arranged around a spacious courtyard. In the courtyard there were three large ponds and statues of honoured Vestals. The circular Temple of Vesta is in the right-hand corner.

◁ The procession of Isis. The figure on the left holds a *sistrum*.

△ A wall painting from Pompeii, depicting ceremonies associated with the worship of Isis.

mother goddess, whose cult object was brought to Rome from Pessinus during the Second Punic War. A temple dedicated to the Magna Mater was inaugurated on the Palatine in 191 BC.

These cults had certain characteristics in common. They required admission by secret initiation rites (hence their definition as 'mystery religions') and promised salvation for believers. Initially both Judaism and early Christianity were regarded by the Romans as mystery religions.

The Hellenised Egyptian goddess Isis also had a cult in Rome. A Temple of Isis was constructed at Pompeii in the late second century BC, and one was built in the Campus Martius by Caligula. From the time of Augustus the cult of Isis became increasingly popular.

Mithras was originally a Persian deity of light, but the Hellenistic and Roman version of Mithras is very different and became associated with the sun. Only men could be initiated, and the cult was particularly popular among soldiers and traders. Mithras is often depicted slaying a bull, as a representation of rebirth and the coming of spring. Many *mithraea* (shrines of Mithras) survive from the Roman world; over fifteen are known from Ostia alone. These were often partly or wholly underground, to recall the cave in which the god was supposed to have been born.

△ A reconstruction of the Temple of Isis at Pompeii.

▽ These two representations are commonly found at the entrance to a *mithraeum*. Left: Cautes with upraised torch, symbolising day. Below: Cautopates with lowered torch, symbolising night.

▽ The *mithraeum* beneath the church of San Clemente in Rome. On either side were benches where the initiated sat or reclined during ceremonies. An altar depicting Mithras slaying the cosmic bull was placed at one end.

A DAY AT THE RACES

Games were held throughout the year in Rome, as part of the religious and political life of the city. The most popular and exciting events, and also the most ancient, were the two, three or four-horse chariot races held in the Circus.

◁ A reconstructed view of the Circus Maximus in the early fourth century AD. The Circus was built in the valley between the Palatine and the Aventine hills. The *carceres* (starting gates) are at the bottom of the picture; Titus's triumphal arch is at the top. The *pulvinar*, or imperial box, is on the left-hand side. The *spina* runs down the centre of the arena, and the chariots raced anti-clockwise around it.

The Circus Maximus

The Circus Maximus was not the only circus in Rome. However, the Circus Flaminius, in the southern part of the Campus Martius, was never monumentalized, and had been mostly built over by the time of Augustus. The emperors Caligula and Nero, who were both fanatical supporters, also developed a circus in the imperial gardens on the Vatican Hill so that they could practise driving chariots. But by the imperial period the Circus Maximus was the only important circus in the city.

The Circus lies between the Palatine and Aventine hills. It is said to date back to the sixth century BC, and for a long time the starting gates and seating remained in wood. The gates were rebuilt in marble by Claudius, but Trajan totally transformed the building. He turned it into a massive monument, with a total length, including arena and steps, of 600 metres, and an average width of 200 metres. The maximum seating capacity is estimated at 385,000 people.

Along the central axis of the Circus was a high, 344-metre long masonry rib (the *spina*). This was decorated with statues, trophies and the seven movable eggs and seven dolphins which were used to count the seven laps of each race. At either end were the turning posts (*metae*) in the form of large gilded bronze cones. Augustus also had erected a 24-metre

◁ An aerial view of the Circus Maximus as it is today. The Palatine is to the right of the picture.

△ A terracotta plaque showing a scene from a chariot race at the Circus, following a collision at the turn round the *spina* (marked by the three columns on the left). The charioteer is lying on the ground behind the vehicle.

△ A terracotta plaque showing *bestiarii* fighting wild animals in the Circus. Wild beast hunts were much more commonly staged in the Circus than in the amphitheatre. In the background are the seven discs or 'eggs' which were lowered as each lap of a chariot race was completed.

▷ A plan of the curved south-east end of the Circus Maximus, showing the substructures of the seating. The black denotes modern remains: the grey is a reconstruction from these remains.

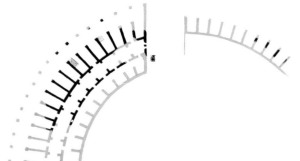

▽ A detail of the curved south-east end of the Circus Maximus. The substructures are built of brick-faced concrete. The staircase gave access to the upper seating from the corridor inside the facade.

▷ Archways between the bays below the second seating section of the Circus Maximus.

▷ Two surviving stone seats of the Circus Maximus. They are not in their original positions. Originally the seating was of wood, but in the first century AD it was rebuilt in stone.

▽ A cross-section through the substructures of the Circus Maximus at the south-east end. Around the top of the seating was a covered portico. The ground floor varies considerably from area to area, depending on whether it is in the valley or built on the bedrock of the hillside.

The structure of the stands

The substructures of the south-east end of the Circus had two functions. They provided a solid support for the seating above, and stairways and gangways for the audience to reach the seating area. The masonry dates from Trajan's reign and is concrete faced with brick. The stairs rested on a substructure made up of three rows of arches built of brick masonry. The facade of the building was arcaded like the facade of the Colosseum.

In the centre of the curved end a triumphal arch, adorned with marble columns, was built in AD 80–81 to commemorate Titus' sack of Jerusalem. This served as the entrance gate and replaced an earlier entrance.

Augustus built the *pulvinar*, a sort of imperial box, on the slopes of the Palatine. This was a sacred area reserved for those presiding over the games.

The starting gates

The starting gates of the Circus, the *carceres*, took the form of stalls or boxes; there were twelve of them. Those in the Circus Maximus have barely survived, but the gates of the circus at Lepcis Magna in Libya survive sufficiently well for us to reconstruct how a race was started. An attendant pulled a lever which operated a catapult system. The catapult jerked out the latches of the gates of each stall, enabling the gates to fly open.

red granite obelisk of Rameses II (dating from the thirteenth century BC), brought to Rome from Egypt in 10 BC.

The excavations

The structure has not been totally excavated. Test trenches have established the overall extent, including a height of about 35 metres for the *cavea* or seating.

In 1936 the south-east curved end of the Circus was excavated. Here the archaeologists found that the seating, instead of being partially supported on the hillside, rested almost entirely on vaulted substructures.

▽ A plan of the south-east end of the Circus Maximus on the Severan marble map of Rome (*Forma Urbis Romae*) of the early third century AD.

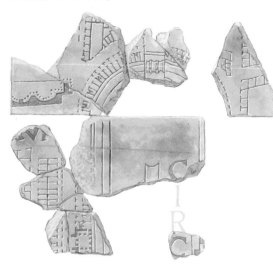

▽ The *pulvinar* of the Circus Maximus.

A A detail of the fragments of the Severan marble map depicting the *pulvinar*

B The restored plan

C A detail of a mosaic from Luni in Northern Italy which depicts the *pulvinar* as a six-column temple facade. The columns were supported on the six bases on the plan.

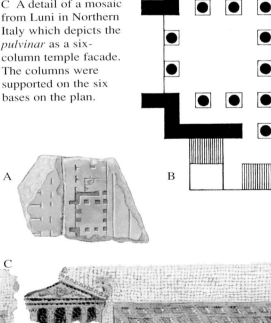

The *carceres* or starting gates.

A A relief from Naples showing the *carceres*. Between the wooden gates and grilles above there is a continuous horizontal architrave. Very tall herms (gate statues) stand in front of and between each gate. Attendants are closing the gates.

B A reconstruction of the *carceres*.

C A detail of the mechanism which opened the gates at the start of the race. This was based on a spring or catapult system, which caused the gates literally to spring open.

△ A fourth-century mosaic from Piazza Armerina in Sicily, showing a victorious charioteer. A prize-giver approaches holding a victor's palm branch. A trumpeter sounding a fanfare stands beside him.

Chariots, horses and drivers

By the time of the Empire chariot racing had become a very professional affair, with large stables supplying the horses, chariots and drivers. All jockeys belonged to teams (*factiones*), and each team had its own colours. From Augustus' reign there were usually four – white worn by the Albata, red by the Russata, blue by the Veneta and green by the Prasina. The *factiones* were virtual companies or corporations under imperial patronage; they supplied teams to the magistrates giving the games and received money prizes in return. The emperors built stables for each of these teams in the Campus Martius with a full staff of coaches, trainers, blacksmiths, vets and grooms. The charioteers by this time were mainly professional, drawn from the lower social classes, freedmen and slaves. As with gladiators, those who succeeded were idolized by the public.

Although many charioteers may have started as slaves, those who were successful could earn enough in prize money to buy their freedom. One such was Gaius Appuleius Diocles, who lived in the first half of the second century AD. A long inscription lists his many victories and huge earnings. The Roman writer Martial tells of another famous charioteer, Scorpus, who won over two thousand races before he was killed in an accident at the age of twenty-seven.

△ A mosaic from the Piazza Armerina. An attendant is handing a charioteer his helmet.

The races

On the day of a race, a procession led into the Circus. The crowd would cheer and place bets. A trumpet would blow and the presiding magistrate would signal the start of the race by dropping a napkin.

At the beginning of the race the competitors entered the arena simultaneously from the twelve starting gates at the northern end of the Circus. They raced anti-clockwise, circling around the *spina* for seven laps. Crashes were common, especially at the start of a race.

A maximum of twelve charioteers could compete. Races had either chariots with two horses or, more commonly, four. Novelty races might also be staged to add variety to the entertainment. Teams of up to ten horses, for example, might be used, or exhibitions of trick-riding, foot races or relays could be put on.

A full day's programme included twenty-four races. Gladiatorial games could also be staged in the Circus. At the end of the games, the victors received prizes – the victor's palm, crowns and neck chains of gold.

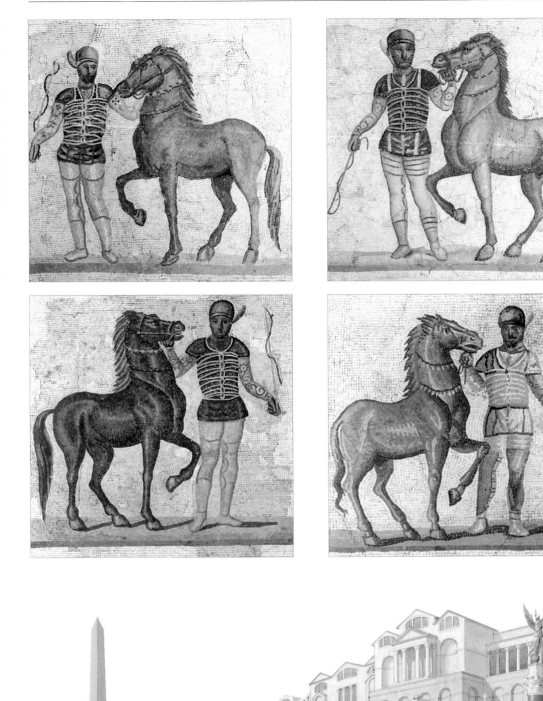

◁ A mosaic from Rome depicting charioteers wearing their team colours with their horses.

▽ A reconstruction of the Circus Maximus during a race. Note the three cone-shaped *metae* marking the turning-point at the end of the *spina*. The *pulvinar* can be seen behind the red column with the winged victory on top.

THE THEATRE

Roman drama was adapted from Classical Greece, but it developed distinctive characteristics of its own, including a great emphasis on farce and parody. Roman theatres were often built on vaulted substructures, with the seating, or cavea, arranged in a semicircle, and an elaborate stage.

▷ A reconstruction of a collapsible travelling stage.

▽ A vase painting from Apulia, showing the old Cheiron being helped up the small flight of stairs to the stage by two servants. All three wear grotesque masks. Two nymphs in the form of ugly old ladies watch the proceedings. Achilles is shown as a modest and gentle youth to the right. This shows a temporary stage from the side, with a roof over it and steps up the front.

Early Roman drama

Early Roman drama was clearly Greek in origin. Dramatic performances, *ludi scaenici*, were originally staged in honour of a particular deity, and there is evidence for them as early as 364 BC. The classical Greek tragedies and comedies, as well as the works of the great early Republican poets (Ennius, Naevius, Pacuvius, Plautus and Terence), reached the height of their popularity in the second century BC.

The performances

Variety was one of the most obvious characteristics of Roman entertainment in the theatre. This reflected the fact that Rome, in contrast to Classical Athens, was offered a huge variety of other types of entertainment, and had a much larger population to keep entertained.

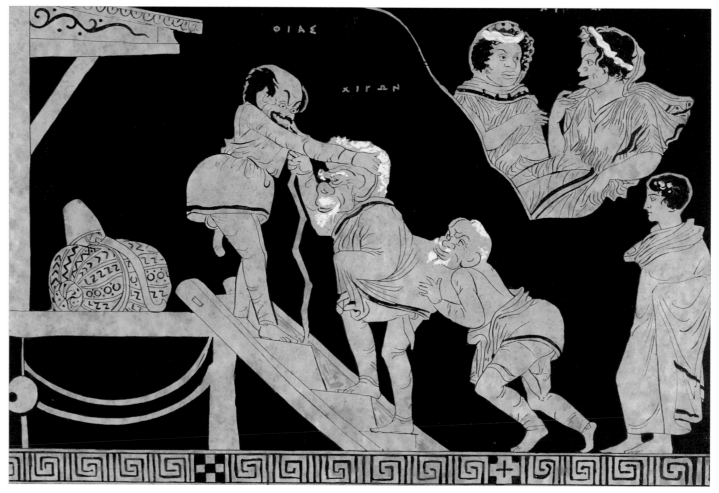

△ A vase painting by Asteas, showing Ajax and Cassandra in the Sanctuary of Athena. Ajax wears a fierce mask. The old priestess of Athena holds an over-size temple key and recoils in horror as Cassandra sets about Ajax. The whole scene is a parody of the original mythological characters.

△ A stage similar to the one shown opposite, but seen from the front. A decorated curtain hides the area beneath the stage, and the roof is supported on columns.

Dramatic performances therefore tended to become less sophisticated over time, in an effort to attract audiences. They were often no more than bawdy farces, providing easy, but vulgar, pure entertainment.

Comedy and bawdy farce in Italy

Two kinds of comic performance which had a great effect on the development of later Roman comedy developed in Southern Italy and Sicily, and were popular in the fourth and third centuries BC. These were the *Phlyakes* and the Atellan farces.

The *Phlyakes* are depicted on contemporary vases. These involved actors wearing masks and padded clothing to give them a grotesque appearance. The plots varied. Some were based on mythological tales, often parodying a tragic story, but everyday life featured prominently too. The main authors of these farces were Rhinthon and Sciras of Tarentum, and Sopater of Paphos.

The second form of comic entertainment was associated with the Campanian town of Atella. The Atellan farces had stock characters, all of them ridiculous in some way: Bucco and Maccus, both fools, Dosennus and Manducus, greedy buffoons, and Pappus, the 'Gaffer'. The action was set in a small Italian town, and often parodied tragedies. Generally, the Atellan farces were a low form of comedy, although many of the dramatic motifs were drawn from Greek New Comedy. They sometimes followed a tragedy, like satyric drama in Classical Athens.

Mime and pantomime

By the first century BC cultural and political changes had transformed the urban population of Rome, and its taste in entertainment. Theatre was geared to suit public taste. The most successful genres were mime and pantomime.

▽ A Roman tragedy depicted on a terracotta relief from a first-century BC tomb in Rome. The relief shows a typical early Roman stage. The columned *scaenae frons,* with a roof above, is already a feature.

△ A reconstructed view over
the Campus Martius, where many
of the entertainment buildings were
constructed. In the foreground is the
Theatre of Pompey with the Portico, and
the Theatre of Balbus beyond. At the top of
the picture, on the banks of the Tiber, is the
Theatre of Marcellus. The Circus Flaminius can be
seen between the Theatre of Pompey and the Theatre
of Marcellus. By this time much of the area would
have been built over.

Mime shows presented undemanding tales of adventure, spiced up with plenty of licentiousness, and later incorporated acts of violence more at home in the amphitheatre. In contrast to other types of Roman drama, female parts in mime were often played by female actors; they did not wear masks, but used heavy make-up. Music and songs were part of the performance.

Pantomime was the most sophisticated of the popular art forms, and was typically Roman. It comprised a display of masked dancers miming the action of a story, often one that was based on some mythological character. The Greeks called it 'Italian dance', despite the fact that two Greeks, Pylades of Cilicia and Bathyllus of Alexandria, are supposed to have introduced it. Performances combined dance and acting, accompanied by music, but most of the action was by a single player, the *panto-mimus* ('one who imitates all things'), supported by a chorus and musicians.

Roman comedy

Greek comedy had a major influence on Roman comedy, as many of the early comedies staged at Rome were Latin adaptations of Greek comedies. But by 100 BC there was a large body of authentic Roman comedy.

The main Roman comic writers were Plautus and Terence. Plautus was born in the second century BC at Sarsina, in Umbria. His work was very popular, and 130 plays were attributed to him in the first century BC. Twenty-one have survived. They are modelled on Greek comedies and are written in verse. Like the Greek comedies they were performed at religious festivals.

Terence (Publius Terentius Afer) was born in about 190 BC in North Africa, and came to Rome as a slave. He adopted the name of his master when he was manumitted (freed). He died on his way to Greece in 159 BC. The six extant plays of Terence were produced at Rome between 165 and 160 BC. Like those of Plautus, Terence's plots were concerned with love affairs and with misunderstandings arising from ignorance. They were also based on Greek originals and were known as the *comoedia palliata* ('comedy in Greek dress'). The *comoedia togata* ('comedy in Roman dress') is a kind of comedy about Italian life and manners which was very popular in the later second century BC.

The first theatres in Rome

In Republican Rome permanent theatres were considered a decadent luxury. They were banned by senatorial decree, until Pompey dedicated his theatre in 55 BC on the Campus Martius. Before that, all theatres built in Rome were temporary wooden structures that were demolished at the end of the festival for which they were erected. In his *Natural History*, Pliny the Elder describes the temporary theatre built by Marcus Scaurus when he was *aedile* in 58 BC. The backdrop to the stage was arranged on three storeys with 360 columns. The lower storey was of marble, the middle of glass and the top storey was of gilded planks. Some 3000 statues adorned the structure. Pliny claims that the theatre was large enough to hold 80,000 people.

We can also get an impression of these stage-sets from Pompeian wall-paintings,

▽ The Theatre of Marcellus. On the right is the Temple of Apollo Sosianus.

particularly those of the Second style. These are not exact copies of theatrical backdrops, but are clearly meant to have a similar effect. They are usually divided into three, with the central area being wider than those on either side. Scenes of gardens, grottoes, houses and other architectural features are shown, divided by columns supporting an entablature and often a pediment. These are decorated with statues, drapes and theatrical masks.

The Theatre of Pompey

Some substructures of Pompey's theatre survive in the basements of buildings, but the plan survives on the Severan marble map of Rome, the *Forma Urbis Romae*. The building was constructed of concrete, allowing Pompey's architects to support the seating on a series of curving and radial vaults. Perhaps because of traditional Roman opposition to permanent theatres, Pompey described his theatre as a monumental stairway to the Temple of Venus Victrix, which was situated at the top of the *cavea*.

The *cavea* was 160 metres (525 feet) in diameter and could seat about 27,000. Associated with the theatre was a large rectangular portico surrounding a garden.

The Theatre of Marcellus

Julius Caesar had planned to build a theatre in the Forum Holitorium, but it was not constructed until Augustus' reign. This was the Theatre of Marcellus, dedicated in 13 or 11 BC in memory of Augustus' nephew and son-in-law, who had died in 23 BC. The structure was 150 metres (490 feet) in diameter, though its seating capacity was probably only 14,000. It was supported on vaulted substructures built partly of cut stone and partly of concrete faced

▽ Second-style wall paintings from the House of Augustus on the Palatine in Rome, showing the form of a temporary stage.

◁ The Theatre of Marcellus, reconstruction and cut-away. The stage-building has not been excavated, but probably took the form shown here. A series of stairs and ramps gave access to the seating via the substructures.

▽ A detail of the facade of the Theatre of Marcellus, showing the upper Ionic architectural order framing the arcades.

▷ The reconstructed *scaenae frons* of the theatre at Sabratha, in modern Libya. This theatre was built in about AD 200 and is the largest in North Africa. The stage-building has three storeys with a total of ninety-six columns: it was typical of Roman theatre design.

with *opus reticulatum*. Concrete was used for the barrel vaults. These were connected by corridors and ramps to allow easy access to the seating. The seats were built in three tiers, the uppermost of timber.

The facade was formed by a system of arcades one on top of the other. There were originally at least two tiers of forty-one arches.

The Theatre of Marcellus: the stage

The stage building still lies buried, but to judge from the Severan *Forma Urbis Romae* it was, and remained through successive restorations, a very simple building. The stage-building rose as high as the *cavea* and was attached to it on both sides, to create an enclosed building.

These large stage-buildings are characteristic of Roman theatres. Some very fine examples survive from the Roman Empire, for example at Aspendos in southern Turkey and at Orange

in the south of France. A particularly good example at Sabratha in modern Libya has been reconstructed to its full height, with marble columns arranged on three levels.

Roman tragedy

By the Empire both comedy and tragedy had for the most part lost their popularity with the Romans. The last writer of tragedy whose plays we know were staged was P. Pomponius Secundus, in the Claudian period.

We have lost all Roman tragedies apart from those of Seneca. However, we know that the earliest Roman writer of tragedy was Ennius, who was born in 239 BC. His work has only survived in fragments, but it is quite clear that he also wrote comedies and satires.

Ten tragedies by Seneca have survived. Again Greek models were followed, but the introduction of gruesome, sensational and extreme situations and characters may owe something to the influence of violent displays in the amphitheatre. Seneca's tragedies were very popular in Elizabethan England.

Actors

Many of the actors were slaves and freedmen, often from the East. In the eyes of the law, acting was a not a respectable profession and its members were banned from holding public office. A top ranking *pantomimus*, however, could become a public idol. L. Aurelius Pylades, who was born a slave and performed as a *pantomimus*, was freed by Marcus Aurelius and Lucius Verus and retired to Puteoli, where he became a prominent local benefactor.

Costumes and masks

Costumes on the Roman stage varied according to the type of drama, but they became more realistic over time. The standard clothes were a tunic with a cloak. Originally masks were commonly worn, as actors played multiple parts, and they were particularly important in mime and pantomime. The masks were often caricatures of the characters being portrayed, instantly recognizable as lower-class figures, including slaves, cooks, soldiers and parasites. The comic masks often had great grinning mouths. In general, the more vulgar and exaggerated masks were used in later Roman comedy.

◁ Masks for a tragic hero (left) and heroine.

△ Masks for stock characters from Roman comedy – an old man (left), a youth (centre) and a slave (right).

△ A bronze statuette of a farce actor, possibly a Dossenus. He is a hunchback with very thin legs. He has a bald forehead, large ears and an enormous crooked nose. His teeth, made of silver, protrude from the corners of his mouth.

△ An ivory statuette of a tragic actor. His sleeves are painted in blue and yellow stripes. He has an exaggeratedly high *onkos* (headdress). The character is probably an elderly woman.

◁ A wall painting in the Naples Museum, showing a tragic actor.

THE COLOSSEUM

The gladiatorial games were the most dramatic manifestation of the Roman taste for public entertainment. From its dedication by Titus in AD 80 onwards, the huge arena complex built to stage the games, the Colosseum, was the centre of an Empire-wide entertainment industry.

Killing as entertainment

Gladiatorial games (*munera*) had a long history. They developed in connection with aristocratic funeral games. In the late Republic, the diffusion of gladiatorial combat and amphitheatres in Italy seems to be associated with the settlement of veterans. Tertullian wrote at the end of the second century AD that 'men believed that the souls of the dead were propitiated by human blood, and so at funerals they sacrificed prisoners of war or slaves of poor quality bought for the purpose'.

The first recorded gladiatorial show in Rome took place in 264 BC, at the funeral of Marcus Iunius Brutus Pera: three pairs of gladiators fought to the death in the Forum Boarium. Over the next two centuries the scale and frequency of gladiatorial shows steadily increased. In 65 BC Julius Caesar displayed 320 pairs of gladiators at elaborate funeral games for his father, who had died twenty years before.

At this time most gladiators were slaves and prisoners of war. They required training, and schools were established, particularly in Campania, where the most famous was at Capua. In 73 BC an uprising by the gladiators at Capua led by Spartacus turned into a nation-wide slave revolt that lasted two years.

In Rome, during the late Republic and early Principate, the religious and commemorative elements of gladiatorial shows began to be overtaken in importance by the political and purely spectacular aspects. The elite began to use the shows as a way of gaining popularity with the people. Over time, gladiatorial shows became entirely separated from their original funerary context.

These displays took a number of different forms: beast hunts (*venationes*), trained gladiator fights, and executions involving condemned criminals. In the case of animals and criminals the combat usually ended in the death of one or other of the combatants. Gladiatorial fights, however, did not always end in fatalities.

A fitting venue

Gladiatorial shows were public performances, and before specific buildings were constructed to house them they were often held in the Circus Maximus and in the social and ritual centre of the city, the Forum. Under the Forum Romanum, archaeologists have found a series

▷ The Colosseum seen from the north-west. Until the eighteenth century the structure was extensively robbed of its building stone. Pope Benedict XIV put a stop to its destruction when he declared it a shrine to the Christian martyrs in 1749.

△ The Colosseum seen from the south-east. The point at which the destruction ceased in effect created a cutaway section of the outer circuit corridors, A1, A2, B1, B2 (see plan on p. 195 for explanation of corridor numbering system). Just visible is the low mezzanine corridor above B2, which gave access to the corridor above A2.

of well-planned corridors with the remains of mechanical hoists that may have been used for the staging of spectacles. Seating would have been temporary and constructed of timber.

The first purpose-built amphitheatres in Rome were wooden, including one built by Caesar on the Campus Martius. These were also essentially temporary structures. The earliest known stone amphitheatre was built at Pompeii in the first century BC. The first one at Rome was erected by L. Statilius Taurus, one of Augustus' generals, but it proved too small to hold the enormous crowds that flocked to the imperial games. Nero built another wooden amphitheatre on the Campus Martius in AD 57, but it was left to his successor, Vespasian, to build the great amphitheatre which was to become synonymous with gladiatorial combat.

The Flavian amphitheatre

Vespasian's amphitheatre was the most famous of all in the Roman world. Over time it became known as the *amphitheatrum Flavium*, a name derived from Flavius, the family name of Vespasian and Titus. It is better known today as the Colosseum. This name is first given to the building in a popular verse quoted by the Venerable Bede in the eighth century; it is probably derived from the enormous size of the

structure itself, rather than from the proximity of a colossal statue of Nero. The Colosseum was begun by Vespasian in the 70s AD on the site of the lake of Nero's Domus Aurea, and was financed from the spoils of the sack of Jerusalem in AD 70. It was dedicated in AD 80 by Titus, after his father's death. It is the largest of all Roman amphitheatres, with outer dimensions of 188 metres by 156 metres, and is by far the most impressive ancient building surviving in Rome.

The Colosseum has survived despite several natural disasters. It was struck by lightning in AD 217 and was so badly damaged that it could not be used for several years. It was again struck about thirty years later, and was damaged by earthquakes during the fifth and sixth centuries.

Arches and vaults

Only the northern half of the building remains intact. After it was seriously damaged in the ninth century by an earthquake, it was much pillaged for building materials. In 1749, Pope Benedict XIV dedicated the Colosseum to the Passion of Jesus and pronounced it sanctified by the blood of the martyrs. This stopped the destruction, but by this time nearly half the southern side had been removed. But enough

△ A sestertius of Titus showing the building completed in every detail. Many scholars believe, however, that construction was not completed until after the death of Titus.

△ The outer circuit corridor at ground level.

survives for us to be able to make an accurate reconstruction of the building, apart from the imperial entrance on the south side.

The framework of the building consists of eighty main, load-bearing, travertine piers. The facade rests on these, rising to a height of over 45 metres. On each level the arches are framed by engaged columns, as in the Theatre of Marcellus. The bottom storey was of the Doric order, the second of the Ionic and the third of the Corinthian. The fourth storey consists of a plain wall with Corinthian pilasters. There is evidence to suggest that when Titus inaugurated the amphitheatre in AD 80 the facade was no higher than the top of the third storey, which is how it is shown in a relief of the late first century AD from the Tomb of the Haterii. However, a coin of Titus shows the complete building, including the upper storey decorated with shields. This may have been part of the projected design which was probably not completed until the reign of Domitian (AD 81–96).

A variety of materials

The foundations of the structure were of concrete about 12 metres deep. The concrete was partly laid in the clay subsoil and partly retained by a brick-faced wall. These foundations supported the framework of travertine load-bearing piers. Tufa was used for the lower radial walls between the piers. In the upper levels these walls were of concrete faced with brick. The vaults were of barrel form and made of concrete. It has been estimated that 100,000 cubic metres of travertine were required to build the facade, with 300 tons of iron to clamp the blocks together.

Many entrances

The compartments formed by the rising network of vaults and passages housed a system of radiating staircases or ramps (*vomitoria*) and four lateral or ring corridors with plastered and

▽ A relief from the Tomb of the Haterii (dating from about AD 100). The Colosseum is shown without its fourth storey, and with a triumphal arch at the main entrance.

△ The main north entrance, with the stucco decoration restored from the existing remains and from Renaissance drawings.

△ The remains of the stucco decoration in the main north entrance.

lettered A–D and the storeys are numbered 1–5 from the ground up.

There were seventy-six public entrances. The Roman numerals can still be seen above the numbered entrances XXIII to LIV (23 to 54). The ceremonial entrance for the emperor was on the south side, on the short axis between entrances I (1) and LXXVI (76). This is in the area destroyed in the Middle Ages, and only the inner portion survives, with no trace of its decoration. The magistrates' entrance, however, which is the unnumbered arch at the other end of the short axis between XXXVIII (38) and XXXIX (39), has survived almost intact. Here, remains of stucco decoration can still be seen on the upper walls and the vaulting. The balustrade above the magistrates' entrance is broken away, suggesting that there may have been a pediment here. The Haterii relief shows the imperial entrance enhanced by a triumphal arch topped with a quadriga (a four-horse chariot), but no evidence remains of this. There are two entrances at the ends of the long axis which led directly into the arena. These were for use by the performers. The entrance at the western end between entrances XIX (19) and XX (20) was directly connected by a tunnel to the gladiator school next door, the Ludus Magnus. This was one of four such schools known in Rome.

Stairs, stairs and more stairs

The outer ring corridors at the first two levels form an open arcade, allowing the spectators easy access to the stairs leading to the individual seating areas. The seating was divided into five levels, the lowest being the ringside seats reserved for senators and other important people. Above these, at increasing heights,

painted walls. The *vomitoria* and ring corridors provided separate access to each wedge of seating (*cuneus*) and to each level within that area. The entrances around the perimeter at ground level are numbered in Roman numerals above each arch. In the ground plan on page 195, these entrances are numbered with Arabic numerals, while the concentric corridors are

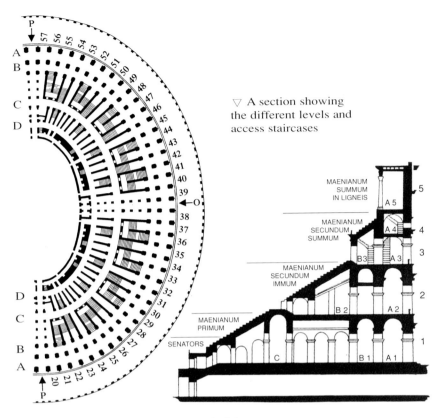

△ A ground plan of the northern half of the Colosseum, showing the entrance numbers 20–57 and the four circuit corridors A, B, C, D. The magistrates' entrance is marked O, and the east and west performers' entrances are marked P.

▽ A section showing the different levels and access staircases

MAENIANUM SUMMUM IN LIGNEIS

MAENIANUM SECUNDUM SUMMUM

MAENIANUM SECUNDUM IMMUM

MAENIANUM PRIMUM

SENATORS

△ The circuit corridor A4 showing steps leading up to the top floor (A5).

△ Another part of circuit corridor A4, showing another staircase leading to the top level (A5).

were the *maenianum primum, maenianum secundum immum, maenianum secundum summum* and *maenianum secundum in ligneis* (the wooden seats at the top of the gallery). Spectators were provided with tokens which gave details of the location of their seats.

To get an idea of the complexity of the access system we can look at just one section, that to the right of the magistrates' entrance, comprising entrances XXXIX (39) to LVII (57). The senators reached their seats via radial passage XXXIX (39) and the innermost ring corridor D. Those with seats in *maenianum primum* used the radial passages XLV (45) or XLIX (49) and ring corridor C and then took one of the four flights of stairs up to their seats. Those with seats in *maenianum secundum* or above had first to reach the second level, which was accessed indirectly by any of the stairs leading off ring corridor B, or directly by any of the stairs leading off the outer side of ring corridor C. From here, they either took a stairway to the upper seats or passed through one of the radial passages to the lower seating of their area. From here there were stairways leading up to the gallery. These were clearly an afterthought, inserted when seating was installed at

▷ The remains of
corridor A4, showing
steps set into the
brickwork of the outer
wall.

▽ The reconstructed
seating of the
*maenianum secundum
immum,* next to the east
entrance.

the upper levels. The stairway led to a low ring corridor above 2B, from which one reached ring corridor 3A by another flight of stairs. The weary climber then either passed into lateral corridor 3B, from which stairs led up to *maenianum secundum summum*, or took the stairs up to ring corridor 4A, from which a further flight of stairs led up to *maenianum secundum in ligneis* – a total of 136 or 138 steps, depending on which way one took to reach circuit corridor 2B. The routes to the upper levels are so complicated that there must have been directions at the foot of each flight of steps.

The seating

Up to the height of the third external level the seating was of marble, carried on the vaulted masonry substructures. Above this, the seating was of wood in order to reduce the downward weight and outward thrust on the outside wall. Below this level, the corridors and vaulted *vomitoria* formed a system of buttressing which supported the seating. The building could accommodate an estimated 45–55,000 spectators.

None of the seating survives. However, many fragments were found during the excavation and some of these have been reassembled to reconstruct a segment of *maenianum secundum immum* at the west end next to the gladiators' entrance. The reconstructed seats are 44 centimetres high by 61 centimetres wide. Spectators were able to get to their seats by steps, half the size of the seats which ran either up or down from the points where the internal flights of steps emerged into the *cavea*.

The *vomitoria* were always a danger point, especially during the crush of spectators trying to leave after the games, for there was a drop of as much as 3 metres into the stairwell from the seats above it. These wells were protected by stone balustrades, of which a number of decorated marble fragments have been found. The balustrade above the portal appears always to have been decorated with spirals of acanthus leaves, flowers and palmettes. Similar balustrade slabs have been found in the amphitheatre at Capua in Campania. Six fragments of these slabs have been found in the Colosseum. Only the side facing the arena is decorated. The categories of spectators allowed in that particular area appears to have been inscribed on the plain side of the balustrade facing the spectators. The balustrades flanking the entrance have various decorations. Two fragments show dogs hunting deer; others have animals such as dolphins, griffins and sphinxes in static positions decorating the end nearest the arena.

From the time of Augustus each section of the theatre seating was reserved by law for a certain sector of the population. This was part of Augustus' wider programme of social

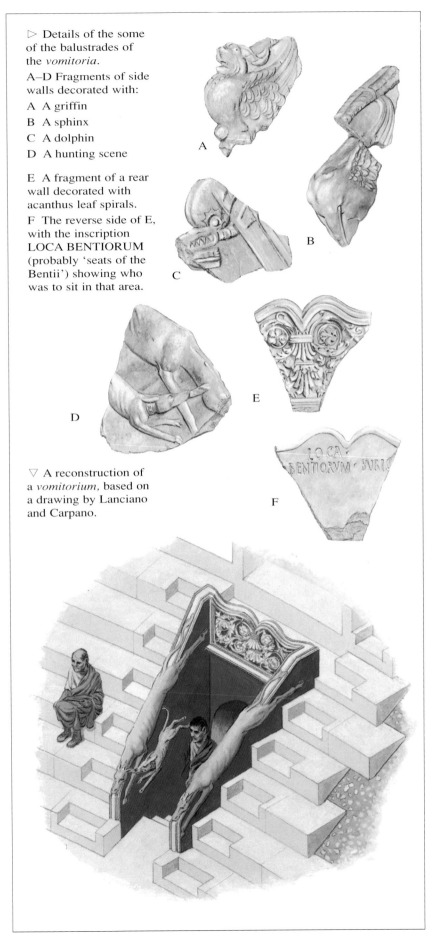

▷ Details of the some of the balustrades of the *vomitoria*.

A–D Fragments of side walls decorated with:

A A griffin
B A sphinx
C A dolphin
D A hunting scene

E A fragment of a rear wall decorated with acanthus leaf spirals.

F The reverse side of E, with the inscription LOCA BENTIORUM (probably 'seats of the Bentii') showing who was to sit in that area.

▽ A reconstruction of a *vomitorium*, based on a drawing by Lanciano and Carpano.

▷ Supports for the masts of the awning on the outer face of the Colosseum. The posts passed through square holes in the cornice above.

▽ Traces of a double flight of steps used by the sailors to reach the top of the colonnade from A5.

reform, intended to reinforce the class structure and promote social stability. The same rule presumably applied to the amphitheatre. Inscriptions indicating section assignments can still be seen on surviving tiers in the Colosseum. Women sat in the highest seats at the back of the amphitheatre (as at the theatre), though in the Republic they sat wherever they liked among the men. Senators would have the grandstand seats at the front. The only women to be reserved seats at the arena-side were the Vestal Virgins.

The topmost seats were covered by a portico, which ran all round the top of the *cavea*. This kind of arrangement is known in other amphitheatres of the Roman world, but it usually forms a covered walkway at the top of the building. In the Colosseum it covers the uppermost tier of seats.

A number of marble fragments surviving from the portico allow it to be reconstructed. The columns were monolithic, of either grey granite or *cipollino*, the green veined marble from Euboea off the eastern coast of Greece. The bases and capitals were of white marble, and the capitals were carved in the Corinthian and composite orders.

The awning

Like other comparable monuments, the Colosseum had a huge canvas awning (*velarium*) to protect the spectators from the sun. A wall painting from Pompeii shows the amphitheatre there in AD 59, at the time of the riot mentioned by the historian Tacitus between rival supporters, with an awning over part of the seating. Awnings were clearly a very attractive amenity; there are graffiti from Pompeii advertising gladiatorial games which include the phrase *vela erunt* – 'there will be awnings'.

Around the topmost part of the facade of the Colosseum are 240 projecting brackets. Masts inserted through square holes in the cornice rested on these brackets and to these was attached the rigging which supported the *velarium*. Sailors from the Misenum and Ravenna fleets were billeted in Rome in order to maintain the rigging. It has been estimated that at least 1000 men would have been required to lower and raise the awnings; they would have operated from the wooden roof above the *maenianum secundum in ligneis*.

On the inside of the north-western end of the uppermost level of the outer wall, above entrances XXVI and XXVII (26 and 27), one can see the remains of the double flight of steps leading up to the roof. A matching set of steps can just be discerned at the other end of the *cavea* above entrances L and LI (50 and 51). These are obviously later insertions as they are built across windows. One may assume that similar flights existed above entrances XII/XIII (12/13) and LXIV/LXV (64/65).

△ One of the stone posts to the north-east of the Colosseum. These probably supported barriers for crowd control.

Outside the amphitheatre is a travertine pavement 17.5 metres wide with a row of stone posts along its outer edge. These have four pairs of square holes cut into the inner face, which has led to the suggestion that they were for the attachment of winches used to raise the awning. However, they can more reasonably be explained as the attachment points for the upper and lower bars of a barrier. Similar posts exist at Capua and they clearly formed a crowd control barrier.

There is no agreement among scholars as to how the Colosseum awning operated. Most envisage 240 ropes extending from the posts on top of the outer wall to an elliptical rope in the centre which formed an *oculus* (opening) through which the sun shone on the arena. The awning itself was somehow stretched out over this. Such a system would have been practical, but would have required considerable discipline among those who operated it. This could explain why sailors from the fleet were employed. A recent estimate by a professional tent and awning manufacturer suggests that the ropes and light linen required to cover the Colosseum in this manner would weigh about 24.3 tonnes. Others have suggested that poles were used; in the amphitheatre riot painting from Pompeii this seems to be the system depicted.

Under the arena

The floor of the arena no longer survives. Beneath the level of the floor is an elaborate system of subterranean passages and chambers

▽ A detail from a painting showing a riot in the amphitheatre at Pompeii in AD 59. The awning here seems to be supported by yard-arms, rather like sails on a ship.

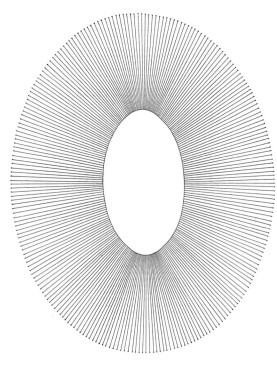

△ A reconstruction, viewed from above, of the rigging for the awning.

▽ A reconstructed cut-away section of the Colosseum showing
the various corridors and *vomitoria*. The corridors and levels are
labelled as on the ground plan on page 195. The emperor's box,
of which nothing remains, is shown in the centre at the far side
of the arena. The senators sat next to the arena. These would
have been broad steps to accommodate their official chairs
(possibly known as *sella curalis*). The trap-doors in the arena are
hypothetical, as nothing survives of them. They are based on the
arena at Capua Vetere. The area below the arena is shown as it
probably was towards the end of the first century AD.

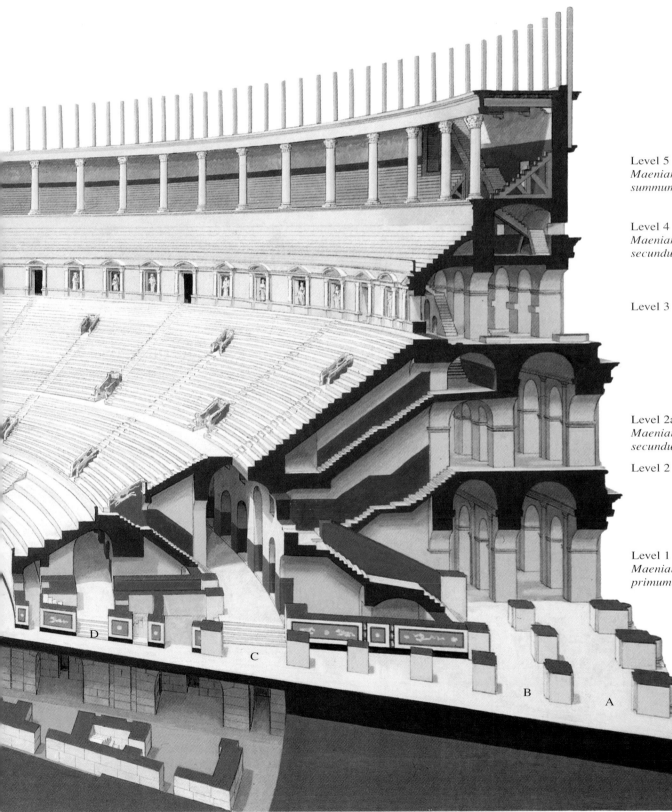

Level 5
*Maenianum
summum in ligneis*

Level 4
*Maenianum
secundum summum*

Level 3

Level 2a
*Maenianum
secundum immum*

Level 2

Level 1
*Maenianum
primum*

where animals and gladiators were kept in readiness. This elliptical area, 75 metres long and 44 metres wide, has a depth of 6 metres below the level of the arena floor. It is entered by an underground passageway from the main gladiator training school (Ludus Magnus) at the east end. There are also stairways down from the ceremonial entrance at the west end. Two more passageways lead out under the emperor's and consuls' boxes on the short axis.

The western end of this area was excavated in the nineteenth century, but the whole area was not cleared until the 1930s. In its present state the area has a main corridor about 4 metres wide (H on the plan) along its long axis flanked by two rows of lifts (G–G) for raising gladiators to the arena. Beyond these are two more corridors (F–F) and another row of lifts on each side (E–E). There are a further two elliptical corridors (C–C) and (B–B) along the perimeter of the ellipse. Beyond the outer elliptical corridor is a very narrow corridor giving access to a series of thirty-two vaulted chambers, generally believed to have been used for housing the animals.

▷ A view of the structures below the arena, seen from the east end. Clearly visible are the three circuit corridors A, B and C. Three of the original central corridors E, F and G, which flanked the central aisle H, were bricked in to form lift shafts at the end of the third century.

A B C D E F G H G F E D C B A

◁ A plan of the structures below the arena. The original walls are shown in black; subsequent modifications are shown in red.

P is the entrance to the underground passage to the Ludus Magnus

The original design

Many aspects of the original design of the Colosseum arena substructures are unclear, because the structure was subject to various modifications and reconstructions in the third and fourth centuries AD. Archaeologists have recently identified no fewer than twelve different building phases, the last being after an earthquake around the beginning of the sixth century AD. Most of these phases are marked by minor functional changes and reinforcements, but after a fire in the mid-third century much of the original structure of the arena substructures had to be encased in brick. This is substantially what one sees today.

We can attempt a reconstruction of the area as it was in the time of Domitian at the end of the first century AD. The original structure was built of blocks of light brown tufa, but much of this original stonework has been destroyed altogether. Added to this, the excavation of the west end in 1874–5 appears to have been hasty, and much of the evidence has been lost forever. However, assuming that the design was symmetrical, it is possible to reconstruct most of it. The best preserved area is in the south-east corner. A study of this portion has recently been published by the Netherlands Institute in Rome.

The original design had five parallel corridors down the centre (H, G, G, F, F), with three elliptical corridors along the perimeter (A, B, C). The walls on either side of the central corridor incorporated eight half-arches, each of which supported a course of masonry sloping down at an angle of about 30 degrees to the horizontal. These are noted by the Italian engineer G. Cozzo in his paper on Roman engineering published in 1928. He believed these walls supported flap-down wooden ramps, onto which large pieces of scenery could be loaded and winched up to the arena level. Cozzo's

△ The remains of the structures supporting the arena at the east end. The original structures were built in light brown stone (tufa). Later modifications are mainly in brick. In the background are the vaulted animal pens built of brick-faced concrete.

▷ The remains of the original curved outer wall of area D on the south side.

▽ The remains of the original inside wall of circuit corridor B in the south-east sector.

▽ The remains of the original half arches and sloping walls on the south side of the central aisle.

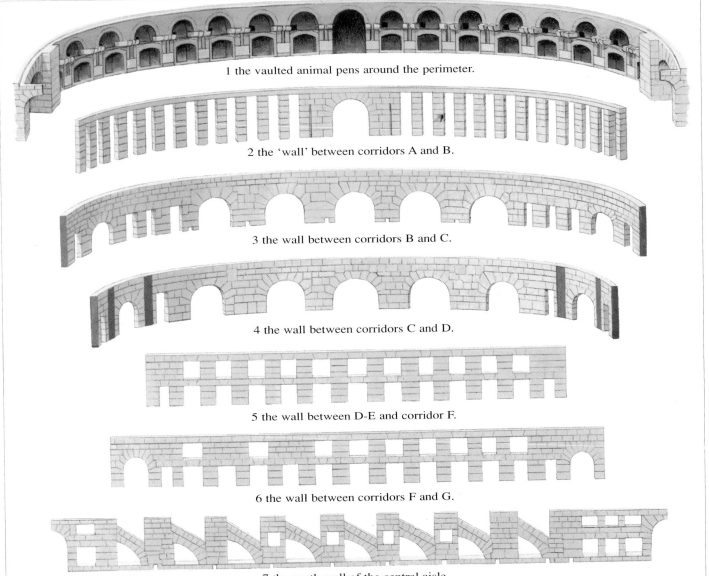

1 the vaulted animal pens around the perimeter.

2 the 'wall' between corridors A and B.

3 the wall between corridors B and C.

4 the wall between corridors C and D.

5 the wall between D-E and corridor F.

6 the wall between corridors F and G.

7 the south wall of the central aisle.

△ An exploded illustration of the south half of the first-century structures beneath the arena.

◁ A reconstruction of the arena substructures towards the end of the first century. Some walls have been cut away, to show the area behind.

study was carried out before the whole area was excavated, and although his basic concept was correct, the detail has to be revised. It can now be seen that these arches supported a series of seven or eight large flap-down ramps, all facing in the same direction.

At the east end of the central aisle on either side are two doorways with windows above, giving access to the corridors (G–G) flanking the main aisle (H). These doorways probably originally gave access to stairs leading to an upper floor, from which the flap-down ramps were operated. Unfortunately corridors G–G were bricked in to form lift shafts in about AD 300, by which time the system of sloping ramps in the central aisle had been abandoned.

The amphitheatre at Capua Vetere

The nearest parallel to the arena substructures of the Colosseum can be found in the amphitheatre at Capua Vetere in southern Italy. The substructures beneath the arena here have an almost identical system of parallel corridors down the centre. The Capuan amphitheatre underwent fewer modifications than the Colosseum, and the floor of the arena is substantially intact.

The arena floor above the central aisle is missing; it too may have had flap-down ramps, but there is no trace of them in the masonry. Above the two corridors (G–G) flanking the

△ The arena of the amphitheatre at Capua Vetere in Campania; the system of trap-doors still survives.

▷ The housing for a trapdoor in the amphitheatre at Pozzuoli in Campania.

▷ A reconstruction of the northern corridors F and G beneath the arena of the Colosseum. Lifts were probably operated in corridor G in both the early and later period. All the trapdoors in the arena floor are shown open. The central aisle with its large sloping trapdoors can be seen in the background.

main aisle in the Capuan amphitheatre there were trapdoors for thirty lifts. There are a further twenty-two trapdoors, four of double size, in corridors (E–E) and ten more, including two double size, in D–D, making a total of sixty-two in all. As the Colosseum is slightly larger, it may have had more than this. The area above corridors F–F at Capua is missing, but it may also have had large trap-doors.

The floor of the arena

The floor of the arena in the Colosseum is generally assumed to have been made of wood, but the original floor above corridors A, B, C and G may very well have been made of slabs of stone. The maximum gap across the crescent-shaped area (D), which is about 6 metres, could

▷ One of the thirty-two vaulted animal pens. Remains of two of the travertine corbels can be seen flanking the brick roof separating the upper and lower chambers.

▽ A reconstruction of an area of the animal pens. Lower right is a cut-away section of the actual remains. The left half shows Cozzo's reconstruction of the animal pens, which may not be correct. However, there is ample evidence for the windlass and lifts in corridor B.

lift

windlass

corridor B

only have been spanned with wooden beams. Near the end of the third century AD another straight wall was inserted to form corridor E, cutting the maximum span to about 4 metres.

The animal pens

When Cozzo published his reconstruction of the arena substructures, more than half the supposed animal pens around the perimeter had already been excavated. They were originally about 4.9 metres high, 3.05 metres wide and 1.75 metres deep at the bottom. Soon after they were built, a brick-faced concrete floor was inserted, forming an upper and lower chamber. This floor had a hole in it, generally about 1.5 metres long and 0.6 metres wide, through which Cozzo suggested a lift operated.

At the back of the upper chamber on the opposite side to the lift hole was another hole about 0.6 metres high and 0.75 metres wide. (This was originally 1.15 metres high, but it was cut in half by the floor separating the upper and lower chamber.) The hole led through to a

▽ A photograph of the excavated area of the Ludus Magnus.

▷ A plan of the Ludus Magnus showing its relative position to the Colosseum and the underground tunnel (only partly excavated) which connected the two.

▽ A multiple leg-shackle found in the gladiator barracks behind the theatre at Pompeii.

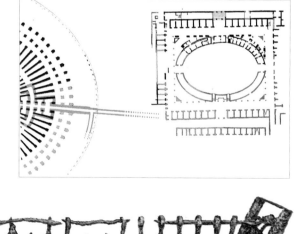

room 1.2 metres square and 2.9 metres high. Cozzo thought that this was used by the man who operated the lift, but he did not explain how.

The chambers are separated from each other by a pier 1.8 metres wide, built mainly of brick-faced concrete with a large block of travertine about 0.81 metres deep set in above the twenty-second course of bricks. The brickwork continues above this in two columns, with a recess 0.45 metres wide and 0.3 metres deep between them. The brick columns finish level with the floor of the upper chamber, and are capped by travertine corbels. Cozzo suggested that the recess between the two columns of brick housed a post, 0.45 metres by 0.3 metres in section, which projected above the level of the arena floor to support a net surrounding the arena. The problem with this suggestion is that such posts appear only to be secured laterally, with nothing to stop them from toppling forwards or backwards. Cozzo also suggested that the corbels supported a wooden walkway by which the animals reached the arena. The animals were driven into a cage in the lower half of the chamber, and hauled up through the hole into the upper chamber. They were then driven, possibly with torches, along the wooden walkway, up a wooden ramp and through a trap-door into the arena. Cozzo's sketches show both the upper and lower chambers closed off with an iron grille.

Unsolved problems

As we have seen, there are many problems with Cozzo's reconstruction. There are no traces of fitting holes for the grilles that he suggests closed the entrances to the upper and lower chambers. The hole in the floor between the upper and lower chambers is generally no more than 1.5 metres by 0.6 metres (5 by 2 Roman feet). Therefore, only such animals as boars, dogs and medium-sized cats, possibly as large as a small leopard, could possibly have fitted in the cages which were hoisted through these holes. Lions, tigers, bears and buffaloes, let alone giraffes and elephants, could not have entered the arena this way. Cozzo's wooden walkway supported by the corbels is also highly suspect. There must have been a simpler and more efficient way of introducing animals into the arena, but present evidence is insufficient for us to specify what it was.

Training schools

The earliest, and most renowned, gladiator training schools (*ludi*) were in Capua, and their rich proprietors profited by their success and popularity. It was at the Capua *ludus* that Spartacus started his revolt in 73 BC. Barracks were comfortable, and good food was provided; gladiators were valuable and had to be looked after. However, the training was very strict and

◁ A reconstruction of the Ludus Magnus, with the Colosseum in the background. Practice stakes (*pali*) are shown set up at the far end of the arena. The bottom righthand corner has been cut away to show the various rooms. Steps led up from the entrance hall to the Via Labicana.

◁ ▽ Two panels from the gladiator mosaic in the villa at Nennig in Germany, showing bear baiting (left) and killing a leopard.

▽ A scene from a fourth-century mosaic from Piazza Armerina in Sicily, showing African animals being loaded onto a ship.

sometimes brutal, and discipline was instilled. Highly-developed fighting skills and great control gave the gladiator the greatest chance of remaining alive in the arena.

The *ludi* in Rome

In the imperial period there were four gladiatorial *ludi* in Rome, the Ludus Magnus, Ludus Dacicus, Ludus Gallicus and Ludus Matutinus. All were probably established by Domitian. Each was under the directorship of a procurator appointed directly by the emperor. He was an equestrian (the class below the senatorial class) and was responsible for the technical and financial administration of the school. Each *ludus* had a full staff of armourers, trainers and doctors. Up to 2000 gladiators were accommodated in these schools in Rome.

The Ludus Magnus

The Ludus Magnus was built 60 metres to the east of the Colosseum. As is name suggests, this was the principal training school for gladiators in Rome.

The exact location of the Ludus Magnus was uncertain until 1937, although its plan was partially known from surviving fragments of the Severan marble plan of Rome, the *Forma Urbis Romae*. It was started by Domitian, but the structure was not completed until the reign of Hadrian. It was constructed throughout of brick-faced concrete.

The main entrance of the building was on the north side, where a wide staircase led down from the Via Labicana. This gave onto a large rectangular courtyard surrounded by porticoes. Behind these were rooms, fourteen on the longer sides and ten on the shorter. The building may have been three storeys high.

In the middle of the courtyard was an amphitheatre in miniature, measuring 63 by 42 metres. There were entrances on the main east-west axis and four more on the curves, two on each side. The seating area (*cavea*) was very narrow, just over 6 metres wide. This was supported on a series of vaulted substructures. It was big enough to hold eight rows of seats, sufficient for no more than 3000 spectators. The arena was surrounded by a wall 2 metres high, topped by a cornice of white marble.

An underground tunnel connected the Ludus Magnus with the Colosseum. To the south of the Ludus Magnus, and of a similar size, was the Ludus Matutinus. This was where the *venatores* were trained. These were the men who fought wild beasts, and so this *ludus* was sometimes called the Ludus Bestiarius. The name Matutinus ('of the morning') reflects the fact that these displays usually took place in the morning, during the gladiatorial shows.

The Ludus Gallicus was probably next door to the Ludus Matutinus and named after the traditional Celtic enemies of Rome, the Gauls.

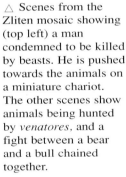

The Ludus Dacicus can be located from the *Forma Urbis* fragments, in the area between the Ludus Magnus and the Baths of Trajan. It was about the same size as the Ludus Magnus, and named after the Dacians, the Danubian people fought by Domitian and Trajan and deployed in large numbers to fight in victory celebrations.

Further east and north of the Via Labicana was the Castra Misenatium, the base for the marines responsible for the *velaria* of the Colosseum. South of this was the Armamentarium, the weapons store for gladiators.

Animals for slaughter

Hunting was much enjoyed by upper-class Romans, and hunting displays (*venationes*) were very popular forms of entertainment. Over time the animals on display became more and more exotic. Full-scale elephant fights were staged in the Circus Maximus in 99 BC. Scaurus, who built the first amphitheatre in Rome, brought hippopotamuses, crocodiles and 150 leopards for beast displays. In 51 BC Marcus Caelius wrote to Cicero, then governor of Cilicia, begging the orator to send panthers for his forthcoming show in Rome. Julius

Caesar imported 600 lions and 400 other large cats, 20 elephants and even a rhinoceros for his *venatio*. The slaughter continued under the empire, as successive emperors searched for ever more exotic animals, and the *venatores* (hunters of the arena) dispatched them in ever more extravagant ways. At the end of the second century AD ostrich hunting was in

△ Scenes from the Zliten mosaic showing (top left) a man condemned to be killed by beasts. He is pushed towards the animals on a miniature chariot. The other scenes show animals being hunted by *venatores,* and a fight between a bear and a bull chained together.

◁ A panel from the mosaic in the villa at Nennig, showing a mock fight.

vogue; the emperor Commodus, who himself fought in the arena, is said to have decapitated a hundred ostriches in one session at the amphitheatre, using arrows with crescent-shaped heads.

The hunters

The hunters (*venatores*) of animals in the arena were recruited and trained in a similar way to the gladiators, though they were always considered inferior to them. *Venatores* are shown on many mosaics and bas-reliefs. They usually wore short, light tunics, sometimes with decorated leggings. Some appear to have fought naked. Normally they wore no armour, but sometimes plates of hide were worn to protect the torso and left arm.

The gladiators

The first gladiators were prisoners of war who had been condemned to death, and slaves. By the imperial period, however, their ranks included free men who voluntarily engaged themselves for a set period, professional fighters, prisoners of war and condemned criminals. There were also some who were slaves bought by trainers (*lanistae*) from dissatisfied owners who looked upon this as a form of punishment. This practice was finally banned by Hadrian. The ban was extended by Marcus Aurelius to include the animal fighters.

On enrolment, a gladiator had to swear an oath of obedience. Petronius records in his *Satyricon* the oath of the gladiators, which committed them body and soul into the hands of the *lanista*: 'We solemnly swear to obey [the *lanista*] in everything. To endure burning, imprisonment, flogging and even death by the sword'. It took years to train a good gladiator; thus very few contests between trained gladiators were to the death. It was possible for a gladiator to gain great popularity and wealth and to retire very comfortably on the proceeds.

Gladiators, along with actors and charioteers, were considered very low in social status. Members of the upper classes were not allowed to appear as gladiators. As early as 38 BC senators and equestrians were forbidden to fight. However, some emperors permitted it, or encouraged and even commanded it. In AD 57 Nero compelled 400 senators and 600 men from the equestrian order to fight each other in the arena. The emperor Commodus fought as a gladiator in the arena. There were also female gladiators. They were less common than male contestants, and in AD 200 women were forbidden to fight in single combat.

Types of gladiator

Twenty or so different types of gladiators are known from literary and epigraphic sources, but few can be described in detail. In some cases the name, such as *provocator*, conjures

▷ A wall painting from a tomb at Pompeii depicting a contest between heavily armed gladiators.

Gladiator armour from Pompeii and Herculaneum.

A Thracian's helmet

B A highly decorated *hoplomachus*, or Samnite helmet

C Thigh-length greaves of the type worn by Thracians and *hoplomachi*

D A short shin greave from gladiator armour found at Pompeii.

△ ◁ Gladiatorial scenes from the Zliten mosaic. The upper scene shows, on the far left, a *retiarius* wearing a shoulder shield (*galerus*) and arm guard (*manica*). He has been disarmed and wounded by a *secutor* and is holding up a finger in a plea for mercy. The next scene shows a fight between two heavily armed gladiators of uncertain type. Next to them is a Thracian with a small shield, who is standing by while his opponent, another heavily armed gladiator, holds up his finger and appeals to the *lanista*.

The lower scene shows a *lanista* restraining a gladiator of uncertain type who is about to render the *coup de grace*.

up a particular image. Others such as the *essedarii*, light chariot fighters from Britain, can be reconstructed with some authority.

The earliest mentioned types of gladiators are the Samnite and the Gaul. The Samnites and the Gauls were Rome's traditional enemies of the mid-Republican period.

The Samnite

The Samnite was probably originally a light-armed gladiator fighting in the Samnite way, but over time he became more heavily armed, and by the end of the Republic he was the standard heavily-armed gladiator. At the beginning of the imperial period he became known by a different name, *hoplomachus* (Greek for 'heavily armed'). He wore a large crested helmet with a visor, and a thigh-length greave on the left leg, and he carried a large rectangular shield of the type used by legionaries. His weapon was the straight stabbing sword of the legionaries (*gladius hispaniensis*).

The Gaul

The Gaul, like the Samnite, was probably originally light-armed, using the traditional Gallic

◁ A bronze statuette of a heavy armed gladiator wearing thigh-length greaves and a *manica* on his right arm.

▷ A *secutor*'s helmet found at Pompeii. This type of helmet has only two small eye holes in its reinforced face piece, which has a flange along its bottom edge to protect the throat. It opened upwards like the visor on a medieval knight's helmet.

▷ A bronze statuette of a *secutor* found at Arles in southern France. He has a laminated arm guard, a large shield and a helmet with the visor raised.

△ A bronze statuette of a *secutor*. His large shield (*scutum*) has broken away.

equipment of a long flat shield with a spindle boss and a cut-and-thrust sword with a straight blade about 60 centimetres long. By the late republic he was armed with a slashing sword and had acquired a helmet.

The Gaul, like the Samnite, appears to have undergone a change of name at the beginning of the empire, when the term *murmillo* appears. In this case the change of name is well-documented. The *murmillo* gets his name from the Greek fish (*murmuros*) which decorated his helmet. The *murmillo*'s helmet had no visor. His shield (*scutum murmillicon*) was long and hexagonal in shape.

The Thracian

The Thracian first appeared in the arena in the second century BC, when Thrace (roughly equivalent to modern Bulgaria) first came into contact with Rome. The Thracian was armed with a broad-brimmed helmet, a small round, or sometimes square, shield and two thigh-length greaves. His sword was the native Danubian curved weapon (*sica*).

The *retiarius*

The *retiarius* or net man (from *rete*, the Latin for net) is probably the most famous of the gladiators. Strictly speaking, as he does not use a sword (*gladius*) he should not be described as a gladiator at all. The *retiarius* wore defensive armour only on his left arm. This armour covered the arm and shoulder and often the left side of the torso as well. Sometimes a large

metal shoulder shield (*galerus*) was added, to protect the neck and lower face. The weapons of the *retiarius* were those of a fisherman: a net and a trident. He also carried a dagger.

The *secutor*

The *secutor* is the most easily identified of the gladiator swordsmen. He was armed with the rectangular legionary shield (*scutum*) and sword (*gladius*) and usually wore a laminated arm-guard (*manica*). His egg-shaped helmet with a metal crest and no brim was unique. This helmet appears to have been specially designed so that it would not be caught in the net of the *secutor*'s main opponent, the *retiarius*.

Armour from Pompeii

More than twenty gladiator helmets and numerous other pieces of gladiator equipment have been discovered at Pompeii and Herculaneum, two of the towns buried by the eruption of Mount Vesuvius in AD 79. This armour is exactly the type worn by the gladiators when the Colosseum was opened in AD 80.

Examples of the Thracian and Samnite type of helmet with a visor and broad brim were found, as well as several of the egg-shaped *secutor* helmets. The *secutor* helmets covered the head completely, leaving only a round hole for each eye.

Examples of the long greaves used by Thracian and Samnite gladiators were also discovered, and a type of short shin greave used by *secutores*. No complete arm-guard (*manica*) was found, but there was more than one shoulder shield (*galerus*). *Manicae* have been found on other Roman sites, in particular at the fort at Newstead in southern Scotland. These were made of thin bronze strips about 3 centimetres wide riveted onto leather straps. The plates overlap upwards to prevent a sword thrust upward between the plates.

The new recruit

There was a constant demand for recruits for the gladiator schools, many of which were state-owned, not only in Rome but elsewhere in the empire. As with the main schools in Rome, the emperor appointed special equestrian procurators specifically to recruit and train gladiators in the provinces.

A novice gladiator was called a *tiro* (plural *tirones*). Training was closely related to military training methods. At the end of the second century BC the consul Publius Rutilius had employed *lanistae* to train his legionaries, using the same methods used for gladiators. This was so successful that it was generally adopted. Gladiators were schooled in sword-play using over-weight wooden swords and wicker shields, and struck at a *palus* or upright stake set in the ground. Only when his technique had been perfected and his worst errors had been eliminated would he begin using proper weapons against an adversary. This advanced training was called *armatura*. Fully-trained gladiators, at least by the time of the opening of the Colosseum, were known as *primi pali* ('first stakes') after the training stakes. Ranks of *secundi pali* and *tertii pali* ('second' and 'third stakes') are also recorded.

Gladiators were known by fighting names, perhaps given to them by the *lanista*. These were often names of mythological heroes such as Perseus and Ajax, or names that described their appearance or performance such as Ursius (bear-like) or Callidromus (speedy).

Away from Rome many gladiators lived an itinerant life as members of a troop travelling from bout to bout. Rapidus, a *retiarius* from the gladiator training school at Aquileia, toured northern Italy and the area of modern Slovenia and Croatia. He fought at Bellunum and Comum, finally dying from wounds received in the amphitheatre at Salonae in modern Croatia.

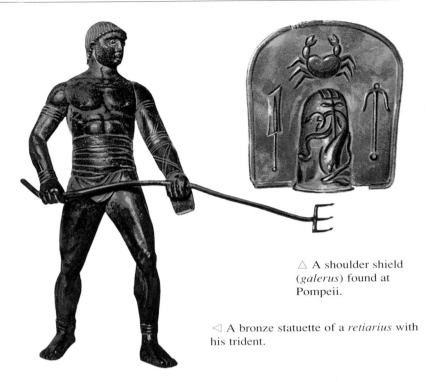

△ A shoulder shield (*galerus*) found at Pompeii.

◁ A bronze statuette of a *retiarius* with his trident.

The opening of the Colosseum

By the summer of AD 80 the building of the Colosseum was far enough advanced for the official opening to be held. At the same time the Roman poet Martial published his *Liber de Spectaculis* (Book on Shows) which described the shows put on by the Emperor Titus in the Colosseum. Suetonius gives little information in his *Life of Titus*, and although Cassius Dio devotes much more attention to it, he was writing 150 years after the event and much of his account is garbled.

▽ A funerary relief from Pompeii showing the *pompa* (procession) with which the gladiatorial games began.

▷ A gladiatorial horn (*cornu*) found at Pompeii.

The festival lasted for one hundred days. The venue included the open area beyond the Tiber where Augustus had built an artificial lake, 'the old naumachia', to stage sea battles and aquatic displays. The festival had several types of entertainment, and Martial seems to imply that aquatic displays also took place in the arena of the Colosseum. The archaeological evidence suggests this may be true: the outer wall of the basement beneath the arena, where the animal pens are, is demonstrably earlier than the internal tufa walls, which show a clear change of plan. Without the internal walls this area could have easily been flooded.

There were also a number of beast and hunting displays. Suetonius says that five thousand animals of every kind were killed in a single day. Dio mentions battles between cranes and between four elephants, and he adds that some of the animals were killed by women. Martial

mentions tigers, lions, bears and a rhinoceros. The aquatic events included a horse race in water. The political use of such displays in the arena is well illustrated by the parade of informers exposed by Titus to the ridicule and hostility of the spectators in order to reinforce the opposition of his régime to the use of such spies.

The entrance of the gladiators

A show began with a parade of the gladiators led by trumpeters (*tubicines*). They would have marched two abreast, carrying their helmets and shields and entering by the west entrance. A musical accompaniment was provided by an orchestra. A mosaic from Zliten in Libya shows such an orchestra.

Beast displays and *venationes* were staged in the morning. These were followed by bouts of single combat between gladiators, each bout

△ A scene from the Zliten mosaic, showing the orchestra, a woman playing the water organ, two horn blowers and a trumpeter, in the arena.

refereed by a *lanista* with a long rod. It was up to the organiser of the games to choose the form these contests took. It was common practice to have contests between differently equipped gladiators, for example a *secutor* against a *retiarius*. Each fight continued until one of the contestants was seriously wounded. The trumpets sounded and the *lanista* restrained the victor. The wounded man appealed for *missio* (a reprieve) by a traditional gesture. The sponsor of the games (*munerarius*) appealed to the crowd to decide whether *missio* should be granted or not. If the defeated gladiator had fought well the crowd would probably reprieve him to fight another day.

Drag out the dead

After a kill, an official (apparently dressed as Charon, the Etruscan demon of the underworld) prodded the vanquished gladiator with a brand to make sure he was dead. The corpse was then dragged out with hooks through the entrance, known as the 'Gate of Execution' (Porta Libitina).

Graffiti (for example from Pompeii) show that results were recorded in a sort of track record for each gladiator: 'Pugnax, a Thracian of the Neronian *ludus*, with three fights to his credit, victorious; Murrans, a *myrmillo* of the Neronian *ludus*, with three fights, killed; Cycnus, a *hoplomachus* of the Julian *ludus*, with eight fights, victorious; Atticus, a Thracian with fourteen fights, reprieved.'

Damnatio ad bestias

Executions took place in the arena at lunch time, between the animal hunts in the morning and the gladiatorial displays in the afternoon. The Zliten mosaic shows prisoners bound to poles on wheeled contraptions. They are being pushed forward towards wild animals to be mauled to death. This form of execution, *damnatio ad bestias*, is famous as a form of punishment for the early Christian martyrs.

◁ A reconstruction of a gladiatorial contest in the arena at Pompeii. In the foreground a *secutor* has managed to wound a *retiarius* and deprive him of his net. The *lanista*, in a long tunic, gets ready to intervene while the official dressed as Charun, sensing the end is near, hovers in the background.

A NEW PALACE

The greatest imperial residence in Rome was built on the Palatine hill by the emperor Domitian, at the end of the first century AD. It was a whole complex of public and private buildings, architecturally innovative and sumptuously decorated.

Aristocratic houses were built on the Palatine hill from the early Republic onwards, including that of Cicero. Buildings from the Republican period were concentrated on the north and west sides of the hill. Augustus chose to live here too, taking over the house of Cicero's rival Hortensius.

The first purpose-built imperial residence was constructed by Tiberius on the western side of the hill; a number of the earlier houses were knocked down to make way for it. The new building was known as the Domus Tiberiana, and was built around a huge peristyle, or courtyard surrounded by columns. Very little of this palace is visible today, as the site is now covered by the Farnese Gardens. Caligula is thought to have added to the palace, on the side of the hill overlooking the Forum.

Nero planned to connect the Palatine to the Esquiline hill with his great palace complexes, the Domus Transitoria (destroyed in the great fire of AD 64) and the Domus Aurea (built to replace it). A monumental fountain from the Domus Transitoria is preserved in the foundations of the Flavian palace on the Palatine. Although Vespasian never lived on the Palatine, his son Titus took up residence there, in the Domus Tiberiana.

The largest and most impressive imperial residence in Rome, however, was built at the end of the first century AD by the emperor Domitian, and covered the whole central portion of the Palatine. This palace became the permanent residence of the emperors for the rest of Roman history. It was never replaced, although Septimius Severus made a number of additions in the early third century.

Domitian's Palace

Domitian's great palace complex was much admired by the ancient authors, though no precise description of it survives. The poet Statius praised its size and decoration, comparing it to the Temple of Jupiter on the Capitoline hill for majesty and dignity. The poet Martial also thought highly of it, referring to the range of imported decorative stones used and to the great height of the buildings. He also praises the architect, Rabirius.

The palace consisted of the state apartments or official area, the Domus Flavia, and the imperial residence, the Domus Augustana. There were also areas for recreation, the stadium

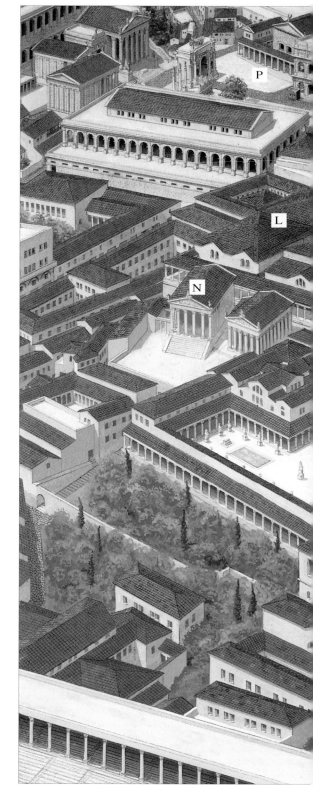

▷ A reconstructed view of Domitian's Palace on the Palatine Hill at the beginning of the third century AD.

A Domus Flavia
B Domus Augustana
C Aula Regia
D Triclinium
E Libraries
F Pedagogium
G Hippodromos
H Baths of Septimius Severus
I Severan addition to the palace
J Extension of the Aqua Claudia
K Temple of Venus and Rome
L Domus Tiberiana
M Temple of Apollo Palatinus
N Temple of Cybele
P Forum Romanum

◁ A view from the
Forum Romanum of
the monumental
vestibule to the
Palatine palace.

or Hippodromos and the baths. An extension of the Aqua Claudia from the Caelian hill provided a private water supply.

The approaches

There were two main approaches to the palace. One was from the Forum Romanum, through a huge monumental vaulted vestibule. This was built of brick-faced concrete, and housed a multi-storeyed ramp to the newly constructed facade of the Domus Tiberiana. The second approach was on the north-eastern side, from the Via Sacra, passing the arches of Titus and Domitian and leading to a large paved area (the Area Palatina) in front of the Domus Flavia

The south-west terraces

The south-west part of the palace overlooked the long valley between the Palatine and Aventine hills, where the Circus Maximus was built. The facade towered up from the terracing on the hill slopes. This was where the servants' quarters were located, and also the Pedagogium — the training school for imperial slaves. A curving facade of columns in the centre gave a glorious view over the Circus Maximus.

△ The Area Palatina in front of the Domus Flavius. This was the second approach to the Palatine complex. The visible structures are the Aulia Regia and the Basilica, the two public reception rooms of the palace.

The Domus Flavia

The official wing of the palace was built on a large platform on the top of the hill. The platform was formed by levelling or filling in earlier buildings (thus preserving them for archaeologists). The various rooms were placed around a huge peristyle. On the north side were three official rooms: a *lararium* (chapel to the domestic gods or Lares), a throne room (the Aula Regia) and an apsed basilica. The whole complex was decorated with mosaic and imported stones. In front of these three rooms was the large paved space of the Area Palatina.

The Aula Regia

The central hall was the Aula Regia, or throne room. This was the largest room of the three, with a diameter of 30 metres. There is much debate about its roofing: modern scholars are divided on whether it was covered by a great concrete vault or by a wooden roof decorated with coffers. The reconstruction here shows a wooden roof.

At one end was an apse, where the emperor received embassies and gave audiences. The splendour of the room was designed emphasise the majesty of the emperor and to impress all

▷ One of the fountains flanking the *triclinium* on the south side of the peristyle of the Domus Flavia.

The Development of the Palatine Hill

▽ **A** The Palatine showing the known late republican buildings (orange). The House of Augustus included libraries and a temple to Apollo. The so-called House of Livia is probably part of the Augustan complex. The position of Tiberius' palace is outlined in black.

◁ **B** The Palatine in the middle of the 1st century AD, showing Nero's extension of the Palace of Tiberius (purple).

B1 Cross-section of the Palace of Tiberius

▷ **C** The Palatine early in the 2nd century. Domitian's palace was built over the Neronian structures. The Palace of Tiberius was remodelled, extending it to the Clivus Victoriae. An entrance hall (C1) was built at the Forum level with a ramp up to the palace. The western corner of the hill (outlined in green) appears to have been terraced at this time.

C1 Entrance hall and
   ramp
C2 Enlarged plan of the
   entrance hall and
   ramp
C3 Cross-section of
   ramp
C4 Lateral section of
   ramp
C5 Ground plan of ramp
C6 Plan of ramp at level
   of Nova Via
C7 Plan of ramp at
   palace level
C8 Section of
   Domitian's palace
C9 Section of
   remodelled Palace
   of Tiberius

▽ **D1** A section of the Palace of Tiberius, which by the 3rd century extended across the Clivus Victoriae to the Nova Via.

△ **D** The Palatine Hill at the beginning of 3rd century. The additions of Septimius Severus are marked in blue.

Key

Late republican buildings

Nero's palace extension

Buildings of Domitian and Hadrian

Third century additions

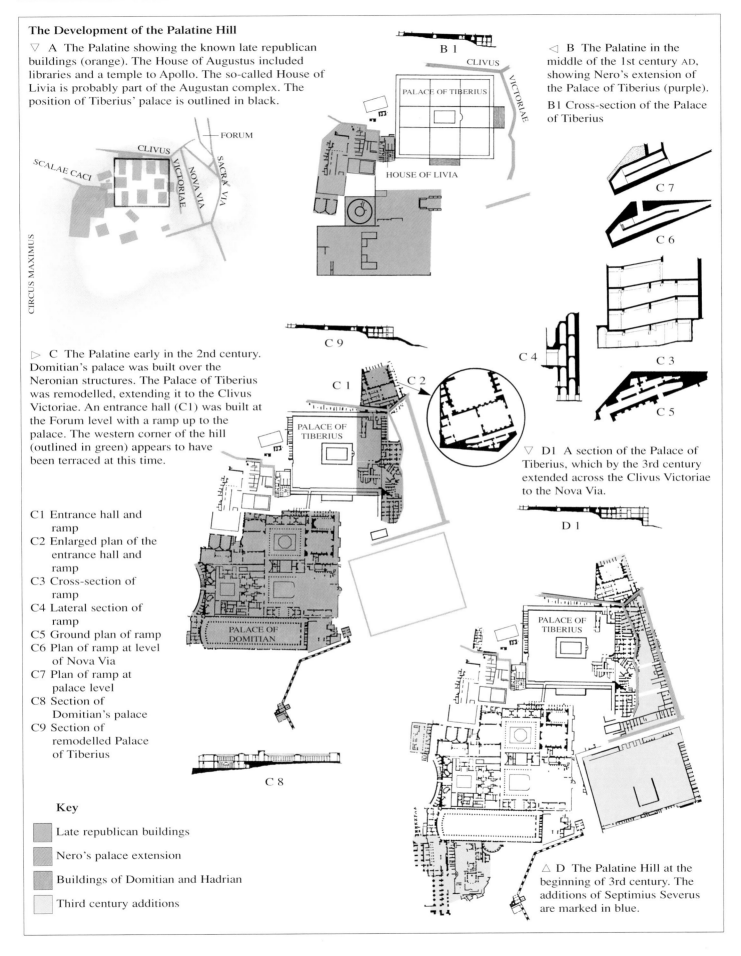

▷ A reconstructed cross-section through the Aula Regia, peristyle and *triclinium* of the Domus Flavia. There is much debate amongst scholars about the form of the roof of the Aula Regia. Here it is reconstructed with a wooden roof.

▷ Fragment of the architectural decoration from the *triclinium*.

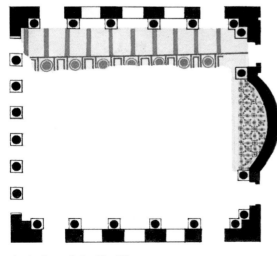

△ A plan of the Basilica
in the Domus Flavia.

who entered. The walls were covered with coloured and patterned marble. There were twelve niches containing colossal statues in black basalt. In the early eighteenth century two statues of Hercules, a statue of Bacchus and a head of Jupiter were removed by the Duke of Parma, who owned the area of the Palatine. Sixteen columns of *pavonazzetto* marble from Asia Minor stood in front of the walls and carried projecting entablatures.

The basilica

The basilica has attracted a great deal of attention from scholars. The building's design had much in common with traditional public basilicas, such as those associated with the Forum Romanum. It was divided lengthways by two rows of columns of Numidian yellow marble. There was an apse at one end, which modern reconstructions show closed off by a marble screen, though there is very little evidence for this. The building may have been used as an auditorium, or a waiting room for those hoping for an imperial audience. A flight of steps led down to the Cryptoporticus, beneath the Flavian Palace. The Cryptoporticus connected with an underground passage that had once been part of the Domus Tiberiana.

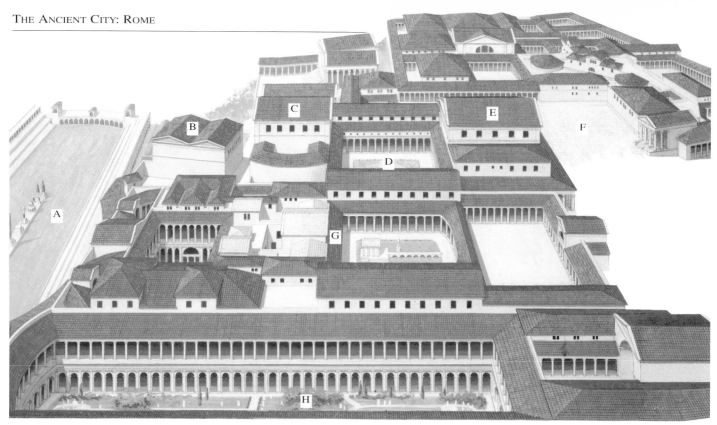

△ A reconstruction of the Palatine palace from the south-east.

A Circus Maximus
B Libraries
C Triclinium
D Domus Flavia
E Aula Regia
F Area Palatina
G Domus Augustana
H Hippodromus

The peristyle

A large peristyle separated this range of rooms on the northern side of the palace from the *triclinium* (banqueting hall). The columns surrounding the peristyle were of pink *portasanta*, and the walls were veneered in marble. Suetonius states that Cappadocian marble was used, polished to a mirror finish so that Domitian could see whatever was going on behind his back. In the centre of the court was an octagonal feature with a labyrinth of low walls and channels, probably for some kind of water display.

The triclinium

▽ The Domus Augustana: a view of the Hippodromus.

On the south side of the peristyle, opposite the Aula Regia, was the state triclinium or ban-

queting hall, probably called the Cenatio Iovis. An apse at one end was raised to accommodate the emperor's table. The hall was paved with coloured marble *opus sectile* of purple and green porphyry from Egypt and Greece, *portasanta* from Chios and *giallo antico* from Numidia. Around the edge of the room, divisions for the positioning of couches were marked out in the floor design. These measured 4 metres by about 2.5 metres, and would have accommodated three couches in the traditional way. Windows looked out on either side onto courts, with a tiered, oval fountain allowing cool, fresh air to circulate in the heat of summer. Behind the triclinium were two apsed chambers approached by a colonnade; they were probably libraries.

The Domus Augustana

The Domus Augustana was the private residence of the emperor, and was similar to a villa in plan and design. It covered about twice the area of the Domus Flavia, but on two levels. The private palace incorporated three peristyles instead of one. The upper level is today poorly preserved, though it is still possible to make out its plan. The lower level survives nearly complete.

Access to this part of the palace was from the Area Palatina, through a monumental entrance. This led to a large rectangular peristyle, and then another peristyle with a sunken pool at the centre. On the south-west side of this court was a maze of rooms whose isolation from the rest of the complex suggests that they formed the emperor's private living area. These

were all vaulted, using many different styles including octagonal vaulting. A staircase led from these rooms down to the lower part of the palace. By the staircase was a handsome, marble-lined *nymphaeum*, and beneath the staircase was a latrine.

The walls of the peristyle have traces of Fourth-style paintings. In the centre was a low platform, with a pool and semicircular niches and channels. A passage led from the peristyle to the Hippodromos.

The Hippodromos

The facade of the Hippodromos facing the Circus Maximus incorporated a nymphaeum, with a logia above it from which the games could be observed. The Hippodromos itself extended to the north-east. Measuring 50 by 184 metres, it was like a miniature stadium or hippodrome in plan, but was actually a walled and secluded garden for the personal use of the emperor, his family and their guests. An arcaded and vaulted portico ran along the two long sides and around the curved end. At either end were two elaborate semi-circular fountains.

Decoration

The Domus Flavia and the Domus Augustana were both richly decorated throughout, with columns, paving and wall veneers of imported marble. The surviving *opus sectile* floors, such as that in the triclinium, are particularly impressive. They are made up of differently shaped and coloured pieces of marble, formed into geometric patterns or pictures. Mosaics and wall-paintings added to the sumptuous overall effect.

△ The Domus Augustana: a view of the sunken peristyle. The concrete vaults of the rooms on the lower level have been preserved.

◁ Architectural fragments from the sunken peristyle of the Domus Augustana.

▽ A reconstructed cross-section through the living quarters around the sunken peristyle of the Domus Augustana.

THE AGE OF APOLLODORUS

A number of major innovations took place in both architecture and building methods in Rome in the first century AD, leading to a recognisably new architectural style. Building in the new style reached a peak early in the second century, during the reign of Trajan. Trajan's architect Apollodorus of Damascus is a key figure, personally credited with the design of the Baths of Trajan and the Forum of Trajan.

△ A relief from the funerary monument of the Haterii, dated to about AD 100. This shows the construction of a temple with the use of a large crane powered by the men turning the great 'squirrel cage' at the bottom of the photo, to lift blocks to the upper levels of the building.

△ The construction of a brick barrel vault on wooden centring or formwork. Brick arches were constructed at intervals along the vault, the individual arches being tied together by larger, 60-centimetre bricks. The spaces between the brick arches were filled with concrete.

The new architecture

The new architectural style was based on the use of concrete faced with brick. Roman concrete was made from an aggregate of stone and/or brick and tile set in a mortar made with water, lime and a special volcanic sand called *pozzolana*. Faced with fired brick, this became the normal material for both public and private construction. The potential of this new material for the construction of vaults was recognised early. From the time of Nero it led to a much greater emphasis on the interior of buildings than had been the case before. The octagonal room of the Domus Aurea is a key milestone in this evolution.

Domes and semi-domes

A feature of the new architecture was the development of new shapes for rooms, both in plan and in elevation. This presented new problems in the roofing of large spaces, but the use of concrete, a flexible and easy-to-handle building material, made a much greater variety of wall and vault shapes possible. Concrete construction and complex vaulting remained features of monumental architecture in Rome into the fourth century AD.

Any vault, whatever it was made from, required a timber framework. This framework, usually known as 'centring', supported the vault during construction and was removed once the mortar or concrete had set enough to allow the vault to remain in place by itself. The centring was the responsibility of master carpenters, who ensured that it conformed exactly to the desired shape of the vault. Depending on the shape required, this centring might be very complicated and require huge amounts of timber.

The highly developed use of the use of domes and semi-domes was particularly characteristic of the new architecture. A dome is a vault of segmental or semi-circular section, usually erected on a circular base, though it can also have a polygonal base, as in the case of the octagonal dome in the Domus Aurea, or even a square base. In the last case, some kind of extra architectural feature had to be added to avoid the difficult transition between square base and circular dome. Instead, it was usual for the Romans to construct a cross vault over a square space. This is how many of the square rooms

◁ A cross or groin vault built in concrete. This was the most common way for builders in Rome to cover a square space.

△ A drawing of one of the octagonal concrete vaults on the lower level of the Domus Augustana. It is made up of eight panels and has an opening, or *oculus*, at the top.

around the sunken peristyle of the Domus Augustana were roofed.

Roman architects built up the haunches of the dome to a great thickness in order to resist the outward thrust of the dome's weight. Without such reinforcement, the weight of the dome would push the supporting walls outwards, causing the whole structure to collapse.

The Pantheon

The Pantheon is one of the great masterpieces of Roman architecture, and is exceptionally well preserved. In AD 608, the Byzantine emperor Phocas gave the building to Pope Boniface IV to turn it into the church of Santa Maria ad Martyres, thus ensuring its survival.

The Pantheon was built by Hadrian between AD 118 and 125, in the Campus Martius. It replaced two earlier buildings on the site. The first of these had been built by Agrippa in 27 BC, and the second was a reconstruction of the original by Domitian after the fire of AD 80. Hadrian's Pantheon records the original builder, Agrippa, in an inscription over its portico, but the plan of the original building was probably completely different.

A temple dedicated to all the gods, the Pantheon was made up of three elements: a porch with columns, a tall intermediary block, and a rotunda that forms the *cella* of the temple.

The porch has sixteen Egyptian grey and red granite columns, each 40 Roman feet in height and weighing about 84 tons. The portico was topped by a pediment. The column bases and capitals, the entablature and details of the pediment were all of white marble from Carrara in northern Italy and from quarries in Greece.

The intermediary block and the rotunda were built of brick-faced concrete. The rotunda was roofed by a concrete dome. The diameter and height of the rotunda are exactly the same, 43.2 metres (140 feet). The span of the dome was not surpassed until modern times; even that of St Peter's is less.

The walls of the rotunda rest on a circular concrete foundation made with aggregate of travertine, 7.30 metres wide and 4.50 metres deep. The walls are 6.15 metres high.

△ An alternative method of covering a square space is to construct curving triangular features to convert the square into a circle and place a dome on this circular base. This was very rare in concrete architecture, but was used elsewhere in the Roman empire in other building materials.

▷ A reconstructed cross-section through the ten-sided Temple of Minerva Medica in Rome. The lower walls incorporated nine projecting apses, above which were ten round-headed windows. The circular dome was formed by merging the angles of the decagon inwards.

▽ A view of the Pantheon today. This building, constructed by the emperor Hadrian, originally stood at the top of a lofty flight of steps dominating a porticoed courtyard.

△ An interior view of the Pantheon. Much of the internal decoration is from a later period.

The dome was built of concrete, with a window opening or *oculus* (eye) at the top, 8.30 metres in diameter. This is open to the sky. The inner surface of the dome is decorated with 140 coffers of diminishing size, arranged in five rows of 28.

The aggregate in the concrete for the Pantheon was carefully graded so that heavier materials were used lower down in the building and lighter materials further up. For the foundations and the walls up to the first cornice, travertine and tufa were used. From the first up to the middle cornice, brick and tufa were used. From the middle to the topmost outer cornice the aggregate is entirely of brick. As the dome rises, so the aggregate becomes progressively lighter, with volcanic pumice being used around the *oculus*.

Some of the marble wall revetment has disappeared from inside the building, but some of the original veneer is still in place. Slabs of purple porphyry and dark green marble are set against yellow Numidian marble. There is also painted stucco decoration, and many of the surfaces are gilded. The floor is also paved with marble *opus sectile*.

▽ Detail of one of the exedrae and the reconstructed Roman marble wall veneer.

In plan the rotunda is designed around eight load-bearing piers which form the framework of the building. Between the piers are eight recesses, or exedrae, which are alternately curved and rectangular. Two columns of yellow marble from Numidia in North Africa screen each recess.

The piers support eight arches which run through the core of the wall, from the inner to outer surface. These are part of a complicated system of relieving arches, both large and small. Their purpose is to buttress the upper walls against the outward thrust of the dome. This complex system of arches extends into the lower part of the dome, helping to stabilise the structure as well as allowing lighter construction, with material-saving spaces.

△ The Pantheon: detail
of the roof of the portico.

◁ The Pantheon: detail
of the marble decoration
of the exterior of the
intermediary block.

▷ A reconstruction of the Pantheon with cutaway of
the dome. This clearly shows the voids in the
thickness of the walls and the stepping on the outside
of the lower part of the dome.

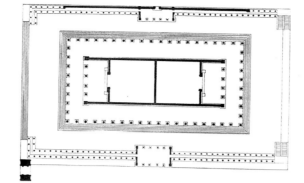

▷ The Temple of Venus and Rome. A plan of the structure as built by Hadrian.

▽ A view of the Temple of Venus and Rome today. The Colosseum can be seen on the far left.

The Temple of Venus and Rome

We do not know whether Hadrian personally designed the Pantheon, but a building that he almost certainly did plan is the Temple of Venus and Rome. This stands on a high piece of ground between the Colosseum and the Temple of Peace. It was built over the atrium of Nero's Domus Aurea, and the Colossus had to be moved to accommodate the huge platform. The form in which we see it today dates to the time of Maxentius (early fourth century). However, it is possible to reconstruct the design of Hadrian's temple. It was designed in the classical Greek style and stood, like the Parthenon, on a stylobate with steps all round. It was an enormous, colonnaded building with ten columns across the facade, 66 metres wide by 136 metres long. On the two long outer sides ran colonnades of Egyptian grey granite, placed on a low stepped platform.

According to the historian Cassius Dio, Apollodorus criticised the design of the temple on the grounds that it should have been placed in a higher position and that there should have been a hollow space beneath it 'to receive machines'. He seems to be referring to the provision of storage space for scenery such as that used in the arena of the Colosseum. Relations between Apollodorus and Hadrian were not as congenial as those the architect had enjoyed with Trajan. Hadrian exiled him in AD 129 and finally had him executed.

Trajan's Forum

One of Trajan's most extensive building projects was the construction of the last and most richly decorated of the imperial fora, to the north-west of the Forum of Augustus. (Vespasian had built the Forum of Peace, and under Nerva the Forum Transitorium had been laid out between it and the Forum of Augustus.)

Trajan's Forum was built between AD 107 and AD 112, paid for from the spoils of his wars

△ A reconstructed general view of the Forum Romanum (foreground) and the Imperial Fora. The huge complex of the Forum of Trajan is clearly visible in the top left-hand part of the illustration.

◁ A marble Corinthian capital from the Temple of Trajan

against the Dacians, and the whole complex was dedicated in AD 113. Apollodorus was the architect.

The complex was vast, measuring overall 300 by 180 metres. The central open piazza measured 200 by 120 metres and was flanked on either side by two large *exedrae* or hemicycles. Placed in the centre was an enormous statue of the emperor Trajan on horseback.

The complex was entered from Augustus' Forum, through a triumphal gate surmounted by a six-horse chariot, depictions of which have survived on coins. The upper storey of the colonnades carried figures of captive barbarian Dacians, sculpted in a variety of decorative stones. There were also gilded statues of horses and military standards.

Opposite the entrance, and closing off the north-western side of the piazza, was the great Basilica Ulpia, the largest such building ever constructed in the Roman period. Beyond this stood Trajan's Column, flanked by two libraries, and then a temple which after Trajan's death was dedicated by Hadrian to the former emperor and his wife Plotina. (It is debatable

△ A statue of the captured barbarian from the Forum of Trajan. Many such statues decorated the porticoes of the Forum and were carved in a variety of different marbles.

△ A sestertius of Trajan depicting the monumental entrance into the Basilica Ulpia from the Forum of Trajan. A quadriga and other figures stand above.

whether this temple was part of the original forum design.) The temple itself now lies partly beneath the church of Santa Maria di Loreto. Representations on coins and the Severan marble map of Rome (the *Forma Urbis Romae*) indicate that it was a huge structure with an eight-column facade, set against a rear wall within a colonnaded enclosure. An Egyptian grey granite column that now lies near Trajan's Column may have come from this temple. When complete, the column would have been 50 feet long, and would have weighed some 120 tons. There are also other architectural fragments from Hadrian's time that are thought to have come from the temple.

The open court of the Forum itself was surrounded by Corinthian porticoes whose columns were of green and white *cipollino* marble from Carystos, on the island of Euboea off the east coast of Greece.

Site preparation

Major engineering works were necessary before construction of the forum could begin. To provide a level site, the slopes of the Quirinal hill had to be cut back, in places up to a height of 38 metres (125 feet), a height marked by the height of Trajan's Column. Until this time, these slopes had probably prevented further major development north-west of the Forum of Augustus.

The Basilica

Rather than a temple as in the other imperial fora, the western side of the Trajan's Forum featured a great transverse basilical hall. This was the Basilica Ulpia (Trajan's family name was Ulpius). It was the largest basilica built in Rome at this time.

The Basilica Ulpia was a five-aisled structure with huge apses at either end. Its total length was about 170 metres. The interior of the building was highly decorated, with the main nave featuring a marble frieze of winged victories. The columns of the central aisle were of grey Egyptian granite; those of the outer aisles were of *cipollino* and smaller in size. The colonnades were continued along the two short sides of the building as well. The floor of the basilica was paved in *opus sectile*, incorporating in particular *giallo antico* and *pavonazzetto*.

The building was 60 metres wide overall. The central aisle was covered by a timber roof with a span of 20 metres. The side aisles are thought to have been topped by galleries, and the interior was lit by clerestory windows.

The entrance of the basilica from the forum is represented on coins. It is commonly shown with six Ionic columns, arranged in pairs, supporting three entablatures joined by blocks of masonry. Above this is a quadriga (a four-horse chariot) and standing figures.

Like the basilicas associated with the Forum Romanum, the Basilica Ulpia had space for both legal offices and shops.

The Libraries

Flanking Trajan's Column were two libraries. These were constructed of brick-faced concrete, vaulted to help protect their contents from damp, and rectangular in plan. The libraries formed an independent complex, accessible from the basilica only by a pair of doors. The scrolls they contained were kept in cupboard-like recesses arranged in two tiers, the upper one accessible from a gallery.

The roofs of the libraries were probably also used as viewing galleries for the lower scenes of the Column spiral.

The Triumphal Column

The most conspicuous surviving monument of the complex is Trajan's Column. It is 39.83 metres high. The shaft itself is 100 Roman feet high, and stands on a pedestal. On top of the column stood a statue of the emperor, but this was removed in the Middle Ages and later replaced by one of St Peter.

The shaft was built of 19 drums of Carrara marble (from Northern Italy), each weighing approximately 32 tons. Each drum was

◁ A view of Trajan's Column. This stood a total of 41.15 metres high. The columns in the foreground are those of the poorly preserved Basilica Ulpia, which stood on one side of the Forum proper.

◁ ◁ Detail of the spiral frieze on Trajan's Column. Carved with over 2600 human figures, it depicts scenes from Trajan's campaigns in Dacia (modern Transylvania)

▽ A reconstructed view of the Forum of Trajan. On the right the porticoes have been cut away to show the wall veneer decoration. The structures beyond are the Markets of Trajan, which would not have been visible from the Forum.

▷ The Great Trajanic Frieze. This comes from an unknown building of Trajanic date and was re-used in the decoration of the Arch of Constantine at the beginning of the 4th century AD. On the left-hand side it shows Trajan being led in to the city and crowned by victory. The other scenes show episodes from the Dacian Wars.

hollowed out, probably initially at the quarry, to form a spiral staircase inside, giving access to a balcony at the top; the interior is lit by forty regularly spaced windows. The outer surface of the shaft was carved with a continuous spiral frieze some 200 metres in length. The frieze and staircase ascend independently, and while the frieze ignores the drum-joints, it does break for the windows. Work on the frieze began after the column was erected, and proceeded from bottom to top.

The sculpted frieze depicts scenes from the two campaigns (101 and 105) which resulted in the annexation of Dacia as a Roman province. It does not form an unbroken narrative, but is made up of a string of generic scenes, such as the emperor sacrificing, addressing his troops, and receiving barbarian embassies and submissions, and the army crossing rivers, marching, building and fighting. The frieze is divided into two equal halves by a figure of Victory flanked by two trophies. These form a link with the Column's pedestal, which is sculpted in exquisite detail to represent a pile of captured barbarian clothing and military equipment.

Trajan's markets

Trajan's reign also saw the construction of a large complex of buildings to the north-east of the Forum, terraced into the lower slopes of the Quirinal hill; it is usually referred to as the Markets of Trajan. This was an elaborately planned quarter, incorpo-

rating over 150 separate office or shop units and a large vaulted hall. These were linked by stairs and streets. The complex was accessible on three levels. At the foot of the hill, a street ran round the outer perimeter of the Forum and gave access to the lower levels. A street, known as the Via Biberatica in the medieval period, gave access at the level of the third storey. At the top of the complex (five storeys in total) was another street giving access from the upper slopes of the Quirinal.

The whole complex was constructed of brick-faced concrete and was built in about

AD 100–112. Although the market complex was close to the Forum, it was separated from it by a high fire-wall of *peperino* tufa blocks.

The Great Hall

A flight of steps leads up from the Via Biberatica to the vaulted hall. This was a rectangular space, 28 metres long and 9.80 metres wide, covered by six cross vaults supported on

▷ A plan of the Forum of Trajan.

◁ A reconstructed cross-section of the Basilica Ulpia. The form of the upper levels of the structure are much debated by scholars and have been reconstructed here after the work of James Packer.

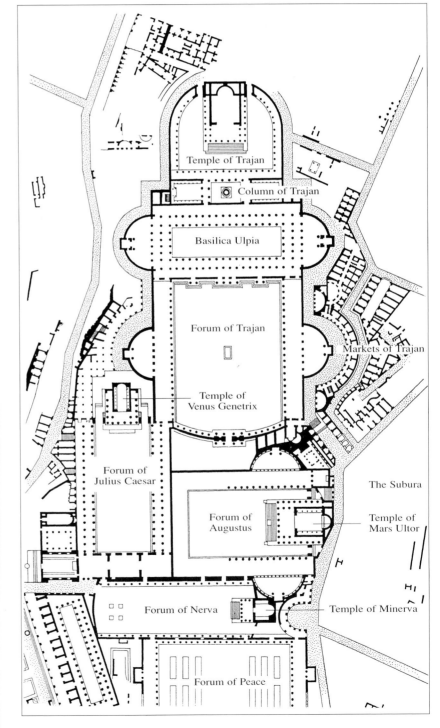

Temple of Trajan

Column of Trajan

Basilica Ulpia

Forum of Trajan

Markets of Trajan

Temple of Venus Genetrix

Forum of Julius Caesar

The Subura

Forum of Augustus

Temple of Mars Ultor

Forum of Nerva

Temple of Minerva

Forum of Peace

235

▷ The Markets of Trajan: a view of the great vaulted hall.

▽ The Markets of Trajan: a view of one of the corridors off which shops and offices opened.

▷ The Markets of Trajan: the Via Biberatica and the exterior of the vaulted hall. The whole complex was terraced up the slopes of the Quirinal and therefore the Roman masonry survives to a considerable height.

△ A reconstructed
view of the Markets of
Trajan.

△ A view of the great
hemicycle of the
Markets of Trajan as it
appears today.

massive travertine brackets. Two rows of six
units opened off either side of the hall on two
levels (making twenty-four units in all). The
upper level formed a gallery that overlooked
the ground floor.

Shopping on four levels

The shop units (*tabernae*) were laid out, for the
most part, in single rows, facing onto the streets
or corridors. The entrance to each unit was
framed by travertine blocks. Above the lintel a
window often lit a wooden mezzanine level.
Interiors would have been plastered, and certainly some *tabernae* were decorated with
frescoes.

At the lowest level, the shops which front
onto the hemicycle have an elaborate facade.
The entrances are framed by pilasters and an
entablature. Every fourth entrance is covered
by a triangular pediment, while the intervening
groups of three have a shallow segmental pediment framed by two triangular half-pediments.

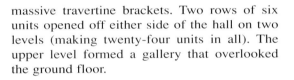

◁ A reconstructed
cross-section through
the Markets of Trajan,
showing how they
were terraced up the
slopes of the hill.

THE GREAT BATHS

The baths were an integral part of Roman urban life. Theatres, amphitheatres and circuses were places of occasional entertainment, but by the late republic bathing had become a daily occurrence for many inhabitants of the Roman Empire. For the Romans, bathing was both a luxury and necessity.

The larger Roman bath complexes served as vast recreation, community and social centres; not only were bathing facilities provided, but also libraries, meeting rooms and gardens for promenading. In the mid-first century AD Seneca in his *Letters* wrote a very lively account of what went on at the baths when he had the misfortune to live above one such establishment. He mentions the noise of people exercising, the shrieks and yells at a thief, "the fellow who likes the sound of his own voice in the bath", and the vendors of sausages and confectionery shouting out their wares.

It was possible to spend several hours at the baths. They were an ideal place to meet one's friends and acquaintances, conduct business meetings, meet one's host before dinner, or indeed acquire a dinner invitation.

The development of the baths from Athens to Rome

It should be remembered that baths and bathing were not invented by the Romans. Bathing was very much part of the ritual of the Greek gymnasium. These complexes provided a social context for exercise and communal bathing, and they exerted a major influence on the subsequent history of bath development.

The first large imperial *thermae*

In the census of 33 BC carried out by Agrippa, there were 170 small baths in Rome; by the early fifth century there were 856 of them, as well as 11 large imperial baths (usually called *thermae*), such as the Baths of Trajan and the Baths of Caracalla.

In Rome the very large, imperially built *thermae* provided space for huge numbers of bathers at any one time. The imperial *thermae* in Rome are some the most sophisticated and ambitious large-scale buildings from the ancient world. They were laid out on a more or less symmetrical plan about the main, short axis formed by the positioning of the *frigidarium* (cold room), the *tepidarium* (warm room) and the *caldarium* (hot room), allowing for the circulation of bathers through the building. There were often a series of subsidiary hot rooms.

The Baths of Agrippa, built on the Campus Martius in 25 BC, provide us with the earliest example of such baths. However, these were rebuilt in the third century AD, and it is not clear exactly what form the original plan took. The same is true of the Baths of Nero. The Baths of Titus, known from the plan of Palladio, are also uncertain in a number of details.

The Baths of Titus

The Baths of Titus (*Thermae Titi*) were hurriedly built to be ready at the inauguration of the Colosseum in AD 80. Titus used ground which had once formed part of Nero's Golden House. The baths were built on the hillside opposite the Colosseum, next to the main domestic wing of the Domus Aurea. Hardly any trace of this building survives. A portico of brick-faced concrete piers with engaged columns which can now be seen across the Via dei Fori Imperiali from the Colosseum has been identified as part of the entrance to the baths. In the later sixteenth century Palladio made a measured sketch of the building which suggests that it was laid out on a symmetrical plan, one

△ Baths of Trajan. Detail of the substructure supporting the semi-circular spectators' seating area in the outer enclosure wall.

which is familiar from the later, and much better preserved, Baths of Trajan and of Caracalla. However, the reliability of the plan is questionable.

Recent excavations on the site have uncovered part of the heated section of the baths, including part of the *caldarium* (hot room). It will be interesting to watch the progress of these excavations in the future, as the details of the buildings become clearer.

The baths built by Trajan

The Baths of Trajan (AD 104–109) are the earliest example of the imperial *thermae* plan of which we can be sure. The baths were opened on 22 June AD 109. They provide a number of features that are seen in all the later baths of this type, both in Rome (Baths of Caracalla, Baths of Diocletian, Baths of Constantine) and elsewhere in the Empire (for example at Trier).

The great imperial baths of Trajan were built on the slopes of the Esquiline Hill and dedicated in AD 109. Work started on the site after a fire in AD 104, which severely damaged the Domus Aurea. The upper floors of the palace were demolished, leaving only the vaulted rooms of the ground floor. The courtyards and gardens were laced with walls joined by vaulted roofs to bring the whole area up to the level of the first floor, 47 metres (154 feet) above sea-level. The rest of the hill was levelled off to the same height to form a huge artificial platform 340 metres by 330 metres (1115 feet by 1083 feet), preserving the main residential wing of Nero's infamous palace almost intact.

The new baths lay to the north-east of those of Titus. The actual bathing block covered three times the area of the Baths of Titus. The baths were oriented so that the main heated rooms received the full strength of the afternoon sun; the afternoon was the normal bathing time for a large proportion of the population.

The baths were almost certainly designed by Trajan's architect, Apollodorus of Damascus, and construction throughout was of brick-faced concrete. The whole area was enclosed by a continuous line of buildings, broken only by a large semi-circular display area with seating on the south-west side. The perimeter buildings included two libraries and two nymphaea. The main entrance was on the north-east side. There was also an entrance on the north-west side, which was probably matched by another on the south-east. Epigraphic evidence tells us that a corporation of athletes was also based here in the mid-second to fourth century AD. The central bathing block is 190 metres by 212 metres (623 feet by 696 feet). It is attached to the outer enclosure on the north-east side; in the Baths of Caracalla and of Diocletian, the block was free-standing and placed more centrally within the enclosure. The open areas between the bathing block and the perimeter buildings were planted out as gardens.

The building is much ruined today, but the plan is partially preserved on the Marble Plan (*Forma Urbis*) and on a remarkably accurate plan drawn by an unknown medieval architect known as the Anonymous Destailler. From these plans and from what remains today, it has been possible to reconstruct most of the baths. It should be borne in mind that the *Forma Urbis* shows the baths at the beginning of the third century AD, whereas the Anonymous Destailler shows it in its final state. This accounts for the discrepancies between the two plans.

Mussolini turned the ruins of Trajan's Baths into a park with huge pieces of brick-faced concrete protruding from the grass. The visible remains consist mainly of four exedrae, half-domed structures of which there were originally six.

△ Reconstruction of the Baths of Trajan. The smaller Baths of Titus are in the bottom left had corner. The reservoir (Sette Sale) is in the top right hand corner.

▷ Reconstruction of the eastern corner of the Baths complex, showing the reservoir R (Sette Sale), with a channel running under building S towards building C. The natatio M and nymphaeum D must also have been supplied from the reservoir. The purpose of Building E is uncertain. The buildings on top of the reservoir were probably domestic quarters for the slaves operating the baths.

Water supply

The Baths of Trajan were supplied with water from two sources. One was the Aqua Traiana. This aqueduct, also built by Trajan, came into Rome on the west bank of the Tiber. The channels radiating from the great terminal reservoir seem to have served every quarter of the city, but especially the Baths of Trajan. The water was carried in pipes over the bridges to the east bank. The course of this aqueduct on the right bank of the river and exactly how it supplied the baths is still unknown. Lead pipes bearing the inscriptions *THERM(ae) TRAIANI(i)* and *AQ(ua) TR(aiana)* have been found on the Esquiline close to the baths, indicating that there was a close connection between the two projects.

The other source of water for the baths was the reservoir known as the Sette Sale. This reservoir was not fed by the Aqua Traiana, as many scholars assert, but by an aqueduct running from the high ground to the east, presumably from one of the aqueducts entering the city in the Porta Maggiore area. This aqueduct entered the reservoir at its north-east corner, where a few metres of its course still remain.

△ Lead pipes from the Baths of Diocletian.

▽ Inside one of the nine cisterns of the Sette Sale.

▽ The reservoir Sette Sale.

The orientation of the Sette Sale has suggested to some scholars that it may have been part of the facilities of the Domus Aurea, but brick stamps confirm its Trajanic construction. The structure was two-storeyed and built of brick-faced concrete. At each level there were nine large, interconnecting 8 metres high (26 feet) chambers, with overall dimensions of 46.6 metres by 37 metres (153 feet by 121 feet). The cisterns, which had a capacity of about 7 million litres (1½ million gallons), were on the upper level. The aqueduct entered the reservoir at a height of just over 8 metres (26 feet) above the level of the baths platform, filling the cisterns to this level and producing sufficient water pressure to supply overhead tanks in the *caldarium* and elsewhere.

The Sette Sale and its surrounding area are the best-studied part of the whole complex. Excavations carried out between 1981 and 1983 established that the water from the reservoir was channelled through a trough along the front of the building and then carried through lead pipes under a partially excavated courtyard building in the direction of a small building C (see plan below). This was on the same orientation as the reservoir attached to the perimeter of the baths, from which it must have fed the main bath buildings.

The half-domed building, exedra D, was a *nymphaeum*. Water, which collected in the curved corridor behind, came through holes in the eleven niches and cascaded into the pool below. Exedra N was also a *nymphaeum*. The partially destroyed two-apsed building E is on the same orientation as the reservoir and should therefore be associated with the water supply.

However, despite the fact that it was excavated, its function has not been established. The northern part of this building is totally missing, but it is shown on the Marble Plan, which also shows a long building at the back of E and two walls heading towards the reservoir. These must represent an aqueduct carrying water to the two *nymphaea* and the bathing pool (*natatio*). This large rectangular pool was about 1 metre (3 feet) deep and surrounded by colonnaded porticoes. It contained cold water and was designed to be a place where bathers could cool off after the heat of the *caldarium*, rather than for swimming.

The *frigidarium*

The *frigidarium*, or cold room, was the focal point of the whole design. This was a large rectangular room delimited by eight piers with huge monolithic columns placed in front. Four cold plunge baths were set one towards each corner.

The eight huge columns of the *frigidarium* appeared to carry the great soaring roof of the structure. In fact, the piers behind the columns were the main load-bearing elements, carrying the three great cross-vaults that formed the ceiling. The underside of the vault would have been richly decorated. The *frigidarium* of the Baths of Diocletian survives intact with its vaults, as it was converted into the church of Santa Maria degli Angeli by Michelangelo in 1563–66 for Pope Pius IV.

▽ Plan of the Baths of Trajan, reconstructed from the Marble Plan and the plan of the Anonymous Destailler.

R Sette Sale
S partially excavated courtyard building
D *nymphaeum* or monumental fountain
N *nymphaeum*
C small building attached to perimeter of the baths
E partially destroyed two-apsed building
B Library
L Library
M *natatio*
F *frigidarium*
T *tepidarium*
A *caldarium*
Y large semicircular area with spectators' seating

known substructures

known remains at or above ground level

details from the Marble Plan

details from the plan of the Anonymous Destailler

remains of the Domus Aurea.

△ Interior of the Church of Santa Maria degli Angeli, converted from the *frigidarium* of the Baths of Diocletian.

The south-west end of Trajan's *frigidarium* was partially excavated in the nineteenth century. Fragments of red and grey granite columns were discovered and the corner of one of the cold plunge baths was uncovered, together with the base of two of the monolithic columns, exactly as shown by the Anonymous Destailler.

On either side of the *frigidarium* was an open colonnaded rectangular area measuring 32 metres by 22 metres (105 feet by 72 feet). The far side was closed in by half-domed exedra H, similar to those at the four corners of the platform. These areas were used for exercise before proceeding to the hot rooms, and each one is usually referred to as a *palaestra*. The imperial *thermae*, because of their symmetrical design, usually incorporated two such areas. Other, asymmetrical bath designs, such as the Forum Baths at Ostia, would have had one larger *palaestra*.

The heated rooms

The main heated rooms of the baths were the *tepidarium*, or warm room, and the *caldarium* or hot room. However, there were at least six other rooms, and those on either side of the *caldarium* were also heated. The *tepidarium* was so placed as to insulate the heated rooms from the cold rooms beyond. The *caldarium* had apses on three sides, each containing a hot plunge pool. The heated rooms could vary quite considerably in design from one bath building to the next. In the Baths of Caracalla, the *caldarium* was circular and covered by a great dome.

The south-east corner of the *caldarium* of Trajan's Baths was partially excavated in 1871. No report of this excavation has ever been properly published, but drawings made by the French architect Leclerc show that the heating system was very similar to examples from Ostia, particularly the more or less contemporary Forum Baths. The hot room was flanked by vaulted underground passageways, often narrow, about 2 metres (6½ feet) wide and

◁ Reconstructed section through the Baths of Trajan, showing from left: main north-east entrance, *natatio*, *frigidarium* (the highest building), *tepidarium*, *caldarium* and semi-circular area with spectators' seating. Beneath this area are the remains of the Domus Aurea.

2.5 metres (8 feet) high, and lit by rectangular holes in the roof. From these passageways slaves operated the underfloor heating system through the numerous stoke-holes that pierced the base of the main walls of the building. The working conditions in these passageways must have been appalling, as the smoke could only gradually escape through the holes in the roof.

The heat provided in the Roman baths was for the most part steam heat. Some baths had another heated room, the *laconicum*, which provided dry heat. Temperatures in this room could rise much higher than in the more traditionally heated hot rooms, so time spent here would have been far less.

The Baths of Trajan, like the other large imperially built baths, provided space for huge numbers of bathers at any one time. As a result, there was often a series of subsidiary hot rooms.

The hypocaust

Traditionally the Romans are credited with the invention of sweat baths and of the hypocaust (underfloor heating). The popular claim, recounted by Pliny the Elder, is that Sergius Orata, Roman entrepreneur of the early first century BC, was the inventor of the system in connection with heating artificial oyster beds on the Bay of Naples.

However, the earliest and clearest archaeological evidence for the true hypocaust comes from the Stabian Baths at Pompeii (Phase IV dated to the late second century BC) and the Greek Baths at Olympia (period IV dated to *c*. 100 BC). The hypocaust could take a variety of forms, but in essence it was a system by which hot air could be introduced under the floor from a furnace area, where the hot water was also heated. The floor was supported on *pilae*, small supporting pillars usually of bricks (though one-piece stone or terracotta *pilae* are sometimes found). The floor itself had to be thick in order to prevent it from becoming too hot to walk on.

△ *Pilae* of the hypocaust under the *caldarium* of the Forum Baths at Ostia.

△ *Tubuli* behind the marble facing of the *caldarium* wall in the Forum Baths at Ostia. These box-tiles lined the walls and allowed the hot air to pass from beneath the floor up to the ceiling, thus heating the walls.

▽ Cutaway section of a hypocaust system, showing how hot air passed from beneath the floor and up the walls.

Below: different tiles used to heat the walls:

A and B – different types of *tegulae mammatae*. C – *tubuli*.

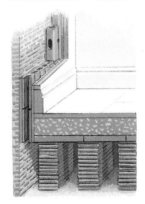

▷ Forum Baths, Ostia. Windows in one of the hot rooms showing a double row of holes, possibly for double-glazing.

▽ Wooden-soled shoes found at Vindolanda in northern Britain. They were possibly for use in the baths, to protect the feet from the heated floor.

Not only the floor, but also the walls and vaults were usually heated. The earliest archaeological evidence for the use of wall heating dates to the early first century BC, when heated hollow walls were introduced into the Stabian Baths at Pompeii and were also used in the construction of the Forum Baths there. A hollow wall can be achieved in several ways. The commonest method was by the use of continuous hollow box-tiles (*tubuli*). These were fastened to the wall using metal clamps and then faced with marble or plastered over. The bottom row of *tubuli* was set so that hot air in the underfloor area could naturally rise up the wall. This is the method used in the Forum Baths at Ostia, and it can still be seen in place today. Another method was to use specially made tiles – *tegulae mammatae* – which created a cavity in the wall up which the hot air could rise. Whatever the method used, the hot air escaped through flues in the roof.

If a heated room was vaulted, as was usually the case by the imperial period, the hot air was channelled around the vault using curved hollow tiles.

The orientation of the baths allowed the heat of the afternoon sun to create a 'greenhouse effect' within the heated rooms. These rooms had relatively large windows (in contrast to Greek and early Roman bath buildings) to facilitate this, and there is some evidence to suggest that they were double-glazed to maximize the effect. This seems to have been the case in the Forum Baths at Ostia.

Heating the water

The furnace area, or *praefurnium*, was not only the source of hot air for the hypocaust system –

it was also where the water was heated. None of the heating systems of the imperial *thermae* in Rome survive enough to reconstruct how they would have worked. However, evidence does survive from many other bath buildings at Ostia, Pompeii and elsewhere in the Roman world, which allow a reconstruction to be made.

In the Forum Baths at Ostia the hot plunge baths were originally flanked by cylindrical boilers, also heated from the passageway. A large L-shaped cavity in walls at the south corner of the *caldarium* of Trajan's Baths was discovered during the excavations of 1871. This space, which could comfortably accommodate two large boilers with a cistern above, opens on to the service corridor.

The Roman architect Vitruvius describes two water-heating systems. One comprises three interconnected tanks, one of which was a boiler placed over the furnace. This system allowed the boiler to be kept topped up with water and allowed cold water to be mixed with hot water actually in the baths and pools.

The second system is the *testudines alveolorum*. This was an ingenious piece of technology and involved a tank (called a *testudo* because of its tortoise-shell like shape) being fitted so that it was a few centimetres lower than the bottom of the bath. The water in the cylinder was constantly heated, the hot water automatically rising to be replaced by the colder water from the bath. In this way hot water was constantly circulating. The fitting for a *testudo* can clearly be seen on the architect's drawing under the semi-circular plunge bath at the south-east end of Trajan's *caldarium*. Similar fittings can be seen in the Forum Baths at Ostia and in the Stabian Baths in Pompeii.

Bathing and massage

Roman bath buildings may vary in detail, but they have a number of characteristic features in common. They are all planned so as to allow logical progression from one room to another. A bather would arrive at the baths and would go to the *apodyterium* (dressing room), where he would leave his clothes. In the Forum Baths

△ The underground passageways of the Forum Baths at Ostia. The rectangular hole in the vaulted roof was the only source of light and ventilation.

▽ Reconstruction of the *caldarium* of the Baths of Trajan.

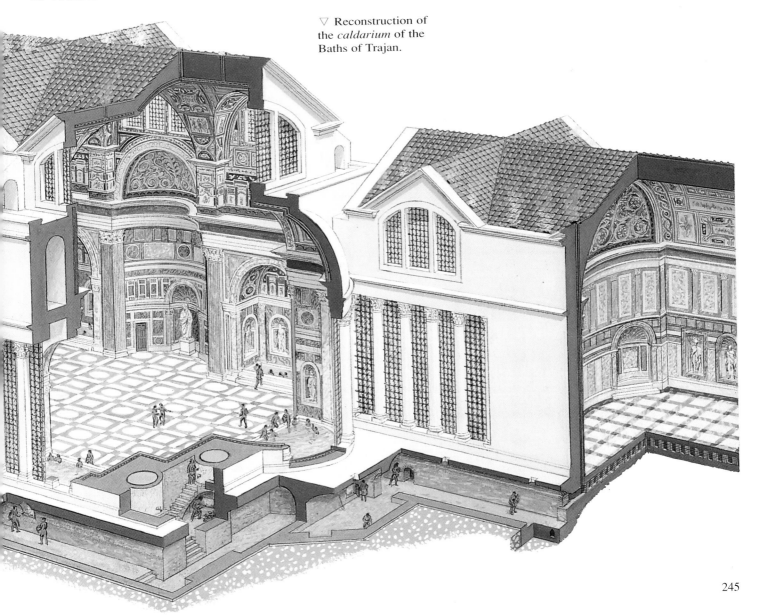

△ Forum Baths, Ostia. The housing for a hot water tank with hearth beneath.

▷ Forum Baths, Ostia. Plan of the *caldarium*. The *tubuli* heating the walls are shown in orange.

Key: 1, 2, 3 – the three hot plunge baths

W–W the hot water tanks

T – the position of the *testudo* of bath 3.

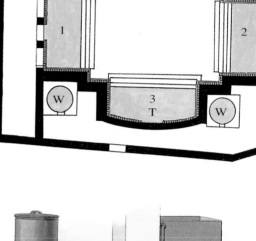

△ Forum Baths, Ostia. Hole for the *testudo* in hot plunge-bath 3.

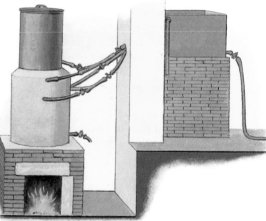

◁ △ Water heating system for a private baths at the Villa Rustica in Boscoreale, near Pompeii. Above: external view. Left: cutaway section.

△ The hole for the *testudo* seen from the service tunnel. The fire was in the trough beneath.

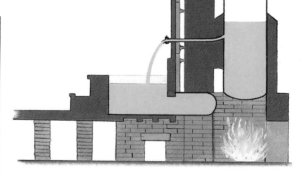

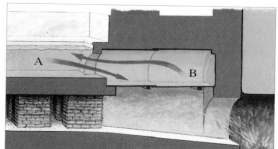

◁ Stabian Baths, Pompeii. Section of the *testudo* in the so-called women's *caldarium*. The cooler water A sinks to the bottom, while the reheated water B rises, making the water constantly circulate.

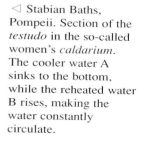

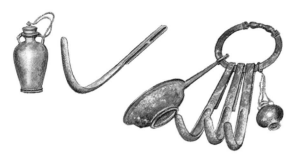

△ Strigils and oil flasks found at Pompeii.

at Pompeii, open-fronted cupboard-like facilities clearly acted as the equivalent of modern-day lockers. (However, instead of a lock and key, a servant or slave was paid to watch over the garments.) From here the bather might follow a number of different courses. He might oil himself (usually with perfumed oil) and exercise in the *palaestra*. From there he would progress to the *tepidarium*, perhaps via the *frigidarium*, and then go on to the *caldarium*. After some time sitting in the steam and immersing himself in the hot-water plunge pools, he would scrape off the oil, along with the dirt and dead skin, using a metal implement called a strigil. (This job might be done by a servant.) He would then make his way back to the *frigidarium* and the *natatio*, where he might take a cold plunge.

The libraries

At the west corner of the enclosure of Trajan's Baths there is a well-preserved semi-circular half-dome building, 28.8 metres (94½ feet) in diameter. This is exedra L and is thought to have been a library. The internal decoration of the dome has now disappeared, but its original hexagonal coffers can be seen clearly on an eighteenth century etching by Piranesi. The interior wall has two rows of hexagonal niches, which probably housed 'bookcases' in two storeys, for storing scrolls. A large niche in the centre probably held a statue of the emperor or of Minerva, the patron goddess of writers. The much-damaged exedra B at the south corner must also have been a library, one probably keeping Latin texts and the other Greek.

△ Reconstruction of exedra L of the Baths of Trajan. This is thought by many scholars to have been a library. If so, it must have had some way of being closed and locked.

▷ Exedra L, view from outside.

▽ Exedra L, view from inside.

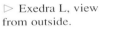

15 16 17 18 19 20 21 22 23 24 25 26 27

A — B — C — D — E — F — G — H — I — J — K — L — M — N — O —

A reconstruction of the centre of
Rome during the reign of the
emperor Severus (AD 193–211).

E 19 Colosseum
B 21 Baths of Trajan
D 3   Forum Romanum
F 26 Temple of Claudius
B 6   Temple of Mars Ultor
B 3   Forum of Trajan
E 12 Temple of Venus and Rome
E 25 Ludus Magnus
H 8   Domus Flavia
K 8   Domus Augustana
P 1   Circus Maximus
I 24 Branch of the Aqua Claudia
C 8   Forum of Peace
F 4   Domus Tiberiana
C 19 Baths of Titus
C 3   Forum of Julius Caesar
C 6   Forum of Nerva
O 21 Septizodium (a 'folly' built by
      Septimius Severus)

15 16 17 18 19 20 21 22 23 24 25 26 27

THE CITY IN LATE ANTIQUITY

After the death of Hadrian, there were far fewer monumental building projects in the City. It was not until the time of the emperor Constantine (AD 312–337) that there was renewed wide-scale urban planning. By then, however, Christianity was beginning to make its mark in the form of large church foundations. The Roman world was changing: although Rome remained important as a religious and symbolic focus it was no longer the political centre of the Roman Empire.

By AD 138 Hadrian had carried out an extensive building programme in the capital. As well as building the Pantheon and the Temple of Venus and Rome, he had added a temple to the Forum of Trajan, dedicated to the deified Trajan himself. Early in his reign he had retraced the sacred *pomerium* of Rome and had inaugurated the Natalis Urbis Romae, an official birthday celebration on 21 April. He had also attended to other less grand but perhaps more important building projects, aimed at improving the daily life of the population of Rome. Among these were various flood prevention measures in the northern Campus Martius and the laying out of a garden around Augustus's Ara Pacis. Across the Tiber he constructed a huge new imperial mausoleum approached by a bridge, the Pons Aelius. Today this building is known as the Castel Sant'Angelo.

The second century AD

Hadrian's ashes were placed in the new mausoleum after his death in 138. His successor, Antoninus, managed to persuade the Senate to grant Hadrian divine honours, earning himself the title Pius ('pious') in the process. He had a temple dedicated to Hadrian in the Campus Martius.

New building in Rome continued under Antoninus Pius, but at a greatly reduced rate. He constructed a temple in the Forum Romanum to his wife Faustina when she died in AD 141. This was re-dedicated to both Antoninus and Faustina after Antoninus's death in 161.

Under his successor Marcus Aurelius, the relative peace and stability that the Roman world had enjoyed for 100 years came to an end. The Rhine and Danube frontiers were increasingly threatened by Germanic tribes like the Marcomanni and the Quadi. The emperor, whose interests lay more in philosophy than warfare, was forced to put most of his energies into fighting off these threats.

His campaigns were commemorated in Rome by the erection of the Column of Marcus Aurelius, which still stands in the present-day Piazza Colonna. The column was modelled on Trajan's Column, and had a shaft 30 metres (100 feet) in height. It also was carved with a spiral relief.

Marcus Aurelius was succeeded by his son Commodus, who by all accounts lived a degenerate and debauched lifestyle. His megalomania led him to change the name of Rome to Colonia Commodiana. He spent money lavishly on public games, often performing in the arena himself.

The third-century crisis

Commodus was assassinated at the end of 192 and (after a brief period of civil war), Septimius Severus, a native of Lepcis Magna in North Africa, emerged as emperor. Severus set about a campaign of restoration and renewal in Rome, restoring aqueducts, the embankments of the river and temples. A triumphal arch was dedicated by the Senate in the Forum to celebrate the tenth anniversary of his accession. This was decorated with sculpted reliefs of Severus' Parthian campaigns in the East. On the Palatine, Severus extended the imperial palace, adding a whole new wing on the southern side.

Septimius Severus' successors made a number of additions to the city, the most important being the huge Baths of Caracalla built in the southern part of the city. However, the third century was a time of political confusion, with at least 25 emperors in the period from 235 to 284. Many of these emperors never visited Rome; they were too busy fighting each other or Rome's enemies on the frontiers.

Diocletian and the Tetrarchy

The chaos came to an end with the accession of Diocletian, who instituted the idea of government by the Tetrarchy ('four rulers'). Under this system, the administration of the Empire was placed in the hands of two *Augusti* assisted by two *Caesares*. Diocletian also attempted many economic reforms.

Although Diocletian spent much of his time away from the city, he was the last of the great builders of Rome. He restored and reorganised the Forum Romanum, which had become cluttered with honorific monuments. He rebuilt the

◁ The Porta Ostiensis, one of the 18 main gates in the walls built by the emperor Aurelian in the AD 270s. These walls enclosed all of Augustus' Fourteen Regions, including the Trans Tiber region.

temples of Saturn and Vesta, along with the Curia, which had recently been destroyed by fire. He constructed the third of Rome's massive bath complexes, on the Quirinal. The scale of this building can be gauged from the *frigidarium*, which was converted into the Church of Santa Maria degli Angeli by Michelangelo and survives to this day.

Constantine and Christianity

A period of unrest followed the abdication of Diocletian in 306; it was not brought to an end until 312, by Constantine's victory at the Battle of the Milvian Bridge over his rival, Maxentius. Constantine quickly made his mark in the city of Rome in the traditional way. He constructed a large set of imperial baths, smaller than those of Diocletian but closer to the centre of the city. Next to the Colosseum he erected a great triumphal arch, much of which was decorated with reliefs taken from earlier monuments (some reworked), presenting a display of Rome's artistic history.

Constantine's greatest contribution was the construction of the first churches. In AD 313 the Edict of Milan officially recognised Christianity as one of the religions of the Roman world, freeing it from the periodic persecution it had suffered in the past. Work began on the great Basilica of St John Lateran, the cathedral church of Rome, at the east end of the Caelian Hill. Across the river a similar basilica was constructed over the tomb of St Peter on the Vatican Hill.

The end of Imperial Rome

Until the later third century AD, Rome had been largely undefended. The ancient Servian walls, built after the sack of the city by the Gauls in the early fourth century BC, had been for the most part demolished, and the city had expanded beyond their line. As conditions became unsettled in the third century AD, however, the emperor Aurelian began the construction of a new set of walls in the 270s. The Aurelianic walls were 19 km (11 miles) long, enclosing an area of 1375 hectares (556 acres). They were built of brick-faced concrete, with much of the fired brick re-used from earlier structures. There were 18 gates and 381 towers along the circuit. With some modifications and repairs (for example, they were doubled in height by Maxentius in the early fourth century), these walls continued to serve as Rome's defences until the late nineteenth century.

From the foundation of Constantinople by the emperor Constantine as a 'New Rome' in 324, imperial prestige was increasingly diverted from Rome. Many of the late Roman emperors did not visit the city at all. The Roman Empire, particularly in the West, became more and more the object of barbarian attacks, and in 410 the Goths under Alaric attacked and sacked Rome itself. Although it was not until 476 that the Western Empire officially ceased to exist, the Gothic sack effectively ended any meaningful Roman administration in the western Mediterranean. Rome was important as a centre of Christendom but no longer of imperial politics.

Athens also suffered from these barbarian invasions. The city was sacked in 267 by the Herulians, and in 396 by Alaric. It recovered to become a centre of learning under Byzantine rule, but in 1456, three years after the fall of Constantinople to the Turks, Athens became part of the Ottoman Empire. A mosque was built within the ruined cella of the Parthenon; in 1687, during a Venetian siege of the city, it was blown up. The Greeks won their independence in 1821, and Athens became the capital of the new Greek state.

GLOSSARY

Acropolis: literally a high city. The citadel of a city. In Athens this was a high flat-topped rocky plateau which from the 6th century BC was increasingly given over to the sanctuaries of the gods.

aedile: a Roman magistrate whose main responsibility from the time of Augustus was the general care of the city.

agora: a market place and open area in a Greek city for public congregation, particularly for the political procedures of the city.

amphora(e): a pottery jar for tranporting wine, olive oil or other foodstuffs.

annona: an annual distribution of free grain to Rome's poor, reorganised by the emperor Augustus.

architrave: a horizontal beam forming the lowest element of the entablature which rested directly on the capitals of the columns.

Areopagus: the Hill of Ares north-west of the Acropolis in Athens and the council associated with it.

atrium: the main central hall in a Roman house.

aulos, diaulos: musical instruments made of one or two (*diaulos*) pipes.

aureus: the standard Roman gold coin, equalling 25 denarii or 100 sestertii.

basilica : a rectangular, usually aisled hall, most often associated with a Roman forum.

boule: the council in Greek states that usually had the day-to-responsibility for the state's affairs.

Bouleuterion: the Greek council chamber.

caldarium: the hot room in Roman public baths.

caryatids: column shafts carved in the form of draped women.

cavea: stepped seating in a Roman amphitheatre, circus or theatre.

cella: the main body of a Greek and Roman temple. It usually contained the cult statue.

chiton: a long tunic dress of linen worn by Greek women

colonnade: a row of columns at regular intervals.

consul : the supreme Roman magistrate of which there were two elected each year

cubit: a unit of measurement used in the classical world equal to the length from the elbow to the tip of middle finger.

Curia: the Roman Senate house.

cursus honorum: the career structure followed by Roman politicians, involving both military and civilian posts.

deme: a village; in the Athenian system it was the basic administrative unit.

denarius: a Roman silver coin, worth 4 sestertii.

ekklesia: the Athenian assembly of adult male citizens.

equites: the middle stratum of Roman society, consisting of both landowners and prosperous businessmen.

Erechtheum: a sacred building on the Acropolis in Athens begun in 421 BC. It housed the wooden cult statue of Athena.

exedra(e): a large recess, often designed to house a statue.

frigidarium: the cold room in Roman public baths.

hemicycle: lare semicircular recess.

Herms: stone shafts or pillars used as boundary stones and milestones. The top of the pillar was usually sculpted with a male bearded head.

himation: a mantle worn over a tunic.

hoplite: a Greek heavily armed soldier.

hoplomachus: the standard heavily armed gladiator.

hypocaust : an underfloor heating system, developed by the Romans around the late second century BC.

imperator: a title given to victorious Roman generals, then later adopted by Augustus and subsequent emperors.

insula : a Roman apartment block several storeys high.

Kerameikos: a large area of north-west Athens based on the potters' quarter.

kithara: a musical instrument similar to the lyre but with a flat, hollow sound-box.

lanista: a Roman gladiatorial trainer. The *lanista* also refereed gladiatorial contests.

lararium : a shrine in a Roman house to the household gods.

Lares: the spirits of a Roman family's ancestors.

metoikoi (metics): an immigrant, foreign, non-citizen resident of Athens.

metope: a rectangular stone panel placed between triglyphs in a Doric frieze.

mina: an Athenian coin worth 100 drachmas.

munera: Roman gladiatorial games.

natatio: the swimming pool in Roman public baths.

nymphaeum: literally a shrine of the nymphs, used to describe elaborate fountains.

omphalos: the navel or centre of a geographical area.

opus reticulatum: a facing which develops at the end of the 2nd century BC for Roman concrete, made up of individual pieces of stone with a square face laid diagonally.

orchestra: the circular area in a Greek theatre where the actors perform.

palaestra: an exercise ground, often attached to public baths.

palla, pallium : a cloak-like garment worn by Roman women (the *palla*) and men (the *pallium*). Similar to the Greek *himation*.

pantheon: literally all the gods.

Penates: the guardian spirits of the Roman family larder.

peplos: woollen dress worn by women.

peristyle: an open courtyard or colonnaded garden in a Roman house.

pilaster: a rectangular column engaged to a wall and only slightly projecting from it.

Pnyx: the hill south-west of the Agora in Athens where the assembly (*ekklesia*) usually met.

pomerium: the religious boundary of a city.

praetor : a Roman magistracy ranked below the consul.

princeps: 'leading citizen' – a title adopted by Augustus and subsequent emperors.

Propylaea: the monumental gateway to the Acropolis in Athens.

retiarius: a type of Roman gladiator, who used a net and a trident.

rostra: the speaker's platform in the Forum Romanum in Rome.

secutor: a Roman gladiator, the traditional opponent for the *retiarius* or net man.

Senator: a member of the Roman Senate.

sestertius: a small Roman silver coin, worth in the imperial period 4 asses, or one quarter of a denarius.

skene: the stage building of a theatre. Originally this was a very simple structure providing a backdrop to the performance in the *orchestra*.

stoa: a colonnade open on one side which carries a roof to a rear wall providing shelter in public areas such as the agora.

strategoi: magistrates and generals. In Athens they were responsible for various military matters, including command of the army.

stylobate: the platform on which a colonnade, particularly one surrounding a temple, stands.

taberna(e): a shop or shops.

tablinum: a large room at the back of the atrium of a Roman house which was both the office and main reception room of the house.

talent: Athenian coin equal to 60 *minas*.

tepidarium: the warm room in Roman public baths.

thermae: large, imperially built, heated Roman baths in Rome.

toga: a Roman formal garment, worn by male citizens.

travertine: a type of limestone quarried near Tivoli.

triclinium: the dining room of a Roman house.

tufa: a volcanic stone of which several varieties were quarried around Rome.

vomitorium: the name given to the points of access for the audience in a theatre or amphitheatre.

BIBLIOGRAPHY

Athens

Bieber, M., *The History of the Greek and Roman Theatre*. Princeton, 1961.

Camp, J. M., *The Athenian Agora – Excavations in the Heart of Classical Athens*. London, 1986.

Economakis, R. (ed.), *Acropolis Restoration*. London, 1994.

Green, R. and E. Handley, *Images of the Greek Theatre*. London, 1995.

Jenkins, I., *The Parthenon Frieze*. London, 1994.

Jones, J. E., *Town and Country Houses in Attica in Classical Times*. Ghent, 1975.

Knigge, U., *The Athenian Kerameikos*. Athens, 1991.

Neils, J., *Goddess and Polis – The Panathenaic Festival in Ancient Athens*. Princeton, 1992.

Oakley, J. R. and R. Sinos, *The Wedding in Ancient Athens*. Wisconsin, 1993.

Pickard-Cambridge, A. W., *The Theatre of Dionysus in Athens*. Oxford, 1946.

Robinson, D. R. and J. W. Graham, *The Hellenic House – Excavations at Olynthus* – Part VIII. Oxford, 1938.

Taplin, O., *Comic Angels and Other Approaches to Greek Drama through Vase Paintings*. Oxford, 1993

Travlos, J., *Pictorial Dictionary of Ancient Athens*. London, 1971.

Wycherley, R. E., *The Stones of Athens*. Princeton, 1978

Rome

General

Richardson, L., *A New Topographical Dictionary of Ancient Rome*. Baltimore and London, 1992.

Robinson, O., *Ancient Rome: City Planning and Administration*. London, 1992.

Stambaugh, J. E., *The Ancient Roman City*. Baltimore, 1988.

Steinby, M., *Lexicon Topographicum Urbis Romae*. Rome, Vol. I, 1993; Vol. II, 1995; Vol. III, 1996.

Architecture

Adam, J.-P., *Roman Building – Materials and Techniques*. London, 1994.

Anderson, J. C., *The Historical Geography of the Imperial Fora*. 1984.

Boethius, A., *Etruscan and Early Roman Architecture*. Harmondsworth, 1978.

Boatwright, M., *Hadrian and the City of Rome*. Princeton, 1987.

Packer, J. E., *The Forum of Trajan in Rome*. Berkeley, 1997.

Reggiani, A. M. (ed.), *Anfiteatro Flavio – Immagine, Testimonianze, Spettacoli*. Rome, 1988.

Ward-Perkins, J. B., *Roman Imperial Architecture*. Harmondsworth, 1981.

Social and Economic Issues

R. Beecham, *The Roman Theatre and its Audience*. London, 1991.

Evans, H. B., *Water distribution in ancient Rome. The evidence of Frontinus*, Ann Arbor, 1994.

Ramage, E., 'Urban problems in Ancient Rome'. In M. Marchese (ed), *Aspects of Graeco-Roman Urbanism*. Oxford, 1983.

Rickman, G., *The Corn Supply of Ancient Rome*. Oxford, 1980.

Packer, J. E., *The Insulae of Imperial Ostia*. Rome 1971.

Scobie, A., 'Slums, Sanitation, and Mortality in the Roman World'. *Klio* **68**, 399–433 (1986).

Wiedeman, T., *Emperors and Gladiators*. London, 1992.

Ville, G., *La Gladiature en Occident des origines a la Mort de Domitien*. Rome, 1981.

Yegul, F., *Baths and Bathing in Classical Antiquity*. New York, 1992.

ACKNOWLEDGEMENTS

The authors would like to acknowledge the help and advice of the following people:

Professor John Camp, American School of Classical Studies, Athens.

Dr Amanda Claridge, Institute of Archaeology, Oxford.

Dr Jon Coulston, St Andrews University, Scotland.

Dr Ian Jenkins, Department of Greek and Roman Antiquities, British Museum, London.

Dr Christopher Smith

La Soprintendenza Archeologica di Roma.

The staff of the School of Classics, Trinity College, Dublin, in particular Professor Kathy Coleman, Professor Brian McGing, Dr Christine Morris and Dr Judith Mossman.

The staff of the British School at Rome, in particular Maria Pia Malvezzi.

PHOTO CREDITS

Page

vi	Scala (Museo delle Terme, Roma)
vii	Index/Archivio Fotografico, Soprintendenza Archeologica, Roma
29 t	Deutsches Archäologisches Institut, Athen
71 t	Bibliothèque Nationale de France, Paris (Jacques Carrey)
112 t	Scala
113 b	Deutsches Archeologische Institut Rom (H. Schwanke)
117	Publiaerfoto
118 t	Index, Firenze
157 b	Index/Publifoto
159 cl	Scala (Galleria Lapidaria, Vatican)
159 cr	Scala (Palazzo Salviati, Rome)
159 bl	Scala (Museo Archeologico, Aquileia)
166 b	Scala (Museo Ostiense, Ostia Antica)
167 b	Scala (Galleria degli Uffizi, Firenze)
174 b	Ancient Art & Architecture Collection Ltd
175	Scala (S. Clemente, Roma)
176 b	Publiaerfoto
180 t	Ancient Art & Architecture Collection Ltd
181	Scala (Museo delle Terme, Roma)
185	Scala
186	Scala
188 t	Ricciarini, Milano
189 bl	Scala (Museo Nazionale Napoli)
193 tl	Index/Archivio Fotografico Soprintendenza Archeologica, Roma
193 b	Scala (Museo Gregoriano Profano, Vatican)
210 b	Sonia Halliday Photographs
211 t,c	Corbis (Roger Wood) (Castle Museum, Tripoli, Libya)
213 t,c	Corbis (Roger Wood) (Castle Museum, Tripoli, Libya)
217 t	Corbis (Roger Wood) (Castle Museum, Tripoli, Libya)
226 t	Werner Forman Archive Ltd. (Museo Gregoriano Profano, Vatican)
242 b	Dr Hazel Dodge, Trinity College, Dublin

Author's jacket photo: Les Prudden

All other illustrations, diagrams and photographs by the author, Peter Connolly.

INDEX